SOVIET-ASIAN RELATIONS

CHARLES B McLANE

Volume Two of
SOVIET-THIRD WORLD RELATIONS

Published by
Central Asian Research Centre
London
1973

Distributed by
Columbia University Press
New York

© *Copyright* 1973 by The Central Asian Research Centre

Published in 1973 by The Central Asian Research Centre,
1B Parkfield Street, London N1 0PR

ISBN 0 903424 07 X

Text set by K. Perlo
Printed by Expedite Multiprint Ltd
51 Tothill Street, Westminster
London SW1H 9LQ, England

CONTENTS

Tables

5079-1

SOVIET - THIRD WORLD RELATIONS

FOREWORD TO THE SERIES

Soviet-Asian Relations is the second volume in a three-volume series of regional surveys of Soviet relations with the countries of the Third World. The other volumes are Soviet-Middle East Relations and Soviet-African Relations.
This series is itself the companion to a comprehensive study of Soviet policies in Asia, the Middle East and Africa since Stalin, Russia and the Third World, which will be completed shortly. This undertaking is the sequel to a more narrowly focused study published by Princeton University Press in 1966, Soviet Strategies in Southeast Asia: An Exploration of Eastern Policy under Lenin and Stalin.
It seemed wise to make the material in this series available separately from the parent study. The latter, already a full length investigation of Soviet Third World policies and of global considerations affecting Russian behaviour in Asia, the Middle East and Africa, would be greatly lengthened by the detail presented in the three volumes. Regional specialists, meanwhile, will find data relating to their areas of concentration more accessible if presented in a regional study instead of a single (and more costly) volume covering Soviet activity throughout the two continents.
It should be emphasized, however, that the material presented in this series is supportive rather than interpretive. I am aware that some readers will be disappointed not to find more analysis here, but it is the record of Soviet ties with Asia, Africa and the Middle East that I am interested in setting straight in these three volumes: the intensity of political and cultural exchange, the extent of Soviet aid, the amount of trade, arms transfers and the general pattern of Soviet commentary on individual states. Russian motives in the Third World, as well as the strategies devised in pursuit of particular objectives, are dealt with more explicitly in the parent study.
The 66 Afro-Asian nations covered in this series are divided into three regions: the Middle East and North Africa (normally referred to here as the Middle East); South and South-East Asia (referred to as Asia); and Africa south of the Sahara (referred to as Africa). Although the assignment of states to one or another region, especially the Middle East, may be contested, the criteria for selecting the 66 nations are the same in the three volumes: all are sovereign; all are underdeveloped; and none are Communist. The dozen or so dependencies in the three regions are accordingly omitted, as are the four Communist states in Asia (China, Mongolia, North Korea and North Vietnam) and developed nations like Japan, Israel and South Africa. This selection admittedly leaves gaps in any comprehensive geographic coverage of Soviet behaviour, especially in Asia, but allows a focus on what is commonly understood as the Third World exclusive of Latin America.
The chronological tables, which bear a heavy burden in the presentation of hard data concerning Moscow's relations with individual Third World states, deserve a word here. These tables were designed initially for my own use, to keep in handy perspective Moscow's intricate dealings with developing nations and major domestic developments in these nations that might affect the course of the relationship. It soon became apparent that the chronologies could be no less useful to readers and they were accordingly refined and rounded out for inclusion in the final text. The data are drawn mainly from Russian sources, supplemented occasionally by Western sources where the former were obscure. Since the data deal for the most part with specific episodes, such as political and cultural exchange and aid agreements, there is little reason to doubt their accuracy; where there is doubt, an appropriate source is shown. Any reader, however, will want a more exacting estimate of the reliability and completeness of these tables. I give mine at an appropriate place below (see Note on Chronologies, in the next section).
I owe a special debt of gratitude to the Central Asian Research Centre in London, where much of the preparation of the present project was undertaken during a sabbatical leave of absence from Dartmouth College in 1969-70. The Centre's library is unique for students of Soviet policies in Asia, the Middle East and Africa (a focus of the Centre that now surpasses its original focus on Soviet Central Asia). David Morison, Director of the Centre, and his staff were stimulating colleagues with whom to debate issues of Soviet behaviour, past and present. The Centre's publications, meanwhile, especially Mizan (the word means "balance" in Arabic), were an indispensable source of documentation and ideas on Russia's Third World policies; it is altogether fair to say that my project could not have been undertaken, at least in its present scope, were it not for the rigorous sifting through of Soviet commentary on the developing nations that is reflected in these publications.
Apart from this particular debt to the Central Asian Research Centre, there is the more general debt to scores of fellow students of Moscow's Third World policies whose studies, often more detailed than mine with respect to given countries, enabled me to carry my investigation forward; these studies are listed, along with relevant Russian and other materials, in the bibliographies at the end of each of the three volumes. I am also grateful to Daniel Stephen Papp, an Honours student at Dartmouth in the class of 1969, who helped me in the early preparation of the chronological tables. To Dartmouth College I am indebted not only for the sabbatical year in London but for grants to cover typing and other expenses. It goes without saying, of course, that none of the individuals or institutions mentioned bear responsibility for any shortcomings in these volumes.

SOVIET - ASIAN RELATIONS

PREFACE

The present volume deals with Soviet relations with 14 developing nations in Asia, stretching from Afghanistan to the Philippines. These states have little in common apart from the fact that they are "developing". Few forces in Asia promote a common sense of identity as is sometimes discerned in other regions of the Third World. In the Middle East religion, and since 1947 fear of Israel, have united the predominantly Arab population of the region; in Africa colour and the common colonial experience have stimulated a sense of unity. In Asia these forces have worked to different effect. Race and religion divide the peoples of Asia; they do not unite them. The common colonial experience ended so differently throughout Asia that there was never a sense, as in Africa, of the process of national liberation itself being a common experience. Burma and the Philippines, for instance, learnt little from each other in the matter of liberation; the conditions of independence in India and Pakistan - that is, the manner of their division - far from creating a bond between them, promoted irreconcilable hostility. It is accordingly difficult, if not impossible, to speak of a Russian Asian policy as one speaks of an Arab policy or a policy in Africa. More than anywhere else in the Third World, Soviet strategies in Asia had to be tailored to individual situations.

The absence of a sensed unity in Asia, however, does not mean that students of Soviet policies there should set aside regional considerations and focus solely on separate states. The impact of China's behaviour, for instance, is central to any appraisal of Russia's; the course of the war in Vietnam inevitably affected Soviet relations with all neighbouring states. Such considerations are explored in some detail in the parent volume to which this one is companion. In Chapter I I try merely to suggest the general scope and profile of Soviet activity in Asia before considering Russia's relations with each of the 14 nations under review.

NOTE ON CHRONOLOGICAL TABLES

The tables which follow represent an effort to chart chronologically all significant milestones in Russia's political, economic and cultural relations with different countries in Asia. The data are taken from Soviet sources in the main, but other sources have been consulted. Activity or episodes which might affect Soviet relations with a given country - such as domestic upheavals or important developments in relations with Russia's rivals (e.g. China after 1960) - are underlined.

Column 1 (Political) includes major landmarks in diplomatic relations, such as recognition, treaties, and major government and party exchanges; exchanges of heads of state and premiers are shown in capital letters. Military exchanges and arms agreements are also included in Column 1 as well as courtesy calls by Soviet naval units.

Column 2 (Economic) shows major developments in economic relations, including the exchange of important trade and aid missions, agreements, protocols and contracts; agreements involving Soviet credits are shown in capital letters. The term "agreement" is normally used to denote an initial commitment, with or without credit, and "protocol" to indicate a supplementary or implementing instrument. Soviet usage, however, is not consistent in this matter. The date given is normally the date of signing, not ratification; the latter date is shown only where there was a significant lapse in time before ratification. The dispatch of Soviet technicians to assist in specific projects is not shown, though the departure of these teams is normally reported in the Russian press. Similarly, the arrival of Asian specialists for further training in the USSR is omitted. The completion date of Russian-aided projects, where reliably reported, is indicated.

Column 3 (Cultural) is limited to the most important exchanges concerned with cultural co-operation and trade union relations, as well as the principal agreements and reported protocols. The following are not included (unless they represent the only activity reported): exchanges of youth, women, athletic, and Friendship Society delegations; the exchanges of performing artists; visits by tourists and individuals (unless of ministerial or other high rank); the arrival and departure of working missions (such as Russian teachers, engineers and doctors) and of Asian students enrolled in educational or cultural programmes in the USSR. The reason for these omissions is twofold: to show this activity would greatly lengthen the tables for many countries; the reporting of cultural exchanges at lower levels is irregular and a fuller listing would still leave many gaps.

Readers using the chronological tables may wish an estimate of the reliability of the data in them. My own estimate is as follows: In the political arena, state and ministerial exchanges shown in the tables may be taken to be nearly 100 per cent complete since these were normally reported in the Soviet press, if not at the time then subsequently; the same is true of major diplomatic agreements. Government exchanges at lower levels were less regularly reported and there are in consequence omissions in the tables - but not, in my view, a significant number. Communist party exchanges in both directions are complete for major conferences and congresses, when lists of the delegations attended are made public, but the periodic visits of party delegations to Moscow between congresses and world conferences are less reliably reported - especially where the party in question is illegal. Military exchanges shown in the tables are probably incomplete before the 1960s, when reporting was irregular; since about 1962 important military exchanges appear to have been regularly noted in Soviet journals (though with little detail). Evidence of arms agreements comes almost entirely from Western sources and both the data and sums involved in the agreements shown should be treated with caution. Exchanges with China indicated in the chronological tables cover only high state and ministerial delegations; evidence of exchanges at this level is reliable, but the tables do not pretend to reflect the full scope of Chinese activity.

In the economic sphere, all major credit and technical assistance agreements may be assumed accurate with these exceptions: the exact date of such agreements is often in doubt, due to uncertainty as to whether the date given represents the signing, ratification or coming into force of the agreement in question; the precise sum involved is sometimes in doubt due to different exchange rates and other considerations. (Where there is wide discrepancy in the sums reported in different sources, the discrepancy is discussed in the text preceding the table.) Protocols and contracts were reported less systematically in Soviet sources and there are in consequence omissions in the tables with respect to these supplementary instruments. The exchange of economic delegations may be considered nearly complete when of ministerial or equivalent rank, but with omissions at lower levels due to irregular reporting. Completion dates of projects are not fully shown in the tables because of the difficulty of verifying Soviet claims in this regard (sometimes anticipating by several years the actual opening of an enterprise).

With respect to cultural co-operation, the data shown in the chronological tables, as indicated above, are more suggestive of Soviet activity than definitive; omissions are therefore the consequence of my selection of what to include or omit, rather than of gaps in reporting of cultural exchange in Soviet sources. Of the activity which I have attempted to cover fully, exchanges of major cultural delegations may be taken as complete, or nearly so. Trade union exchanges were undoubtedly more numerous than shown, since many such exchanges – especially in the 1960s – were reported only in trade union journals which I covered less systematically than others. There are similarly gaps in professional exchanges – that is, of lawyers, doctors, journalists, educators, and the like.

It is worth noting, finally, that the principal defect in the chronological tables is omission, not padding; the tables may omit activity – even some activity of significance – but they do not show exchanges that never occurred or agreements that were never negotiated. The Russians, in short, were at least as active as the tables show them to have been and in most countries more so.

A conscious Russian policy towards the Third World in the post-war era, it may be said, began in Asia. There was activity here some years before a general shift in Soviet attitudes towards developing nations could be detected - that is, by 1955. At this time Russia had six embassies in Asia, where 11 countries were independent, as compared to three in the Middle East, where 10 countries were independent, and a single mission in Africa south of the Sahara. Moreover, relations were considerably more active by 1955 with countries like India, Afghanistan and Burma than with Turkey, Iran and Egypt (the three Middle East nations with which Moscow had diplomatic ties). Trade, too - if one excludes Iran, a traditional trading partner - was more extensive with developing nations in Asia than with those elsewhere. The first Soviet credits in the Third World in the post-war years were extended to an Asian state: to Afghanistan, in 1954. It was therefore natural that the famous expedition by Khrushchev and Bulganin in 1955, the first state visit by Russians in the Third World, should be in Asia and that the itinerary should include the three countries with which Moscow had already developed cordial relations.

Cordial relations with India, Afghanistan and Burma had not been cultivated by chance. Soviet diplomacy in these three nations after Stalin was motivated, as it was subsequently in the Middle East, by the threat of a military alliance directed against the USSR. American interest in such an alliance became increasingly apparent to the Russians, especially after the end of the Korean War in 1953 and the termination of hostilities in French Indochina a year later. The alliance which in due course emerged, the South-East Asia Treaty Organization (SEATO), never posed a significant threat to Russia, but while it was being negotiated there was reason for concern. Were India, Burma or Afghanistan to adhere to this security system, American influence in the sub-continent would be greatly extended at Russia's expense; moreover, India, Burma and Afghanistan would create a bridge between SEATO and any parallel treaty organization to emerge in the Middle East. Such a linking of two American-dominated security systems would limit Russia's manoeuvrability south of its borders for some years to come. Soviet activity in South Asia in the mid-1950s must be seen against this background. The early diplomatic overtures to India, Afghanistan and Burma, capped by the Khrushchev-Bulganin expedition of 1955, were designed to strengthen the neutrality of these crucial states. Since these nations, meanwhile, were already inclined towards non-alignment - more so than the Russians apparently appreciated - they reacted warmly to the Soviet overtures and relations flourished.

As the danger, or imagined danger, of American-oriented alliances receded, the Soviet Union could, and did, devote more attention to developing Asian nations in their own right. This is reflected in the widening of contacts throughout the continent, the growing preoccupation with political and cultural exchanges, the development of trade, the maturing of economic co-operation, and in other activities discussed in the country studies below (see also the Tables at the end of this volume). During the period 1955-1971, for instance, there were nearly as many head of state exchanges between the USSR and the developing nations of Asia as between the USSR and all other nations of the Third World. Soviet economic aid to Asian states to the end of 1971 accounted for more than a half of all Soviet credits extended to Asia, Africa and the Middle East. Soviet trade with developing Asian states also was greater than with Middle East and with African states over the years under review (though exports to Arab nations for several years after the Six Day War of 1967 produced higher annual totals in the Middle East). Soviet activity in Asia, in short, measured by such criteria, did not decline as the initial reasons for the commitment in Asia lost their urgency.

If expanding Soviet interest in Asia after the 1950s is best seen in the context of expanding interest in the Third World as a whole, the reasons for demonstrably greater activity in Asia than in Africa and the Middle East must be sought elsewhere. Rivalry with China was clearly a central consideration. The dispute between Russia and China was inevitably carried on with more intensity in South and South-East Asia than in regions more remote from one or both, such as the Arab world or Africa south of the Sahara. Moscow's relations with nearly every developing state in Asia were affected after 1960 by this spiralling conflict with Peking. A Chinese advantage in Ceylon or Nepal, for instance, stimulated Russian strategies to overcome it. Peking's influence in Karachi led to a major shift in Soviet policies in India, which for some years altered the course of events in the sub-continent (these developments are discussed in some detail below, in the sections dealing with India and Pakistan). In South-East Asia the rivalry was particularly keen, and it may be useful to focus attention briefly on Soviet strategies in this complex region, the more so since regional strategies are easily overlooked in a study that concentrates on individual countries.

China had a natural advantage over Russia in South-East Asia because of proximity, a certain cultural affinity in some areas, traditional commercial ties in others, the presence everywhere of overseas Chinese, and other factors. Early Soviet gains in countries like Burma and Cambodia, for instance, were quickly neutralized when China began its diplomatic thrust in earnest and the Russians were discouraged from developing more intimate ties with these two states. Peking's radical influence in Djakarta in the early 1960s wholly frustrated Moscow's efforts there and left the Russians powerless to moderate Sukarno's disastrous policies, despite the fact that Indonesia at this time was one of the principal beneficiaries of Soviet economic and military aid. In Laos and Vietnam the inevitably greater voice of the Chinese in revolutionary formations like the Pathet Lao and Viet Cong, as well as in Hanoi, reduced the Russian role at times to that of mere observer. Khrushchev, in consequence, preferred to disengage from costly commitments in Indochina rather than stand by and see Russian influence slowly eroded. In 1961-62 he worked for the "neutralization" of Laos, even though "neutralization" was not necessarily in the best interests of the well-placed and well-organized Laotian rebels under Prince Souphanouvong. Thereafter he deliberately curtailed Moscow's role in Vietnam: aid fell off and diplomatic relations were barely cordial as the North Vietnamese relied increasingly on China; during the Tonkin episode of August 1964 the Russians appeared relatively indifferent, in sharp contrast to the Chinese, to American bombing of coastal installations in North Vietnam – an act that served as a prelude to escalation of the Vietnamese war.[1] Khrushchev's successors, to be sure, could not avoid Soviet re-engagement in Vietnam when escalation became a reality during Kosygin's visit to Hanoi in February 1965. Ties were greatly strengthened with the North Vietnamese during the succeeding years and Russia became Hanoi's principal supplier of arms, valued at approximately $1 billion annually by 1968 and including sophisticated anti-aircraft systems and advanced aircraft. Still it may be questioned whether renewed Soviet activity in Vietnam, in fulfilment of an obligation Moscow could not easily escape, led to increased influence throughout Indochina or South-East Asia generally. The Russians were surely less active during the Paris peace talks (from 1968 to 1973) than during the earlier conferences on Indochina (1956 and 1961–62) and were probably less influential than the Chinese in bringing the long Vietnam war to an end.[2]

In 1969, in a thinly disguised effort to contain China, the Russians proposed a new "collective security system" in Asia. The idea was put forward on the eve of the world Communist conference in Moscow in June and formally stated by Brezhnev himself in his address to the conference on 7 June;[3] Gromyko dealt with the proposal in a major report on foreign policy before the Supreme Soviet in July.[4] The Russians hesitated to spell out their proposal in any detail, apparently waiting for a favourable reaction in Asia. Reaction, however, was mixed. The Russians had too long denounced regional pacts of all sorts in Asia – not merely military alliances like SEATO but economic unions such as the Association of South-East Asia (ASA), the Asian Pacific Council (ASPAC) and the Association of South-East Asian Nations (ASEAN)[5] – to win wide support for a similar venture of their own. The Indians favoured the idea, out of deference to their allies in Moscow, and a few states (Thailand and Malaysia, for instance) expressed polite interest in the Soviet proposal. Most Asian leaders, however, were sceptical. The Pakistanis, seeing the security pact as an instrument directed against their ally China, were the most adamantly opposed. Why, a high Pakistani official asked, should Asian nations join a new regional security system when earlier systems such as SEATO and CENTO had been so thoroughly discredited?[6] – largely as a result of Soviet propaganda, he might have added. The Russians none the less explored the idea relentlessly for some months before quietly relegating it to the background in their policy pronouncements; Brezhnev did not mention the Asian security pact in his report to the Twenty-fourth Party Congress in March 1971. The idea was revived, however, following the Treaty of Friendship with India in 1971, a pact which the Russians chose to consider as the first step in the elusive security system they sought. "Collective security in Asia", Brezhnev stated in March 1972, "should be based on the principles of renunciation of force in relations between states, respect for the sovereignty and inviolability of borders, non-interference in internal affairs, the broad development of economic and other co-operation on the basis of complete equality of rights and mutual benefit."[7] He pledged Russia's continuing support for a collective security system of this sort.

By 1972, however, there was less reason than ever for a security pact directed against China – assuming this was still the Russians' concealed intent. Chinese diplomats had returned to their posts in Asia and informal missions were exchanged with nations like Malaysia and the Philippines with which Peking still had no diplomatic ties. In short, apart from some lingering (and, as a rule, perfunctory) support for Maoist factions in Asia,[8] there was little to distinguish Chinese diplomacy from Russian.

If Soviet policies towards the developing countries of Asia since 1955 are considered in a broad perspective, most observers will conclude that security and national advantage predominated in Moscow's calculations. Initially the Russians were concerned about the possibility of an American-supported alliance directed against the USSR; after 1960, while this concern did not entirely disappear, a greater concern was felt over expansion of Chinese influence at Russia's expense. Soviet strategies varied in this search for security and national advantage. At the outset the Russians tended to reward non-alignment and punish alignment (with the West, that is) by providing or witholding aid, arms, friendship and support for local national objectives – such as India's claim to Kashmir. Subsequently the Russians became less partisan: they distributed aid more widely, they sought political and economic relations with all states, and they refrained from taking sides in local disputes. In short, they sought to stimulate as well as to fortify neutralist tendencies in Asia. The principal focus of their attention in these endeavours was the Asian sub-continent, a region that ranked second only to the Middle East in the perspective of Russia's Third World policy over the years reviewed (if we exclude Moscow's brief, though intense, preoccupation with Africa early in the 1960s).

The Russians were also motivated in part, in their behaviour in Asia, by a sense of the historic force of the national liberation movement. They wished not only to keep abreast of it but to claim its affinity to the socialist bloc. This was reflected, for instance, in enthusiastic responses to the Bandung conference of Afro-Asian leaders in 1955 and in lip-service regularly paid to the virtues of the national liberation and anti-imperialist movement, even where a number of the states identified with this movement held views on international affairs at variance with Moscow's. The Russians did not trouble much about evidence in this respect: they did not require rigorous proof of anti-Western attitudes to affirm their existence at one level or another in all, or nearly all, developing Asian states.

Closely related to the idea of national liberation as a "historic force" was the idea that the developing nations in Asia would in due course become socialist. This too was a motive for Soviet behaviour. Russian commentators never tired of pointing out the virtues of the "non-capitalist" course; Soviet aid was explicitly earmarked, in the nations that received it, for enterprises that would enhance the state sector and encourage the development of socialist economies. In nations where considerations of Russian security were insignificant, this motive was often dominant: in Indonesia, for instance, Khrushchev's infatuation with Sukarno's regime seems to have grown from a vaguely ideological hope that Indonesia would develop into Asia's Cuba, like Ghana and Guinea in Africa or Algeria and the UAR in the Middle East. Soviet interest in Burma after 1963

had a similar origin. The Russians were never so pro-
pelled by their ideological object, it should be noted,
that they allowed it to interfere with diplomacy: socialism never stood in the way of cordial relations with states
Moscow considered "bourgeois"; nor did the Russians
make special efforts to use local Communist parties as
instruments of their designs - although they took an
interest in these parties where conditions permitted it.

Purely ideological motives, then, appear to have
been marginal in Soviet behaviour in Asia and the best
proof of this is the ease with which the Russians turned to
other objectives when ideological goals were frustrated.
Sukarno abandoned his pro-Soviet orientation and was
eventually overthrown; Burma remained perversely bank-
rupt; India stubbornly clung to a predominantly capitalist
economy despite eloquent claims of moving towards socialism. The Russians responded to these disappointments with
a certain equanimity and pragmatism, especially after the
fall of Nikita Khrushchev. They patched up as best they
could relationships that had grown strained. They adjusted
their diplomacy to the requirements of the status quo.
They became the apostles of political stability and cau-
tious economic development. In short, the most persistent
Soviet objectives in Asia after the mid-1960s were conservative. The image of Russia as peace-maker at Tashkent
was persistently recalled after 1966; in Singapore,

Bombay and Bangkok the Russians posed as neutral traders;
the strategy recommended to Asian Communists was not
insurrection, but coalition and united front.

The Russians' benign behaviour suggests that they
had another motive in Asia, related neither to ideology
nor specifically to security. That is, simply to maintain
a presence in the region. It was an imperative of their
foreign policy, the Russians may increasingly have felt,
that the USSR be represented in all parts of the world to
play whatever role the occasion required. It was this
consideration, rather than specific political or economic
advantage, that sent Soviet diplomats and trade missions
to remote parts of Asia, as of Africa and Latin America.
The build-up of Russian naval power in the Indian Ocean
after 1968 may also be understood in this light: although
the number of Soviet vessels there has been exaggerated,[9]
their presence was a reminder that Russia was not to be
excluded from any developments or settlements in South
and South-East Asia.

The Soviet Union, to judge from the foregoing,
had varied motives and objectives in Asia. They did
not, of course, have equal force at all times; nor do
all apply to every country on our list. Soviet relations
with the 14 Asian states to which we now turn, however,
reflect at one time or another each of the motives and
goals discussed above.

References

[1] Compare, for instance, the official TASS communiqué
on the incident in Pravda, 6 August, 1964 and the official Chinese reaction in a New China News Agency
release of the same date; the episode, along with others,
is discussed in my article "The Russians and Vietnam:
Strategies of Indirection", International Journal, Vol.
XXIV, No. 1 (Winter 1968-69), pp. 47-64.

[2] The impact of Soviet policies in Vietnam on Soviet Third
World policies is discussed in more detail in Russia and
the Third World, but the policies themselves are not sys-
tematically reviewed in this series (as explained in the
Foreword above). They have, however, been the subject
of extensive research and commentary by Western scholars.
See, inter alia, Donald S. Zagoria, Vietnam Triangle:
Moscow, Peking, Hanoi (New York: Pegasus Books,
1967); Robert A. Rupen, ed., Vietnam and the Sino-
Soviet Dispute (New York: Praeger, 1967); Joseph G.
Whelan, "Soviet Aid to the Vietnamese Communists",
Library of Congress, Legislative Reference Service,
JX1435, F-211 (19 December, 1966); Jan S. Prybyla,
"Soviet and Chinese Economic Aid to North Vietnam",
China Quarterly, No. 27 (July-September 1966); and
Allen W. Cameron, "The Soviet Union and Vietnam:
the Origins of Involvement", chapter in Duncan, ed.,
Soviet Policy in Developing Countries (see Bibliography
for full listing), pp. 166-205.

[3] See V. Matveyev in Izvestiya, 29 May, 1969 and
Brezhnev's speech in Pravda, 8 June, 1969, p. 9.

[4] Pravda, 11 July, 1969.

[5] See Peter Howard's article, "Regional Co-operation in

South-East Asia: Soviet Misgivings", Mizan, November-
December 1967, pp. 252-57; also, Marian P. Kirsch,
"Soviet Security Objectives in Asia", International
Organization, Summer 1970, pp. 469-70.

[6] M.A.H. Ispahani, "Pakistan and New Regional Ar-
rangements", Pakistan Horizon (Karachi), Third Quarter,
1969; see also Peter Howard, "A System of 'Collective
Security'", Mizan, July-August 1969, pp. 199-204,
and Lawrence L. Whetton, "Moscow's Anti-China Pact",
World Today, September 1969, pp. 385-95, and Marian
Kirsch's article cited above, pp. 464ff.

[7] Pravda, 21 March, 1972.

[8] Communist schisms are touched on in this volume where
they are relevant to the course of Soviet policies, but
they are not treated systematically; the impact of the
Sino-Soviet dispute on Third World Communist parties is
discussed more fully in the parent volume Russia and the
Third World.

[9] Western sources in 1970 and 1971 estimated as many
as 100 ships in Russia's Indian Ocean "squadron"; see
Marian Kirsch, op. cit., p. 473 and Neville Brown's
article in New Middle East, March 1971, p. 19.
A subsequent and more exacting count, however,
shows that while the Soviet "presence" did indeed
grow from 1968 to 1971, the total number of capital
ships in the Indian Ocean at any one time never exceeded half a dozen; Geoffrey Jukes, "The Indian
Ocean in Soviet Naval Policy", Adelphi Papers, No.
87 (May 1971), pp. 15-16 (based on Australian
Intelligence sources).

2. RELATIONS WITH AFGHANISTAN

The long, continuous diplomatic relationship between the Soviet Union and Afghanistan, dating from 1919, facilitated improved relations after 1955 when Russia's policies in the Third World shifted. The relationship had not been particularly cordial since the Second World War, but neither had it been particularly strained. The Friendship Treaty of 1921 and the Neutrality Pact of 1931 continued in force. Trade between the two countries increased fourfold from the end of the war to the early 1950s and as early as 1950 kits for entire factories were reportedly being exported to Afghanistan.[1] The credits extended in 1954 (see Chronology) were the first since the Second World War to any non-Communist regime in the Third World. Afghanistan was in a sense the proving ground of changing Soviet policies.

Developments in 1955 accelerated better relations between the two countries. In the spring a new crisis in Afghan-Pakistani relations over Pashtunistan led to Pakistan's closing the border for the second time (the first closing, over the same issue, was in 1949-50).[2] This prompted a Soviet-Afghan transit agreement in June and made Afghanistan immediately dependent on Soviet oil and other supplies normally received from, or through, Pakistan. A new trade agreement in August spelt out these needs in some detail and projected a significant rise in Soviet exports to Afghanistan.

It was natural in these circumstances for Afghanistan to be placed on the Bulganin-Khrushchev itinerary in South Asia at the end of 1955. This visit stimulated further economic and political ties, which were in turn cemented by the return visits of Prime Minister Daud and the King in 1956 and 1957. From 1955 to the end of 1970 there were more state exchanges between Russia and Afghanistan than between Russia and any other Third World nation except India and a corresponding number of exchanges at lower levels. In the 16 years under review there was no significant break in this pattern of cordiality. Indeed, there is no country in Asia or Africa where the course of diplomatic relations with the USSR, to judge from outward indications, ran so smoothly.

The Russians were helped in their efforts to woo the Afghans, especially in the latter half of the 1950s, by American intransigence in Afghanistan. Until the mid-1950s, American influence in Kabul had been stronger than Russian, but with the signing of the Baghdad Pact in 1950 this situation changed. Pakistan now became the central focus of Washington's policy in South Asia. Accommodation with Afghanistan became secondary. The Afghans' repeated requests for American arms were turned down, in consequence of which the Russians concluded an arms agreement with Kabul in 1956 (their first in Asia); the Americans procrastinated so long over loan requests for paving the streets of Kabul that the Afghans turned finally to the Russians; a similar delay in responding to Kabul's request for American aid in developing an alternate overland route through Iran during the Pashtunistan crisis of 1955 hastened the transit agreement with Moscow (see above). The Afghans, meanwhile, conscious of the vulnerability of their long exposed frontier with the USSR and desirous of a neutral foreign policy, resented American efforts to draw them into the Baghdad alliance.

The Russians profited from these tendencies, or blunders, in American policy.[3]

Afghanistan, in return for its promise of neutrality, gained Russia's support - and this was almost the only international support it received - on the Pashtun issue. Pashtun aspirations, a Soviet scholar wrote in 1957 in a long and detailed analysis of the problem, are "part of a common liberation struggle against colonialism and oppression". Pashtunistan had been linked to Pakistan through a historical accident and it should now be liberated "according to the principles of self-determination".[4] The Soviet-Afghan communiqué following Khrushchev's visit to Kabul in 1960 affirmed that "the proper and sensible way to lessen tension and to guarantee peace (in the Pashtun issue) is to apply to the solution of this problem the principle of self-determination".[5] This continued to be the Soviet position when a new crisis over Pashtunistan flared up a year later, leading to a break in Afghan-Pakistani relations.[6]

One might have expected a cooling of Soviet-Afghan relations in the mid-1960s when Russia's relations with Pakistan improved. This did not in fact occur. The Russians of course no longer took sides on the Pashtun issue - but there was presently no need to do so for the issue ceased to be critical in South Asian diplomacy. Afghan-Pakistani relations gradually improved (reflected, for instance, in a sizeable increase in their trade by 1965)[7] and it is not improbable that the Russians played a part in the rapprochement. By the end of the 1960s "constructive co-operation" between Afghanistan and Pakistan was a major theme in Soviet policy in South Asia, as Kosygin emphasized during his tour of the area in the spring of 1969.[8]

The Russians did not, in their very considerable coverage of Afghan developments after 1955,[9] attempt to paint Afghanistan as a modern or progressive state. A 1960 study, for instance, called Afghanistan "semi-feudal" and noted that most of the peasantry, which constituted 80 per cent of the population, was landless; tribalism was said to predominate and the role of the clergy was everywhere strong; foreign investment was still encouraged. This did not, however, hinder cordial relations with socialist states, the authors noted: Soviet-Afghan relations "bear witness to the fact that differences in the social structure of states constitute no obstacle to the peaceful coexistence and friendly co-operation of their people".[10] This theme was repeated endlessly in Soviet commentaries, the most saccharine of which were normally on the occasion of Afghanistan's national day in May of each year. Kosygin, who was in Kabul during the 50th anniversary of Afghan independence in 1969, called Soviet-Afghan relations "a convincing example of peaceful coexistence between states with different social systems"; he ascribed the success of the relationship largely to "Afghanistan's policy of neutrality and non-alignment".[11] King Mohammed Zahir Shah, in Moscow on a state visit 16 months later, echoed Kosygin's words: Soviet-Afghan relations were "a vivid example of fruitful peaceful coexistence in the field of international ties, especially between countries that have different political and social systems".[12]

The Chinese posed no serious challenge to Russian diplomats in Afghanistan during the years under review. Peking established diplomatic relations with Afghanistan in 1955 and during the next decade exchanged a number of high-ranking missions with Kabul (as well as many lesser delegations not shown in the Chronology); the Chinese also extended a modest credit to Afghanistan in 1965 for projects in the second Five-Year Plan. Sino-Afghan relations did not develop significantly, however, before the Cultural Revolution. China's friendship with Pakistan was proof against Afghan enthusiasm for closer ties with Peking at Moscow's expense while the Pashtunistan issue remained active; when this issue receded, unrest in China during the Cultural Revolution acted as a barrier to improved relations. By 1970, when relations again improved between Kabul and Peking, the Russians' advantage in Afghanistan was so great that a challenge from the Chinese would not be felt for many years. Neither increased exchanges from 1970 on nor a generous Chinese loan in 1972 for the fourth Five-Year Plan[13] appeared to affect Russia's confident posture in Kabul. The Chinese effort in Afghanistan, it could be said, was to maintain a listening post over Soviet activity - in much the same way that Russia's effort in certain Asian nations where Chinese influence was pre-eminent, as in Nepal, was limited to surveillance of the actions of Peking.

Economic, Military and Cultural Relations

Soviet economic aid to Afghanistan through the 1960s greatly exceeded that from any other nation. The nearest competitors were the United States and West Germany, which provided respectively 23 and nine per cent of Afghanistan's foreign credits during the second Five-Year Plan (1962-67) as compared to Russia's 65 per cent.[14] The precise total of Soviet credits is unclear, estimates ranging from slightly over $500 million to as much as $700 million by the end of 1970.[15] The reasons for this large discrepancy go beyond the usual problems of exchange rates and multiple reporting of single credits; they centre instead on the existence and size of a reported gift for the Hindu Kush highway and the inclusion, or non-inclusion, of a military credit in 1957 among the loans for economic development. The credits appear to have been expended reasonably promptly and new loans provided. At the end of 1971 the Russians claimed that 49 enterprises built with Soviet aid were in operation and another 27 in progress.[16]

A detailed description of Soviet aid projects in Afghanistan would be out of place here, but a brief catalogue of the major undertakings suggests the range of Russian activity.[17] Of greatest significance to the Afghans (and perhaps also to the Russians) was the Hindu Kush highway, linking Kabul with North Afghanistan; though less than 100 miles in length, this route shortens motor connexions with the north by several days and makes travel possible all the year round. The project was completed in 1964. Another, longer highway (525 miles) was completed in 1967, linking Kushka on the Soviet-Afghan border to Kandahar, where it ties in with the American-built roads southwards from Kabul to Pakistan. These highways provide Afghanistan with a modern road system into all important sectors of the country. An irrigation system at Jalalabad, together with a dam and power station, was begun in 1964 and the first portion of it - the canal - was completed in 1965; four mechanized farms were constructed in this area. Additional power stations were completed at Mazar-i-Sharif and Naglu. Airports were constructed at several towns and an international airport was built at Kabul. Of the early projects undertaken in Kabul, the combined flour mill-bakery-granary, a motor repair works and an asphalt factory were in operation as early as 1960. In addition to the above, there were either under construction or in operation by 1970: a fertilizer plant, a nuclear reactor, a technical institute, a gas pipeline to Uzbekistan spanning the Amu Darya, and a number of lesser undertakings. In May 1969 a permanent Soviet-Afghan Economic Commission was set up in Kabul to supervise on-going and future projects.

Trade between Russia and Afghanistan grew steadily until the mid-1960s, when it levelled off. During the latter half of the 1960s Afghanistan ranked persistently among the top six of Russia's trading partners in the Third World. Russia had for many years ranked first among Afghanistan's partners; in 1967, for instance, the Soviet Union provided 63 per cent of Afghan imports and took 38 per cent of Afghan exports - accounting for approximately 50 per cent of Afghanistan's total foreign trade.[18]

From 1956 on Russia was the sole supplier of arms to Afghanistan. The total value of arms transfers by the end of 1967 has been estimated at $260 million, including small arms, tanks, and jet aircraft of various advanced designs;[19] the frequency of high level military exchanges to the end of 1971 (see Chronology) suggests that collaboration between the two nations continued to expand.

Cultural relations were also active, reflected in a steady exchange of educational, performing and other delegations from 1955 on; many of these exchanges took place between Afghanistan and the Central Asian republics. In 1970 an estimated 720 Afghan students were at universities in the USSR, not counting another 200 trainees on technical courses.[20] It was said that 46,000 Afghans had been trained in Soviet programmes in the USSR and in Afghanistan.[21]

It is apparent from this survey that a strong and stable relationship existed between the Soviet Union and Afghanistan during the years under review. One should not, however, read more into the relationship than was there. Russia and Afghanistan were cordial, but not necessarily intimate, neighbours. The Russians, so far as is known, did not intervene actively in Afghan politics or try to transform Afghanistan into a socialist state. They made little of the small Communist Party in Kabul and did not cultivate special relations with any other faction or party, as they did in many favoured countries in the Third World; when a severe government crisis occurred in 1965, Moscow remained aloof. Ideology, meanwhile, played a negligible part in Soviet attitudes towards Afghanistan. The Afghan leaders were never described as "progressive" - any more than the leaders of other Northern tier states (Pakistan, Iran and Turkey) - nor were they seen as contemplating the "non-capitalist path of development". The Soviet-constructed road network in Afghanistan, it is true, gave the Russians a certain mobility in this strategic region and provided direct overland access for the first time to the sub-continent. Russian commentators called attention to the economic value of the new Afghan roads, but there is no evidence that Russia used the network to gain a military advantage. Afghan neutrality, not military advantage, was the Russians' central object in Afghanistan. This was the condition of Moscow's good will and for neutrality the Russians were willing to pay handsomely. It is an illustration of the pre-eminence of national considerations over ideological in Soviet policy - for nothing in Afghanistan's semi-feudal social structure and outlook would seem to justify outlays which made this nation Russia's principal beneficiary on a per capita basis in all of Asia and Africa. The Afghans, for their part, mindful of their long and vulnerable frontier with the USSR, took easily to neutrality and the relationship accordingly prospered.

Chronology

(See explanatory note on tables, p. 6.)

	Political		Economic	Cultural
Pre-1955				
1919	Independence: diplomatic relations established			
Feb 1921	Friendship treaty			
June 1930	Non-aggression, neutrality treaty			
Jan 1950	Afghanistan recognizes CPR			
		July 1950	Trade agreement	
		Apr 1953	Aid mission in Afghanistan	
		Jan 1954	Credit agreement for flour mill, granaries ($3.5m)	
		Oct 1954	Additional credit for road construction ($2.1m)[22]	
1955				
Jan	- Embassies exchanged with CPR			
May	- Emergency declared during Pashtunistan crisis	May	- Economic delegation in USSR for aid talks	
		June	- Transit agreement	
		Aug	- New trade agreement	
Dec	- KHRUSHCHEV, BULGANIN IN AFGHANISTAN for 4-day visit: 1931 treaty extended 10 years			
1956		Jan	- CREDIT AGREEMENT for various projects ($100m)	

AFGHANISTAN

	Political		Economic		Cultural
1956 (cont.)					

		Mar	– Air space agreement
			– Technical co-operation
			  protocol on January
			  credit: power plants,
			  Hindu Kush highway,
			  airfields, repair shop,
			  irrigation		

				Apr	– Medical delegation in Afghanistan
				May	– Educational delegation in USSR

		July	– Protocol on Soviet
			  technicians for
			  aid projects		

Aug	– Military delegation
	  in USSR: first arms
	  agreement ($25m)
		Aug	– Further protocol
			  on 2 power plants
			– Air services agreement
				Aug	– Medical delegation
					  in USSR

		Sept	– Agricultural delegation in Afghanistan		
Oct	– PREMIER DAUD IN USSR on 15-day visit				
				Nov	– Journalists in USSR
1957					
Jan	– Chou En-lai in Afghanistan	Jan	– Trade protocol for 1957		
		Mar	– Flour mill completed	Mar	– Press delegation in USSR
				May	– Cultural delegation in USSR

July	– KING IN USSR on
	  18-day official visit,
	  holiday
		July	– CREDIT AGREEMENT
			  for oil prospecting
			  ($15m)		

Aug	– Reported arms agreement
	  ($60m credit)[23]
				Aug	– Journalists in
					  Afghanistan

Oct	– Daud in CPR for
	  economic talks
		Oct	– Agricultural delegation
			  in Moscow for conference		

1958					
Jan	– Frontier agreement	Jan	– Contract for oil prospecting		
		Feb	– Trade protocol for 1958		
		May	– Gift of hydro- turbines		

		June	– Agreement on
			  joint use of
			  Amu Darya		

		Sept	– Commercial dele- gation in USSR		

	Political	Economic	Cultural
1958 (cont.)			
Oct	– PRESIDENT VOROSHILOV IN AFGHANISTAN for 6-day visit		
Nov			– Journalists in USSR
Dec	– Foreign minister Naim in USSR		
1959			
Jan		– Agreement on sale of commercial aircraft, equipment for domestic air service	– Gift of books to Kabul university
Feb		– Communications agreement	– Soviet Orientalists in Afghanistan
Mar		– Gift of wheat after crop failure	
Apr		– Trade minister in USSR: protocol for 1959	
May	– DAUD IN USSR on 4-day visit	– Agreement on Kandahar highway (reported gift of $129m)[24]	
June		– Economic delegation in USSR: further protocols on power stations, canals, etc.	
Aug			– Artists in Afghanistan
Sept	– Foreign minister Naim in CPR		– Writers in Afghanistan
Oct		– Public works minister in USSR	– Central Asian artists in Afghanistan
Nov	– Parliamentary delegation in USSR		– Journalists' delegation in USSR
1960			
Jan		– Trade protocol for 1960	
Feb			– Education delegation in USSR
Mar	– KHRUSHCHEV IN AFGHANISTAN for 3-day visit	– Gift of additional wheat	– Cultural agreement
Apr	– Daud in USSR for 5-week rest cure		
May		– Protocol on river port construction	
June			– Artists in USSR
Aug	– Friendship treaty with CPR		

AFGHANISTAN

	Political		Economic		Cultural
<u>1960</u> (cont.)					
		Nov	– Protocol on geological survey		
		Dec	– Trade delegation in USSR: protocol for 1961		

<u>1961</u>

	Political		Economic		Cultural
				Jan	– Doctors in Afghanistan to combat cholera
Apr	– DAUD IN USSR	Apr	– Medical aid promised	Apr	– Locust control specialists in Afghanistan
Sept	– Foreign minister Naim in USSR – Afghan–Pakistan <u>relations broken</u> over Pashtunistan issue				
Oct	– Parliamentary delegation in Afghanistan – Marshal Sokolovskiy in Afghanistan	Oct	– Economic delegation in USSR: CREDIT AGREE-MENTS for second 5-year plan ($195m) – Agricultural delegation in Central Asia		
				Nov	– Teachers in Afghanistan – Musicians in Central Asia

---

<u>1962</u>

	Political		Economic		Cultural
		Jan	– 5-yr trade agreement – Protocol on hydro-meteorology project		
				Feb	– Cultural protocol
		Apr	– Protocol on Kabul housing project		
		May	– SUPPLEMENTARY CREDIT ($20m)[25]	May	– Press chief in USSR – Kabul university professors in USSR
Aug	– King in USSR for 10-day holiday				
				Sept	– Musicians in Central Asia
Oct	– Foreign minister Naim in USSR				
Nov	– Supreme Soviet delegation in Afghanistan	Nov	– Protocol on enlargement of flour mill		

<u>1963</u>

	Political		Economic		Cultural
		Feb	– Commerce minister in USSR: trade protocol for 1963 – Protocol on airports		
Mar	– <u>Jusuf replaces Daud as premier</u>	Mar	– Protocol on mechanized farms		

Political	Economic	Cultural
1963 (cont.)		
		Apr – Cultural protocol
		June – Red Cross delegation in USSR
	July – Protocol on 1961 credit	
	Sept – Agreement on nuclear reactor ($17m)	Sept – Musicians in Central Asia
Oct – BREZHNEV IN AFGHANISTAN for 5-day visit	Oct – CREDIT AGREEMENT for natural gas extraction ($39m) – Protocol on poly-technical institute	
Nov – Frontier agreement with CPR		
1964		
		Jan – Cultural protocol
	Feb – Agreement on nuclear co-operation	
Mar – Jusuf in USSR for 3-month medical care		
July – Mikoyan in Afghanistan – Defence minister heads military delegation to USSR		
Aug – Parliamentary leaders in USSR	Aug – Further protocol on housing projects	
Sept – Deputy premier Kosygin heads delegation to Afghanistan for opening of Hindu Kush highway		
Nov – King stops in USSR en route to CPR – Deputy foreign minister Lapin in Afghanistan		
		Dec – Cultural delegation in USSR
1965		
Jan – Deputy premier in USSR on unofficial visit	Jan – Trade protocol for 1965	
		Feb – Cultural protocol
Mar – Polyanskiy heads delegation to Afghanistan for canal opening – Chen Yi in Afghanistan	Mar – CPR credit ($28m)	
Apr – JUSUF IN USSR for 9-day visit	Apr – Protocol on river development	
	July – Protocol on chemical plant	July – Afghan actors perform in Tadzhikistan

	Political		Economic		Cultural
1965 (cont.)					
Aug	– KING IN USSR for 11–day state visit: 1931 treaty extended 10 years	Aug	– Transit agreement extended		
		?	– Reported credit ($11m)[26]		
Nov	– Maiwandwal replaces Jusuf as premier after post–election riots				
	– Deputy premier Mazurov in Afghanistan for highway opening				
1966					
Jan	– Kosygin stops in Kabul en route from India			Jan	– Expanded cultural agreement
Feb	– MAIWANDWAL IN USSR for 10–day visit				
Mar	– Foreign minister in USSR for medical treatment				
Apr	– Liu Shao–chi, Chen Yi in Afghanistan				
		May	– Trade protocol for 1966	May	– Artist delegation in Afghanistan
June	– Government delegation under Mazurov in Afghanistan				
		?	– Reported credit ($1m)[27]		
July	– Crown prince in USSR			July	– Information chief in Turkestan
	– Defence minister in USSR				– Artists in USSR
				Aug	– Artists in Afghanistan
Nov	– Government delegation in Afghanistan for opening of another highway				
1967					
		Feb	– Protocol on 400–bed hospital	Feb	– Mukhitdinov in Afghanistan: cultural protocol
May	– PODGORNYY IN AFGHANISTAN for opening of power station				
June	– Kosygin meets Afghan prime minister at UN in New York				

	Political		Economic		Cultural
1967 (cont.)					
		July	- Gas pipeline completed from Afghanistan to Uzbekistan	July	- Musicians perform in Tadzhikistan
		Aug	- SUPPLEMENTARY CREDIT for irrigation project ($5m)		
Sept	- Military delegation in USSR				
Nov	- Government delegation in USSR for 50th anniversary - Etemadi replaces Maiwandwal as premier				
1968					
Jan	- Municipal delegation in USSR				
Feb	- Kosygin stops in Kabul en route from India				
				Mar	- Education officials in USSR
				May	- Gift of technical book to Kalid university
June	- KING IN USSR for 10-day state visit			June	- Tadzhik actors in Afghanistan
				Sept	- Muslim delegation in USSR
		Oct	- CREDIT AGREEMENT for third 5-year plan projects ($127m)	Oct	- Cultural delegation in USSR - Musicians in USSR
Nov	- ETEMADI IN USSR				
		Dec	- Trade protocol	Dec	- Red Cross delegation in Afghanistan - Medical delegation in USSR
1969					
Jan	- Defence minister in USSR on holiday				
		Mar	- Foreign office official in Afghanistan to inspect aid projects		
Apr	- King stops in Khabarovsk en route to Japan			Apr	- Cultural protocol
May	- Kosygin meets Afghan premier in Delhi - KOSYGIN IN AFGHANISTAN for 5-day visit on 50th anniversary	May	- Soviet-Afghan economic commission established - Technical institute opens	May	- Meteorology delegation in Afghanistan: agreement on weather stations

	Political		Economic		Cultural
1969 (cont.)					
				June	– Agreement on degrees equivalency – Journalists, actors in Afghanistan for Soviet culture week
July	– Military delegation in Afghanistan				
		Sept	– Agricultural minister in USSR	Sept	– Editors in USSR
				Nov	– Agreement on joint archaeological expedition
Dec	– Defence minister Grechko in Afghanistan	Dec	– Contract for road construction – Protocol on diesel power station – Power station opened at Jalalabad	Dec	– Cultural delegation in USSR
1970					
		Jan	– Protocol on gas deliveries to USSR		
		Feb	– Deputy minister of chemical industry in USSR – Protocol on sugar sales to Afghanistan – Section of Kabul–Shibarghan highway completed		
Mar	– Army commander in USSR to observe manoeuvres – Chief of Staff in USSR	Mar	– Trade delegation in USSR: protocol for 1970		
		May	– Agreement on agricultural laboratories		
		June	– Protocol on cotton pest control		
		July	– Transport delegation in Afghanistan: new transit agreement – Another flour mill completed in Kabul		
Aug	– Premier stops in Moscow en route to Yuyoslavia	Aug	– Minister of mines in USSR – Protocol on Kandahar irrigation project – Minister of communications in USSR to discuss expanded services		
Sept	– King, Queen stop in USSR en route to Czechoslovakia	Sept	– Planning minister in Tadzhikistan for seminar		

Political	Economic	Cultural
1970 (cont.)		
Oct – Deputy premier stops in Moscow en route to New York	Oct – Veterinarians in Moscow for conference	Oct – Cultural protocol for 1971
	Nov – CPR loan for consumer purchases ($2.4m) – Agreement on Soviet advice in drafting new five-year plan	Nov – Agreement on malaria control programme
Dec – Defence minister in USSR on holiday	Dec – Trade protocol for 1971 – Irrigation minister in Afghanistan for opening of a Soviet-built state farm – Chinese-built farms, textile factory completed – Protocol on oil and gas college in Mazar-i-Sharif – Agreement on oil sales to Afghanistan – Contract for gas pipe-line across Amu Darya – Trade delegation in CPR: new agreement	Dec – Education delegation in Afghanistan: new exchange agreement
	? – Reported credit ($3m)[28]	
1971		
	Jan – Trade delegation in Afghanistan: transit protocol – Agreement with CPR on hydro-electric station	
Feb – Exchange of delegations on 50th anniversary of friendship treaty		
	Mar – Soviet motor show opens in Kabul – Protocol on power line	
	Apr – Agreement on wheat deliveries to Afghanistan	
May – Defence minister again in USSR	May – Chinese-built poultry farm opens	
June – Deputy foreign minister Smirnov in Afghanistan		
	July – Sale of aircraft to Afghan airlines	
	Aug – Shibarghan highway completed	Aug – Chinese aid to flood victims – Public health official in CPR

	Political		Economic		Cultural
1971 (cont.)					
Sept	– Infantry commander in USSR – KING, QUEEN IN USSR for 10-day state visit before holiday in Crimea	Sept	– USSR agrees to help in 4th five-year plan	Sept	– Aid to flood victims
		Oct	– Protocol on veterinary co-operation		
				Nov	– Further aid to flood, drought victims
Dec	– King again in Moscow on unofficial 2-day visit	?	– CREDIT AGREEMENT for road construction ($5m)		

References

[1] Christopher D. Lee, "Russian Trade with Seven Countries of Central Asia and the Middle East, 1945-1953", Mizan, July-August 1968, p. 131.

[2] The Pathans, kinsmen of the Afghans living in the frontier province in north-west Pakistan known as Pashtunistan, had been agitating for independence since 1947 and Afghanistan supported their demand for a plebiscite.

[3] For a fuller discussion of American policy in Afghanistan, as it related to Soviet-Afghan relations, see Louis Dupree, "Afghanistan's Big Gamble", American Universities Field Staff, IV, 4 (2 May, 1960) and William Ballis, "Recent Soviet Relations with Afghanistan", Bulletin, Institute for the Study of the USSR, June 1966, pp. 3-13.

[4] R.T. Akhramovich, writing in Sovetskoye Vostokovedeniye, No. 4, 1958 (summarized in Central Asian Review, No. 3, 1959, pp. 291-97).

[5] Pravda, 4 March, 1960.

[6] See, for instance, Pravda, 24 March and 3 April, 1961; also K. Smirnov, in Izvestiya, 9 September, 1961.

[7] Afghan imports from Pakistan doubled between 1960 and 1961 (on the eve of the last Pashtun crisis) and 1964 and 1965; over-all trade increased by 50 per cent. See Louis Dupree, "Afghanistan: 1966", American Universities Field Staff, X, 4 (July 1966), p. 30, citing official Afghan sources.

[8] Pravda, 1 June, 1969.

[9] Bibliografiya Afganistana (1965) lists about 1,000 Russian monographs and articles on Afghanistan from 1955 to the end of 1964; the most significant of these – including the works of R.T. Akhramovich, the most eminent Soviet student of Afghanistan – are reviewed in quarterly issues of Central Asian Review from 1956 on (in a section entitled "Borderlands in the Soviet Press").

[10] Sovremennyy Afganistan, 1960, p. 275 (reviewed in Central Asian Review, No. 2, 1961, pp. 206-19).

[11] Pravda, 27 May, 1969.

[12] Pravda, 15 September, 1971.

[13] The loan, according to Afghan sources, was for $40 million; Radio Kabul, 22 May, 1972.

[14] The Far East and Australasia, 1970, p. 146.

[15] The total given in the U.S. State Department estimate up to the end of 1971 is $705 million (RECS-3, 15 May, 1972, p. 7). A 1965 Russian estimate, brought up to the end of 1971 by reported loans since 1965, is $621 million (USSR and the Developing Countries, p. 55). Two estimates by American scholars, updated to the end of 1970, are respectively $520 million and $521 million (Janos Horvath, "Economic Aid Flow from the USSR: A Recount of the First Fifteen Years", Slavic Review, December 1970, p. 625 and Goldman, Soviet Foreign Aid, p. 116. The estimates in the Chronology above total $673 million.

[16] Radio Moscow, 28 December, 1971.

[17] For greater detail on Soviet programmes, see L.B. Teplinskiy, Sovetsko-afganskiye otnosheniya, 1919-1960, 1961, especially Chapter VI; Yu.M. Golovin, Sovetskiy soyuz i Afganistan, 1962; Goldman, Soviet Foreign Aid, Chapter 5; Welles Hangen, "Afghanistan", Yale Review, October 1966, pp. 66-68; and R.K. Ramazani, "Afghanistan and the USSR", Middle East Journal, Spring 1958, pp. 144-52.

[18] U.S. Department of State, RSE-65, 5 September, 1969, p. 8. According to Afghan sources, the Soviet Union accounted for 50 per cent of total Afghan trade as early as 1960; see Louis Dupree, American Universities Field Staff, IV, 4, p. 3.

[19] Joshua and Gibert, Arms for the Third World, p. 73, citing Western news sources; see also Adelphi Papers, No. 28 (October 1966), p. 36.

[20] U.S. Department of State, RSES-35, 12 August, 1970, p. 79 and RSES-34, 30 August, 1971, p. 18.

[21] Pravda, 24 August, 1970.

[22] Sources vary on Soviet credits in 1954. The two credits indicated are reported in Afganistan (spravochnik), 1964, p. 201. Afghan sources, however, show the

credits in 1954 as high as $17.3 million. American Universities Field Staff, South Asia Series, IV, 4 (2 May, 1960), pp. 9-10.

[23] Oriente Moderno, August-September 1957, cited in Central Asian Review, No. 1, 1958, p. 74.

[24] Goldman, op. cit., p. 118.

[25] Ibid., p. 116, citing Afghan government sources;

Soviet sources note a credit at this time but do not show the amount.

[26] U.S. Department of State, RSB-50, 17 June, 1966, p. 2.

[27] U.S. Department of State, RSB-80, 21 July, 1967, p. 4.

[28] U.S. Department of State, RECS-15, 22 September, 1971, p. 6.

Soviet economic relations with Burma between 1952 and 1955 paved the way to closer political relations. A number of trade delegations were exchanged after the Moscow Economic Conference of March 1952, leading to a three-year agreement in mid-1955. The good will generated in these negotiations led to an invitation to U Nu to visit the USSR in October 1955 – the first Third World leader after Nehru to do so – and to the inclusion of Burma on the Bulganin-Khrushchev tour of South Asia a month later. Mikoyan, leading a high-level delegation to Rangoon in early 1956, extended the 1955 trade agreement to 1960 and negotiated an aid agreement, the first in the Third World after the agreements with Afghanistan. Other economic and political exchanges followed.

Soviet commentaries on Burma during these early years were cordial but on the whole superficial and, compared to coverage of developments in India, Indonesia and the Middle East, not especially voluminous. An article marking the ninth anniversary of Burma's independence in January 1957 noted gradual economic growth in the ex-colony and ascribed this to the government's role in developing a "state-capitalist sector" – seen in this instance as a healthy trend.[1] An article marking Burma's 10th anniversary reviewed developments over the decade, accenting the cordial relations between the two countries, but showed little insight into Burma's problems; it virtually ignored, for instance, the various insurrections that continued to harass the government.[2] The first serious and sustained treatment of Burmese developments in a Soviet publication appeared only at the end of 1958, in a volume that carried an Introduction by U Nu and included articles by both Russian and Burmese scholars.[3]

The political crisis in Burma during the summer of 1958 was the first such crisis in a developing nation befriended by the USSR since Moscow's shift in Third World strategies after Stalin. The question of how properly to respond caused the Russians some perplexity. Vladimir Kudryavtsev, the Izvestiya commentator and often a tester of diplomatic waters for the Russian Foreign Ministry, saw the split in the Anti-Fascist People's Freedom League (AFPFL) as a consequence of "American intrigue", seeking to divert Burma from its neutralist course; U Nu, in Kudryavtsev's view, was the Burmese leader most identified with this course, but he did not suggest U Nu was the only one who could maintain it.[4] When General Ne Win assumed control in September, at the request of the government, the Russians maintained a discreet silence for some months. Their coolness towards the "caretaker" regime was made clear during the following year. A.S. Kaufman, for instance, in a pamphlet that went to press in May 1959, noted that the "favourable basis for negotiations" with Communist insurgents which U Nu had established in January 1958 had been rejected by Ne Win when he came to power; Ne Win refused "equal negotiations".[5] In July, a writer in Pravda noted reactionary tendencies in Burma – such as the attitude of the three major Rangoon newspapers (the Nation, Guardian and Tribune) towards Burma's entry into SEATO and the presence of a Burmese observer at a recent SEATO conference – and remarked that these tendencies "meet no opposition from the side of ruling circles in Burma".[6] An article by Kaufman in October was more explicit: Burma, he wrote, was one of the few

Asian countries which had not regained pre-war levels in its economy; the current economic plan was criticized for curtailing, not expanding, industrial production; foreign investments were still being sought; American loans had been accepted for arming the police; the civil war (this was the first mention of it in Soviet journals in some years) dragged on; arrests were increasing; the motive in splitting the AFPFL had been to remove the neutralist U Nu and pave the way for the militarists, whom U Ba Swe, U Nu's opponent and the architect of the split, supported. U Nu was sympathetically quoted as saying that the situation in Burma was "many times worse than it might seem at first glance".[7]

The Russians, it appears from these commentaries, had become unambiguously hostile towards the "caretaker government" by the end of 1959 and sympathetic towards U Nu. They had undoubtedly been helped in this direction by awkward incidents involving Soviet personnel in Burma earlier in the year: the attempted escape in April, for instance, of a Soviet military attaché and the defection in June of a diplomat, Aleksandr Kaznacheyev, who subsequently revealed much of the inner workings of the Soviet embassy in Rangoon.[8]

U Nu's return to power following the elections of February 1960 (the month of Khrushchev's second visit to Burma) prompted less rejoicing in the Soviet press than might have been expected. To be sure, commentaries on Burma were less critical than during 1959, but the enthusiasm of the pre-"caretaker" era was not recaptured. Continued investments by foreign capital were criticized;[9] American influence and growing separatist tendencies among the non-Burman peoples (e.g. the Shan and Karen) were deplored.[10] The two years of U Nu's second government, in short, were marked by a lingering malaise in the Burmese-Russian relationship.

U Nu himself was not accorded the favour shown him in Soviet commentaries after 1955. Articles marking the 14th anniversary of Burmese independence in January 1962, for instance, applauded Burma's neutralism and spoke approvingly of the development of a "state sector" in the economy but made little explicit reference to the Burmese premier.[11] U Nu, it is clear, was not a Third World leader the Russians could easily embrace during an era when they were affirming Marxist doctrine with greater force (as, goaded by China, they were at this time). His mysticism had grown with the years as his professed Marxism declined. His extraordinary return to power in 1960 on a predominantly Buddhist platform had made him even more of a religious fanatic than he had been before. The Russians accordingly were undismayed when Ne Win, in March 1962, resolved the problem of mounting chaos in Burma by seizing power in the name of a Revolutionary Council and arrested political leaders of all persuasions.

The Soviet response to the new regime, given the cool appraisal of the "caretaker" government two years earlier and continuing doubts in Moscow about the character of military regimes in general, was surprisingly warm. Russia recognized the Ne Win government immediately[12] and by May Soviet observers had begun to report favourably on its initial steps, especially the proclamation on "positive neutrality" and the decision to terminate the activities in Burma of two American institutions, the Ford and Asian Foundations.[13] Articles marking the 15th anniversary of Burma's independence, in January 1963, commended the Revolutionary Council for its economic reforms, in particular the nationalization of certain private trades and industries.[14]

It is probable that the views of R.A. Ul'yanovskiy, a Party official and Deputy Director of the Institute of the Peoples of Asia, had an important influence on the Soviet reappraisal of Burma in 1963 and 1964. Although Ul'yanovskiy apparently never visited Burma, he made a detailed study of the April 1962 programme of the Revolutionary Council, "Burmese Way to Socialism" (BWTS), and concluded that such a programme held forth prospects for an early transition to socialism. An article by Ul'yanovskiy in Pravda in early 1963 argued that Burma not only sought a socialist course but as a result of measures taken by the Revolutionary Council stood an excellent chance of achieving socialism.[15] In another article at the end of the year he considered that a confluence of circumstances - the alliance of workers and peasants under the "progressive" leadership of the Revolutionary Council, the nationalization measures already adopted, and Burma's traditional neutrality - allowed this country to set forth immediately on the "non-capitalist path of development".[16] Burma henceforth was listed in most Soviet commentaries as one of the half a dozen model states in Asia and Africa, along with Ghana, Guinea, Mali, Algeria and the UAR. It is easy to imagine that the endorsement of so influential a figure in the Orientalist community had as much to do with Burma's elevation in Soviet esteem as any economic measures undertaken by Ne Win. For Burma was in no sense "socialist" in 1963; or if it was, this was obscured by poverty and economic chaos.

Shortly after Ne Win came to power the Russians, for the first time in many years, appeared to take an interest in the Burmese Communists - or more correctly the White Flag Communists, whom Moscow supported over the Red Flag Communists after their split in 1946. The White Flag Communists had been in rebellion against the government since shortly after independence. Moscow accordingly ignored them during the period of rapprochement with the U Nu regime after 1955, except to note their periodic appeals for peace.[17] In 1963 prospects of a settlement excited Moscow's interest. Pravda, in June, reported new Communist proposals sympathetically and noted the government's pledge of safe-conduct for rebel negotiators,[18] including the White Flag leader, Than Tun. In November Ul'yanovskiy called the current talks "realistic" and a reflection of the improved atmosphere in the country with respect to the Communist issue.[19] The enthusiasm was short-lived. By the end of the year negotiations had broken down entirely and the Russians thereafter showed little interest in the fate of White Flag Communists in Burma.

Moscow's attitude towards the Burmese Communists was certainly affected by Sino-Soviet rivalry. During the 1950s there had apparently been a tacit understanding between the Russians and Chinese that the latter should advise the White Flag Communists (the Red Flags were of interest to neither side).[20] As the dispute between Moscow and Peking intensified, however, the Russians could not have been indifferent to who controlled the Burmese Communists; their sudden interest in the 1963 negotiations between Ne Win and Than Tun, at a time when Sino-Soviet rivalry was most critical, must be seen in this

light. The Russians had meanwhile been openly interested for some years in the legalized front organizations of the White Flag Communists, such as the Burma Workers' and Peasants' Party (BWPP) and the National United Front (NUF). In 1963 the Russians presumably felt that the best course for the Communists in Burma was to leave the jungle and, if possible, enter into an alliance with the Ne Win government - in much the same way that the Pathet Lao in 1962 had formally agreed to collaborate with the neutralists in Vientiane (see below, under Laos). Moscow, in short, stood a better chance of gaining influence in the BCP if it were in the open. The collapse of the negotiations with the Revolutionary Council meant the end of Moscow's project and the inevitable return of the Burmese Communists to the jungle - and, of course, to Chinese control. From 1963 on Peking's influence was clearly dominant in the BCP.[21]

Peking's ties with the Burmese Communists did not seriously strain diplomatic relations with successive governments in Rangoon, at least until the Cultural Revolution. A disagreement over the Sino-Burmese border in 1959 threatened for a time to cloud the relationship, but the successful resolution of the issue and the accompanying non-aggression treaty of 1960 led to even closer ties in the next few years. Indeed, to judge from the frequency of high diplomatic exchanges in the early 1960s, Peking's stature in Burma - despite its known support of the rebellious Burmese Communists - was higher than Moscow's. The impression is strengthened by the greater volume of trade between the two countries (nearly two and a half times greater than Soviet-Burmese trade during the five-year period 1962-66) and the larger credits offered (the Chinese credit of $84 million in 1961 - though not more than a third of it was used - was six times greater than known Soviet credits to Burma in the 1960s).

The apparent warmth of the Sino-Burmese relationship may explain a growing reserve in Soviet commentaries on Burma after 1963. Although Burma had now been acknowledged as a "progressive" state, well launched on the "non-capitalist path", the Burmese were not above criticism. The mounting national debt, for instance, was viewed with alarm by Soviet economists and ascribed to "immense expenditures in maintaining the state apparatus and armed forces"; the solution, A.N. Uzyanov wrote in September 1964, was to end civil strife in the country.[22] In early 1965, Kaufman spoke of "hasty nationalization" in Burma and consequent unemployment, shortage of consumer goods and declining GNP.[23] At the end of 1966 the same writer noted a drop of 4.6 per cent in agricultural production during the preceding year and laid this in part to shortcomings in the work of Ne Win's Burma Socialist Programme Party (BSPP), which "functions only in certain districts"; the chief difficulty, Kaufman wrote, was that "the organization of the masses lags behind the creation of a new social and economic structure".[24] A 1966 volume on socialist development by A.A. Galkin departed from the usual practice of linking Burmese socialism to socialism in Guinea, Mali and the UAR and likened it instead to Indian "socialism"; Galkin categorically rejected the claim of one Burmese that socialism in Burma was "a third path in the organization of life, the refuge of a new civilization" - in short, neither Communism nor Capitalism. Egyptian socialism, Galkin wrote, had evolved (as it properly should) from Right to Left;

"the concepts of Burmese socialists have evolved from Left to Right".[25] It was some years since remarks so unflattering to the Burmese had appeared in Soviet publications.

During 1967 Sino-Burmese relations deteriorated sharply. Efforts by the Chinese Embassy to extend the Cultural Revolution to the overseas Chinese community in Rangoon led to rioting and fierce anti-Chinese demonstrations in May, which in turn brought all activity between the two nations to a standstill. Chinese advisers were sent home and correspondents expelled. Skeleton staffs maintained the embassies in each country. The Chinese press meanwhile mounted a vitriolic campaign against the "fascist" government in Rangoon and against Ne Win, the "Chiang Kai-shek of Burma".[26] Chinese Army units, meanwhile, were reported to have set up bases in Burmese territory south of the border and to have actively aided the various insurgent groups; rebel leaders appeared publicly in Peking and used Chinese press and radio facilities to denounce the Rangoon government.[27]

The 1967 crisis in Sino-Burmese relations led to an improvement in Russia's relations with Rangoon, just as cordial Sino-Burmese relations a few years earlier had affected the Soviet-Burmese relationship in an opposite sense. Exchanges were stepped up and press coverage of Burma became less critical. An article by V. Vasil'yev, marking the 20th anniversary of Burma's independence in 1968, noted continuing economic difficulties and the low participation of the masses in economic life, but the tone of the article was sanguine.[28] A series of articles by Yu. Lugovskoy, following a second visit to Burma in 1968, noted many improvements since his 1961 visit (see reference 10); he commended in particular recent moves to nationalize additional sectors of the economy.[29] In June 1969 the reported end of Karen and Shan resistance was applauded as a step towards "national stability"; henceforth the "main task" was to persuade "the several thousand extremists, and those among the national minorities misled by them, to return to their normal everyday occupations".[30] The "extremists" were of course the remaining Communist guerrillas under Maoist influence. Ul'yanovskiy, writing on the occasion of the 22nd anniversary, accented the gains of the Burmese revolution – such as the control by the state sector of 80 per cent of the extractive industries and 60 per cent of the processing industries – and minimized the shortcomings; he believed that the long drawn out insurrection of "feudal separatists" and "insurgent organizations like the 'Red Flag' and 'White Flag'" was at last on the decline.[31] Two Pravda correspondents at the end of 1970, while acknowledging the continuing difficulties of the Ne Win regime, blamed them on agitation from outside the country, especially by the former premier U Nu, rather than on incompetence and confusion at home.[32]

A. Malov, the foremost specialist on Burma among Soviet correspondents, was not altogether sanguine about the quality of the Burmese Socialist Programme Party as "the leading force in Burma", but he hailed its first congress in June 1971 as a major landmark in Burmese political life.[33] Podgornyy, on a state visit to Burma later in the year, said that the "conversion of the BSPP to a mass party and its implementation of a consistently revolutionary-democratic course" guaranteed Burma's steady progress in the years ahead.[34] Commentaries during 1971 were normally in this more charitable vein.

More charitable commentaries, however, and

improved relations with Rangoon during an era when Sino-Burmese ties were strained did not guarantee a Russian advantage when relations between Peking and Rangoon were normalized after the Cultural Revolution. The return of ambassadors and full embassy staffs early in 1971 paved the way for Ne Win's state visit to China in August, which in turn paved the way for the resumption of Chinese aid projects and renewed trade agreements in the months following.[35] China again became Burma's principal economic partner, and the importance the Burmese attached to this restored relationship is indicated by the government's forbearance with respect to the Burmese Communist radio station in China that continued to excoriate Ne Win's regime.[36] Why indeed the Chinese themselves tolerated this clandestine radio is unclear, but one reason was doubtless Peking's assurance that the Ne Win government did not greatly mind. The White Flag remnants posed no grave threat to Rangoon by 1971 and both Chinese and Burmese may have felt it to be less trouble to humour the Burmese Communists than to silence them. The double aspect of Chinese behaviour, in any case, is a reminder to Western analysts that relations between Asian states are not always conducted on a single plane: China was able to resume diplomatic ties with Burma while maintaining contact with Burmese Communists in a way that Russia surely could not.

Aid and Trade

Soviet aid to Burma appears to have been parsimonious, especially in view of the persistent listing of Burma after 1963 as one of the half a dozen "progressive" states in Asia and Africa. Apart from the initial credits of 1956-57, extended in the form of an exchange of gifts and totalling an estimated $15 million, no other credits have been identified. Several of the early projects – for instance, a stadium, conference hall and luxury hotel – seem trivial. Later projects, such as the dam and irrigation system on the Kyetmauktaung river, were more relevant to Burma's needs, but proceeded slowly. In 1971 the Russians were said to have no more than 18 aid technicians in Burma, participating in two projects – a river valley development programme and mine rehabilitation – although they had proposed assistance in many others.[37] No military aid was received from the USSR, though Burma received American arms in some quantity during the 1960s.[38]

Trade between the two countries was also slight. Burma ranked 22nd in Soviet trade with 43 Afro-Asian nations during the period 1965-68; Chinese trade with Burma, except during the years of the Cultural Revolution, appears to have remained significantly higher than Russian. Russia's share of Burmese trade in 1967 was about four per cent, a trifling proportion when compared to Russia's share of the foreign trade of other favoured nations in Asia and the Middle East: 50 per cent of Afghanistan's, for instance, or 23 per cent of Egypt's.

Soviet policy in Burma was paradoxical, it is clear from the foregoing record. On the one hand, Russian spokesmen expressed persistent ideological sympathy towards Burma after 1963 (punctuated to be sure by occasional criticism, but persistent none the less); on the other hand, Russia's outlay in Burma was negligible. So wide a discrepancy between what the Russians said of Burma and what they did there raises questions about the efficacy of Soviet strategies. Why, except during the Cultural Revolution and its immediate aftermath, were Burma's relations with Moscow no more cordial than with Peking despite China's constant support of the White Flag Communists? How was it that Americans rather than Russians sold arms to the "socialist" Burmese? Why were Russia's relations with Burma so much less intimate than with other "progressive" nations favoured in Moscow?

The answer to these questions lies in part in the stubborn quality of Burmese neutrality and isolationism. Burma was a reluctant ally of all Great Powers and all had difficulties with Rangoon at one time or another. Soviet strategies, therefore, were not necessarily at fault if the Burmese deliberately kept the Russians at arm's length. But the Russians, just as deliberately, appear to have wanted a low-keyed relationship with the Burmese once Burma's neutrality was assured. A defensive relationship – as with the Afghans, for instance – was impractical in Burma given the distance separating the two countries and Russia's inability to guarantee Burmese security. An extensive financial commitment, given the uncertain state of Burma's economy and the political instability in the nation, was also unwise. Meanwhile, too great a show of interest in Burma might cause resentment in New Delhi, where there was already uneasiness after 1965 over Soviet attention to Pakistan. The Russians accordingly chose the relatively innocuous course of showing good will towards Rangoon by professing enthusiasm for Burma's "way to socialism", but without staking too much on its success. If the enthusiasm was premature and sometimes too shrill for Burmese realities, this was of no great consequence. Delays and set-backs could always be explained away as the consequence of "imperialist" manoeuvre and the Russians in the meantime gained credit in Rangoon for their sympathy.

Chronology

(See explanatory note on tables, p. 6.)

	Political	Economic	Cultural
Pre-1955			
Jan 1948	Independence; diplomatic relations with USSR		
Dec 1949	Burma recognizes CPR		
		Apr 1954 — Trade agreement with CPR	
June 1954	Chou En-lai in Burma		
Dec 1954	U Nu in CPR		
1955			
Apr	— Chou En-lai in Burma en route to and from Bandung		
		July — 3-year trade agreement with USSR	
Sept	— General Ne Win heads military delegation to CPR		
Oct	— U NU IN USSR for 2-week visit	Oct — Trade delegation in USSR: protocol on July agreement	
		Nov — Air service agreement with CPR	
Dec	— KHRUSHCHEV, BULGANIN IN BURMA for 7-day visit	Dec — Aid promised for industrial, agricultural projects	

BURMA

	Political		Economic		Cultural
1956					
		Mar	– Mikoyan in Burma for aid talks; AGREEMENT ON GIFT EXCHANGE: technical institute, hospital, stadium for Burmese rice[39]; 1955 trade agreement extended to 1960		
		May	– Economic delegation in USSR		
				Oct	– Dancers in USSR
Nov	– U Nu in CPR for talks on Kuomintang troops in North Burma	Nov	– Contract for tractor plant, irrigation system: Soviet experts to work in Burma		
Dec	– Chou En-lai in Burma	Dec	– CPR promises aid for textile mill	Dec	– Academicians in Burma
1957					
		Jan	– Economic delegation in USSR: protocol on 1956 agreement		
		Feb	– Trade protocol for 1957		
Mar	– U Nu in CPR for holiday and border talks				
June	– Parliamentary delegation in USSR				
Nov	– Deputy prime minister in USSR				
		Dec	– CREDIT AGREEMENTS for tractor plant and irrigation system[40]		
1958					
Jan	– Supreme Soviet delegation in Burma	Jan	– CPR credit for textile mill ($4.2m)		
		Mar	– Agreement on construction of hotel in Rangoon		
May	– Parliamentary delegation in USSR				
				Aug	– Cultural delegation in USSR
Sept	– Ne Win forms caretaker government in Burma after preelection crisis			Sept	– Co-operative delegation in USSR

	Political	Economic	Cultural
1959			
Jan	– CP delegation in USSR for XXI congress		
June	– Soviet diplomat defects in Rangoon		June – TU delegation in USSR
Oct	– Parliamentary delegation under Mukhitdinov stops in Burma en route to Indonesia		
Dec	– Supreme Soviet official in Burma		
1960			
Jan	– CPR military delegation in Burma – Ne Win in CPR: border agreement, non-aggression treaty		
Feb	– KHRUSHCHEV IN BURMA en route to Indonesia – Elections in Burma: U Nu returned to power		
Apr	– Chou En-lai in Burma en route to India		
		June – Trade protocol for 1960	
Sept	– U Nu, Ne Win on separate visits to CPR		
Oct	– Sino-Burmese border treaty		
			Nov – Cultural delegation in USSR
1961			
Jan	– Chou En-lai heads delegation to Burma	Jan – CPR credit for 6 years ($84m)	
Apr	– Ne Win to USSR via Peking – U Nu in CPR on holiday – Foreign minister Chen Yi twice in China on trip to Indonesia		
		June – Trade protocol for 1961	June – Medical delegation in Burma
July	– Government delegation in Burma for opening of hospital, technical institute, hotel		July – Buddhist delegation in USSR
Oct	– U Nu, Ne Win again on separate visits to CPR	Oct – Aid to flood victims	

BURMA

	Political		Economic		Cultural
1962					
		Feb	- Economic delegation in USSR: protocol on irrigation project and theatre - Civil aviation delegation in USSR to open Rangoon–Moscow air route		
Mar	- U Nu overthrown; revolutionary council under Ne Win takes power				
Apr	- Revolutionary council releases programme "Burmese way to socialism"				
June	- Air force chief Vershinin stops in Burma en route to Indonesia			June	- Education delegation in USSR - Journalists in USSR
		Aug	- Further protocol on irrigation and dam project at Kyetmauktaung		
		Oct	- Rice sales agreement		
Dec	- CPR delegation in Burma to explain Sino-Soviet dispute				
1963					
				Jan	- Gift of books to technical institute
				Feb	- Education delegation in USSR - Cultural delegation in Burma: expanded programme planned
		Mar	- Trade protocol for 1963 - Contract for tractor deliveries - Contract for oil delivery		
Apr	- Defence minister Malinovskiy in Burma - Liu Shao-chi, Chen Yi in Burma				
Sept	- Foreign minister in USSR - Secretary of United Workers party in USSR on holiday			Sept	- Writers in USSR - Education delegation in USSR
Oct	- Revolutionary council delegation in USSR				

	Political	Economic	Cultural

1963 (cont.)

Nov - Abortive talks between Burmese government and White flag communists

Dec - Technical mission in Burma to survey Kyetmauktaung projects

---

1964

Jan - Rice sales agreement

Feb - Chou En-lai, Chen Yi in Burma

Mar - Gift of smallpox vaccine

May - Air service agreement

July - Supreme Soviet delegation under Mikoyan stops in Burma on visit to Indonesia

Aug - Supplementary protocol on Kyetmauktaung projects

Nov - Deputy foreign minister Firyubin in Burma

Dec - Chen Yi in Burma on trip to Indonesia

1965

Apr - Chou En-lai twice in Burma on trip to Pakistan

July - Ne Win in CPR

Aug - Chen Yi in Burma on trip to Indonesia

Sept - NE WIN IN USSR for 10-day visit

Nov - Protocol on irrigation projects

Dec - Rice sales agreement
- Bridge built by CPR opens

1966

Jan - Aid to flood victims

Mar - Deputy foreign minister Firyubin in Burma

Mar - Soviet industrial fair opens in Rangoon

Mar - Ballet dancers in Burma

Apr - Liu Shao-chi, Chen Yi in Burma

BURMA

	Political		Economic		Cultural
1966 (cont.)					
				Aug	– Journalists in USSR
Sept	– Ne Win in United States				
Oct	– Firyubin again in Burma	Oct	– Burma withdraws from sterling bloc		
Dec	– Supreme Soviet delegation in Burma en route to Cambodia	Dec	– Economic delegation in USSR		

	Political		Economic		Cultural
1967					
				Jan	– TU delegation in Burma – Journalists in USSR
				Apr	– Delegation from technical institute in USSR to study university system
May–June	– Anti-Chinese demonstrations in Rangoon; Chinese advisers expelled				
				July	– Welfare workers in Moscow to study social programmes
				Aug	– Red Cross delegation in USSR
				Sept	– Soviet art exhibition opens in Rangoon
				Dec	– Cultural delegation in Burma

	Political		Economic		Cultural
1968					
Jan	– Chinese correspondents expelled				
		May	– Aid to flood victims	May	– Radio delegation in Burma – Science professors in USSR to study teaching techniques
June	– Deputy foreign minister in USSR	June	– Trade delegation in USSR	June	– Gift of additional smallpox vaccine – Editors in USSR – Education delegation in USSR
				Aug	– Film delegation in USSR
Sept	– CP leader Than Tun assassinated				
				Nov	– Red Cross delegation in Burma

	Political		Economic		Cultural
1969					
		Apr	– Soviet civil pilots demonstrate aircraft in Burma		

Political	Economic	Cultural
1969 (cont.)		

		June - TU delegation in USSR
		        - Film and radio delega-
		          tion in USSR

		July - Information ministry delegation in USSR

	Dec - Agreement on
	       opening of mine
	       at Mawkhi	

1970		
		Jan - Radio, TV delegation in Burma
		Mar - Film delegation in Burma

	Apr - Civil aviation delega-
	       tion in Burma: new
	       air agreement
		Apr - Gift of smallpox
		       vaccine
		       - TU delegation in
		         Burma

		Sept - Baptist delegation in Burma

	Oct - Industrial development
	       leader in Tashkent
	       for conference
	       - Trade delegation
	         in CPR	

		Nov - Cultural delegation in USSR
1971		

Apr   - Clandestine CP
       radio station
       opens in CPR
		Apr - Gift of medical equipment

May - First congress of BSPP		

	June - Offer of oil refinery
	       in exchange for rice
	       - Technical delegation
	         in USSR
		June - Gift of additional vaccine

Aug - Ne Win in China on 6-day state visit		
		Sept - TU delegation in USSR

Oct   - Podgornyy stops in
       Rangoon en route
       to and from Hanoi
	Oct - Agreement with CPR
	       on resumption of 1961
	       aid programme
	       - Chinese minister of
	         economic relations
	         in Rangoon for aid
	         talks
		Oct - Red Cross officials in USSR

BURMA

Political	Economic	Cultural

1971 (cont.)

	Economic	Cultural

	Nov - Deputy trade minister
	       in Rangoon for
	       exhibition
	     - Trade minister in CPR
	       for Canton fair: trade
	       agreement
		Nov - Cultural delegation
		       in Burma

	Dec - Chinese light industries delegation in Burma	

References

[1] A.S. Kaufman, writing in Sovetskoye Vostokovedeniye, No. 1 (January–February), 1957, pp. 36–49.

[2] A.N. Uzyanov, in Sovetskoye Vostokovedeniye, No. 1 (January–February), 1958, pp. 10–17.

[3] Birmanskiy soyuz, 1958. The Russian contributors included specialists such as Kaufman, Uzyanov, and V.F. Vasil'yev; among the Burmese contributors was U Thant.

[4] Sovremennyy Vostok, No. 8 (August), 1962, p. 62.

[5] A.S. Kaufman, Gosudarstvennyy stroy Birmy, 1959, p. 19 (cited in Yuva Newsletter, April 1962, p. 11).

[6] I. Mairov in Pravda, 30 July, 1959.

[7] International Affairs, No. 10 (October), 1959, pp. 96–100.

[8] Kaznacheyev deals with the episode of the military attaché, Colonel Strygin, as well as his own escape, in his book Inside a Soviet Embassy, pp. 182ff.

[9] E.g. A. Lavrent'yev, writing in Vneshnyaya torgovlya, No. 1 (January), 1961, pp. 24–25; G. Klimko, in Mirovaya ekonomika i mezhdunarodnyye otnosheniya, No. 5 (May), 1961, pp. 105–10.

[10] See articles by Yu. Lugovskoy in Aziya i Afrika segodnya, No. 12 (December), 1961, pp. 36–39 and New Times, No. 36, 1961, pp. 24–28; the articles were based on a recent visit to Burma.

[11] E.g. Pravda, 4 and 5 January, 1962, and Trud, 4 January, 1962.

[12] TASS, 9 March, 1962.

[13] M. Aleksandrov, in Pravda, 13 May, 1962.

[14] E.g. Pravda Vostoka, 4 January, 1963 and Pravda, 17, 20, 23 and 28 February, 1963.

[15] Pravda, 15 March, 1963.

[16] R. Ul'yanovskiy, "Birma na novom puti razvitiya", Narody Azii i Afriki, No. 6 (November–December), 1963 (reviewed in Yuva Newsletter, May 1964, pp. 13–16). Another important article on Burmese socialism by Ul'yanovskiy, co-edited with N.P. Anikeyev, is "Programma natsional'nogo vozrozhdeniya (filosofiya partii 'Birmanskiy put' k sotsializmu')", Narody Azii i Afriki, No. 4 (July–August), 1964, pp. 3–11.

[17] Communist peace feelers in 1956 were reported in For a Lasting Peace, For a People's Democracy!

16 March, 1956, p. 4; proposals in 1958 were referred to, inter alia, in Kaufman's 1959 study, cited above.

[18] Pravda, 16 June, 1963, citing a TASS report from Rangoon.

[19] Narody Azii i Afriki, No. 6 (November–December), 1963, p. 43.

[20] Such an understanding is reported in Kaznacheyev, op. cit., pp. 143ff (as well as in an interview with the author in 1960). He notes that on at least one occasion the Russians made direct contact with Burmese Communist leaders to assure them Moscow had not forgotten them while cultivating better relations with the Burmese government; this was during the visit to Rangoon in January 1958 of B.G. Gafurov, a high Party official and Director of the Institute of the Peoples of Asia.

[21] For a fuller treatment of the Burmese Communists and their relations with Moscow and Peking through the mid-1960s, see the chapter by John H. Badgley in Scalapino, ed., The Communist Revolution in Asia, pp. 290–308.

[22] Aziya i Afrika segodnya, No. 9 (September), 1964, p. 17.

[23] International Affairs, No. 2 (February), 1965, p. 69.

[24] Izvestiya, 27 December, 1966.

[25] A.A. Galkin, Stroitel'stvo kommunizma i mirovaya revolyutsiya, 1966, p. 275.

[26] For a discussion of Sino-Burmese relations during this era, see W.A.C. Adie in Mizan, November–December 1967, pp. 238–41; also Frank N. Trager, "Sino-Burmese Relations: the End of the Pauk-Phaw Era", Orbis, Winter 1968, pp. 1039–45.

[27] These denunciations appear in regular coverage of the Chinese radio and press (as in Mizan or daily Foreign Broadcast Information Service bulletins). The clandestine activity of the Chinese, however, is more difficult to verify, especially during the leadership struggles triggered by the assassination of Than Tun by a disgruntled colleague in September 1968. Coverage of Western intelligence reports is given in Robert A. Holmes, "China-Burma Relations since the Rift", Asian Survey, August 1972, pp. 688ff; see also Trends and Highlights, especially Nos. 280, 283, 290 and 292.

[28] Aziya i Afrika segodnya, No. 1 (January), 1968, pp. 2–3; see also Pravda, 31 May, 1968.

[29] Aziya i Afrika segodnya, Nos. 11 and 12 (November and December), 1968 and New Times, Nos. 26, 27 and 29, 1968.

[30] Z. Novikova, "Moving Towards National Stability", International Affairs, No. 6 (June), 1969, pp. 96-97.

[31] Pravda, 4 January, 1970.

[32] A. Filippov and N. Novikov, Pravda, 16 December, 1970; U Nu was released from detention in 1969 and thereafter attempted in London and Bangkok to organize resistance to the Ne Win regime.

[33] A. Malov in Aziya i Afrika segodnya, No. 4 (April), 1971, pp. 28-31; Pravda, 28 June, 1971; and Aziya i Afrika segodnya, No. 11 (November), 1971, pp. 4-7.

[34] Pravda, 4 October, 1971.

[35] An agreement signed in Rangoon in October 1971 provided for the use of the balance of the 1961 loan, of which there was $56.7 million left when Chinese aid was suspended in 1967; payments on the loan were deferred to 1980. A trade agreement signed in Peking in November opened up the borders of the two countries which had been closed for several years.

[36] The "Voice of the People of Burma" radio station was inaugurated in March 1971, apparently near the Burmese border in China. Its goal, according to a broadcast on the day of inauguration, was to fight the twin evils – "Soviet revisionism" and "Ne Win's Burmese Way to Socialism"; Trends and Highlights, No. 311 (1 August, 1971), p. 5. Broadcasts from this station monitored in the following months underscored this goal: Ne Win, for instance, was castigated as a "reactionary" during his visit to Peking in August and Podgornyy was condemned as a "revisionist" of the Khrushchev mould during his visit to Rangoon in October (broadcasts of 5 August and 21 October, respectively – these clandestine broadcasts are reviewed periodically in Trends and Highlights and USSR and Third World).

[37] USSR and Third World, No. 6, 1971, p. 288, citing Western sources; also U.S. Department of State, RSES-34, 30 August, 1971, p. 92.

[38] See New York Times, 25 August, 1970, reporting American arms sales of an estimated $80 million from 1958 to the end of 1969. These purchases were terminated in 1970, either out of deference to China or because Ne Win felt they jeopardized Burmese neutralism; see Robert A. Holmes, "China-Burma Relations since the Rift", Asian Survey, August 1972, p. 692.

[39] No credit figure was indicated for this agreement; Goldman, Soviet Foreign Aid, p. 142, estimates the construction cost of the projects at $5-10 million.

[40] Again, no figure was given for these agreements at the time. Subsequent Soviet sources show a credit at this juncture of $4-5 million; Krasnaya zvezda, 4 January, 1964.

4. RELATIONS WITH CAMBODIA

The course of Soviet-Cambodian relations ran smoothly from the establishment of diplomatic relations in 1956 to Sihanouk's fall in March 1970. Political relations were correct (with one brief exception, noted below); cultural relations were friendly; economic relations were sustained, if modest. As was the case in Burma, there was some slackening of Soviet interest in Cambodian affairs after the first flush of enthusiasm following Sihanouk's 1956 visit to the USSR, but interest revived during the 1960s as the war widened in Vietnam.

Cambodia, in Soviet eyes, was a model neutralist state in the Third World - that is, independent enough to resist being drawn into Western alliances, yet cordial towards the USSR. Sihanouk's refusal to join SEATO, a Pravda correspondent wrote after interviewing him in March 1956, established his credentials as a neutralist.[1] Cambodian neutrality was the central theme of another Pravda article two months later, marking the establishment of diplomatic relations between the two countries.[2] On the occasion of the fifth anniversary of Cambodia's independence, in 1958, a Soviet commentator predicted that "Cambodia will continue unswervingly to conduct a policy of peace and non-participation in aggressive blocs and military ventures".[3] On the sixth anniversary, Pravda's Viktor Mayevskiy wrote that cordial Soviet-Cambodian relations, despite differences in the social systems of the two countries, reflected "the policy of peaceful coexistence in action, the policy to which the future belongs".[4] Observations such as these - none of them especially edifying - predominated in Soviet commentaries on Cambodia during the latter part of the 1950s.

There was no significant shift in Soviet commentaries during the 1960s. Cambodia's patriarchal system and semi-feudal economy might well have been the target of Soviet commentators early in the decade, when Third World doctrines were more taut, but political tension in South-East Asia was too real to encourage ideological irrelevancies. Cambodia's continuing neutrality mattered more and, to ensure it, the Russians gave eloquent verbal support to Prince Sihanouk's repeated calls for a conference on the neutralization of Cambodia - calls which were especially insistent after the Geneva conference of 1961-62 on Laos. Khrushchev personally endorsed such a conference on several occasions;[5] the Soviet government officially did likewise.[6]

No conference on Cambodia was held in the end and one must question whether the Russians seriously wanted one. During the last years of Khrushchev's rule, the Soviet Union appeared to disengage somewhat from South-East Asia and this undoubtedly lessened Moscow's interest in another full-scale conference like the Geneva conferences of 1954 and 1961-62; if Cambodian neutrality could be assured by other means, that was preferable. Khrushchev's heirs, meanwhile, were more reserved than he in responding to Cambodian calls for a conference, especially after their decision to support the North Vietnamese more vigorously. Mikoyan, for instance, replied politely but evasively to another appeal by Sihanouk for a Cambodian conference in late February 1965.[7] Gromyko, six weeks later, was even more evasive.[8] The Russians evidently felt that a conference devoted solely to Cambodia would distract attention from the central problems in South-East Asia and engage energies needlessly. It was more prudent to wait until

a wider settlement in the area could be negotiated - while paying lip service, of course, to the idea of Cambodian neutralization and protesting against violations of the nation's security. The "provocation" and "criminal military aggression" against Cambodia by Thailand, South Vietnam and the United States were persistent themes in Soviet commentaries on Cambodia during the latter half of the 1960s and the subject of occasional official protests to the governments concerned.[9]

The sole episode which momentarily cast a shadow over Soviet-Cambodian relations arose because of Moscow's postponement of Sihanouk's scheduled visit to the USSR in November 1965. The Prince, used to more deferential treatment by Khrushchev, felt slighted by the postponement and cancelled his visit entirely. The Russians promptly explained that the postponement was due solely to a conflict in the schedules of the Soviet leaders; they charged the Western press with exaggerating the incident in an effort to damage Soviet-Cambodian relations.[10] Sihanouk's visit to Moscow was not rescheduled until 1970, but the 1965 episode was quickly forgotten. Soviet-Cambodian relations returned to normal, to judge from the tone of press commentaries both in Phnom Penh and Moscow. Indeed, it is a reflection of the unusual stability of this relationship that in 15 years the Russians had only this one minor brush with the mercurial Prince.

Peking's relations with Cambodia were closer than Moscow's, and this is one of the few nations in the Third World where this was unambiguously so. By the end of 1969 Sihanouk had made five state visits to China as against two to the USSR, and at least as many Chinese state visits were made to Cambodia; Chinese aid to Cambodia, according to some estimates, was nearly twice as generous as Russia's, and, unlike Chinese programmes in other countries (for instance, Burma), those in Cambodia appear to have proceeded well; Sino-Cambodian trade from 1964 to the end of 1967 was seven times greater in volume than Soviet-Cambodian trade. Cambodia stood with Peking on important issues in foreign policy - for instance, the test ban treaty of 1963, at the peak of the Sino-Soviet dispute.[11] Sihanouk's sons, meanwhile, were sent off to study in China in 1959. There is abundant evidence to suggest the outward warmth of this relationship and indeed little to suggest evil designs or persistent subversive activities on China's part - at least before the Cultural Revolution.[12]

The Cultural Revolution inevitably had repercussions in Cambodia. Maoists, working through the embassy in Phnom Penh, sought to extend the Cultural Revolution into the 320,000 overseas Chinese community in Cambodia - a group previously left alone by Peking, at Sihanouk's insistence - and immediately encountered the Princely displeasure. Sihanouk first cautioned the Chinese, then in September 1967 threatened to close the Cambodian embassy in Peking and suspend all Chinese aid and other programmes, as Ne Win had done in Burma. Chou En-lai's prompt assurance that Peking desired, in truth, its traditional friendly relationship with Phnom Penh and his promise of additional arms (including jet fighters) mollified the Prince and relations subsequently improved.[13]

At the end of the 1960s it was neither China nor the United States and its allies who most threatened Cambodia, but the North Vietnamese. As the war in South Vietnam dragged on, the relatively empty and ill-consolidated territories of north-east Cambodia became increasingly vital to the North Vietnamese, both as a supply line to the Viet Cong and as sanctuary for hard-pressed guerrilla forces; by 1969 many thousands of North Vietnamese were using this area.[14] Sihanouk's fateful visit to Moscow and Peking in March 1970 had as its chief purpose Soviet and Chinese intervention in Hanoi to end this situation. It was Kosygin who informed Prince Sihanouk in Moscow of the coup in Phnom Penh which had toppled him from power (see below).

The success or failure of Soviet policies towards Sihanouk's Cambodia is not easy to assess. To the extent that Russia and Cambodia shared the common objective of limiting American influence in Indochina, Soviet strategies enjoyed some success. Moscow's steady support of Prince Sihanouk was undoubtedly a factor encouraging him to resist American advances in the 1950s and eventually to break relations with the United States in 1965; thereafter the Russians applauded each time Sihanouk decided loudly not to resume relations with Washington.[15] Though relations were in due course re-established, the inconvenience caused to the Americans by Sihanouk's intransigence over many years served Moscow's purposes. Any irritation to the United States in South-East Asia was a gain for Russia.

From Cambodia's view-point, the relationship with the USSR was not so simple. Friendship with the Soviet Union was manageable, Sihanouk appears to have felt, because of the distance that separated the two countries. He was under no illusion as to how things might have been were Russia closer. "We have not quarrelled with the Soviet Union because Russia is too far away from us", the Prince said in August 1968, "but ... if we become disunited and follow the Reds, then they will lead us to the same fate as Czechoslovakia."[16]

China, closer to Cambodia than Russia, was always foremost in the Prince's calculations, though it is safe to say that he feared the Chinese more than the Russians – and perhaps more than the Americans. "We shall never abandon China", Sihanouk asserted early in 1969. "Cambodia under the Sangkum will always maintain friendship first with China, second France and third the Soviet Union."[17] One need not, of course, accept this priority as a fixed thing in Sihanouk's restless mind to appreciate that so long as he remained in power relations with China, good or bad, played a larger part in Cambodian foreign policy than those with the USSR – or indeed with any other power.

The Russians responded cautiously to the coup of 18 March, 1970 in Phnom Penh. The first substantive commentary, based largely on Western news reports, appeared only a week after the coup and after Soviet officials had speeded Prince Sihanouk on his journey to Peking. Americans were behind the coup, Viktor Mayevskiy wrote in Pravda, and their object was to destroy Cambodian neutrality; Sihanouk was acknowledged as the architect and "over a period of many

years" the most active defender of neutrality, but Mayevskiy gave the impression that his fall meant less to Moscow than the loss of Phnom Penh's "peace-loving, neutralist course".[18] Yuriy Zhukov, Pravda's senior political analyst, wrote in similar vein some weeks later, arguing that it was Cambodia's persistent neutrality in the Vietnam war that prompted "those boys from CIA" to organize the plot; Sihanouk's efforts to regain power were noted, but this was not the main thrust of Zhukov's analysis.[19] In Peking, meanwhile, Sihanouk was accorded the amenities due any chief of state and he appeared frequently in public with Mao and other Chinese leaders.

The Russians also reacted cautiously to the "summit" conference of Indochinese leaders held in South China at the end of April, which brought together Prince Sihanouk, Prince Souphanouvong of the Pathet Lao, North Vietnamese and Viet Cong leaders and, as a special guest, Chou En-lai. Kosygin sent greetings to the conference in which he expressed support for a "united anti-imperialist front of the peoples of Indochina",[20] but the Soviet Union did not otherwise commit itself to the strategies adopted at the conference. On 10 May Kosygin sent a telegram to Sihanouk in Peking welcoming "the creation of the National United Front of Cambodia", which was one outcome of the "summit" conference, but he made no mention of Sihanouk's government-in-exile announced a few days earlier and already recognized by Peking and Hanoi as the sole government of Cambodia;[21] the Soviet embassy remained open in Phnom Penh.

The American-South Vietnamese invasion of Cambodia, which began on 1 May, was meanwhile receiving extensive attention in the Soviet press. Kosygin, in a live TV broadcast on 4 May, denounced the invasion as a major and deliberate escalation of the Indochinese war and "a crude repudiation of the 1954 and 1962 Geneva agreements to which the United States is a signatory". During the next two months all Soviet journals and publications kept up a bitter assault on the policies of the Nixon administration in Cambodia. The assault continued even after American troops were withdrawn at the end of June. Vladimir Kudryavtsev, for instance, writing on American Independence Day, called US policies "frankly racist", because of the large numbers of Cambodian civilians indiscriminately slaughtered during an invasion that was supposed "to preserve the lives of American soldiers".[22] Viktor Mayevskiy doubted that the troop withdrawal would end American intervention in Cambodian affairs, since Washington's purpose was to establish a Rightist axis across South-East Asia embracing Bangkok, Vientiane, Phnom Penh and Saigon.[23]

As the dramatic events in Cambodia during the first half of 1970 receded somewhat into the background, the Russians were able to appraise their posture in Cambodia more deliberately and they appear to have been satisfied with it. The posture, to be sure, was ambiguous, but until it became clear how matters would turn out in the battered kingdom, the Russians felt it prudent to keep all their options open. They kept their mission in Phnom Penh, but in low profile and without an ambassador; they permitted the former Cambodian ambassador in Moscow, who remained loyal to Sihanouk, to stay on in the embassy premises, obliging the new representatives from Phnom Penh to find other quarters;

and they received unofficially periodic delegations from the "National United Front of Kampuchea" in exile. The Soviet government continued to withold formal recognition of Prince Sihanouk's exiled regime in Peking, but Russian commentators carefully refrained from criticizing it.

This situation could not endure indefinitely. Sihanouk was of course grateful for his continued cordial reception in Peking,[24] and for the 25 nations that followed Peking's lead in recognizing his regime, but he came more and more to identify the Soviet government as the cause of his frustrations. At the end of 1971, after several veiled complaints against Moscow's attitude toward the Royal government-in-exile,[25] the Prince delivered a bitter attack on Soviet policies throughout South-East Asia. In an interview carried in the Far Eastern Economic Review, he charged the Russians with deliberately witholding recognition of his government, which "is the only thing we want from them"; with maintaining a mission in Phnom Penh on the pretext of gathering intelligence for the "Indochinese popular forces" - intelligence that was never received; and with having provided the North Vietnamese with inadequate arms out of a desire to keep them from a clear victory. "The Russians want to keep Asians in a state of subservience", Sihanouk said. "There is in the Russian mind a neurotic fear of an imaginary 'yellow peril' embodied by China."[26] The Russian reply came in an unsigned editorial in Literaturnaya gazeta which refuted all of Sihanouk's charges and in turn charged the Prince with propagating racism and applying a "special 'royal' logic" which placed his own personal interests in the monarchy higher than those of the Khmer people.[27] There could be no turning back after this sharp exchange. Sihanouk was now ignored

in Soviet commentaries on Cambodia. Articles marking the second anniversary of the National United Front, for instance, which was enthusiastically reported to control 80 per cent of Cambodian territory, made no reference whatsoever to the exiled Prince.[28] The Front, in Soviet eyes, was a suitable vehicle for the Khmer national liberation movement, but not for the restoration of Sihanouk or the monarchy.

The exact amount of Soviet economic aid extended to Cambodia is unclear. Russian sources do not indicate the total and Western sources give varying estimates.[29] The initial project was the Soviet-Khmer Friendship Hospital, completed in 1960 at an estimated cost of $10,700,000; funds were raised from the sale of Soviet commodities given to the Cambodian government. Other projects included a technical institute (completed in 1963) and a power station on the Camachai River (originally scheduled for completion in the 1970s). All projects were apparently suspended following the coup of March 1970. In addition to economic aid, an estimated $10 million in arms had been delivered to Cambodia by the end of 1971. These included an anti-aircraft defence system, trucks and a few aircraft.[30] Soviet trade with Cambodia, meanwhile, was meagre - less in the period 1965-69 than with any of Russia's regular trading partners in Asia except Nepal; even trade with Thailand exceeded that with Cambodia. Cultural exchange was continuous from 1957 to the end of 1969. Except in the field of medicine, however, where co-operation was stimulated by the Friendship Hospital, the cultural programme played a relatively modest role in Soviet-Cambodian relations.

Chronology

(See explanatory note on tables, p. 6.)

	Political	Economic	Cultural

Pre-1955

Aug 1953	Independence		

1956

	Political		Economic		Cultural
Feb	– Sihanouk in CPR				
		Apr	– Trade agreement with CPR		
May	– Diplomatic relations with USSR				
		June	– CPR credit for textile, cement and paper works ($22.4m)		
July	– SIHANOUK IN USSR for 7-day visit	July	– USSR promises hospital to Cambodia		
Nov	– Chou En-lai in Cambodia				

1957

	Economic		Cultural
		Apr	– Artists in Cambodia
May – Trade agreement		May	– Cultural agreement

1958

	Political		Economic		Cultural
		May	– Agreement on 800-bed hospital ($10.7m)[31]		
July	– Parliamentary delegation in USSR after visit to CPR – Diplomatic relations with CPR				
Aug	– Sihanouk in CPR			Aug	– Journalists in USSR
Sept	– Government delegation in USSR	Sept	– Trade protocol		
		Nov	– Chinese-built radio station opens		

1959

1960

	Political		Economic		Cultural
May	– Chou En-lai, Chen Yi in Cambodia	May	– Chinese-built textile plant opens		
				July	– Sihanouk sons in CPR for study
		Aug	– Soviet-built hospital completed		

CAMBODIA

	Political	Economic	Cultural

1960 (cont.)

	Political	Economic	Cultural
Nov	– SIHANOUK IN USSR and CPR: friendship, non-aggression treaty with CPR (Dec)		
		Dec – Technical assistance agreement on power station, mining survey – CPR credit ($26.5m)	

1961

	Political	Economic	Cultural
		May – Chinese-built plywood factory opens	
June	– Sihanouk aide Chau Seng in USSR	June – Agreement on construction of technical institute as gift	
		July – Gift of helicopter to Sihanouk	
		Aug – Chinese-built hospital opens	Aug – Information exchange agreement
			Sept – Writers in Cambodia
			Oct – Cultural delegation in USSR

1962

	Political	Economic	Cultural
		Feb – Chinese-built paper mill opens	
Mar	– Kazakh delegation in Cambodia		
Apr	– Premier in CPR on private visit		
			May – Protocol on hospital staff: 25 Soviet aides for 2 years – Writers' delegation in USSR
			Sept – Journalists in USSR – Red Cross delegation in Uzbekistan
		Oct – 1957 trade agreement extended	Oct – 1957 cultural agreement renewed

1963

	Political	Economic	Cultural
Feb	– Sihanouk in CPR on 3-week visit		Feb – Soviet film festival in Phnom Penh
Apr	– Deputy premier in USSR	Apr – Economic delegation in USSR; protocol on power station (reported $12m)[32]	
May	– Liu Shao-chi, Chen Yi in Cambodia		

	Political		Economic		Cultural
1963 (cont.)				Aug	– Cultural protocol
Sept	– Agreement on air defence	Sept	– Technical institute opens in Phnom Penh		
			– Chinese-built road, bridge completed		
		Oct	– Contract for dam, power surveys		
		Nov	– Cambodia renounces US aid		
Dec	– First arms agreement with CPR				

	Political		Economic		Cultural
1964					
Feb	– First Soviet arms delivered to Cambodia				
Apr	– Defence minister heads military delegation to USSR and CPR				
May	– Parliamentary delegation in CPR				
				July	– Royal ballet in USSR
Sept	– Government delegation in Cambodia for opening of institute	Sept	– Chinese-built cement works opens		
	– Sihanouk in CPR: promise of arms				
Oct	– Cambodian military delegation in CPR: arms agreement				
Nov	– Government delegation in Cambodia for anniversary	Nov	– Reported Chinese credit ($5–10m)[33]		
	– Chen Yi in Cambodia				

	Political		Economic		Cultural
1965					
Jan	– Komsomol delegation in Cambodia				
Apr	– Cambodia breaks relations with USA				
June	– Parliamentary leader in USSR				
		July	– Aid pledged for river development		
				Aug	– Cultural protocol for 1965
Sept	– Government delegation under deputy premier in USSR after visit to CPR				
	– Sihanouk in CPR for fifth official visit				

	Political		Economic		Cultural
1965 (cont.)					
		Oct	– Trade protocol – Protocol on power plant (possible supplementary credit of $4m)[34]		
Nov	– Sihanouk cancels USSR visit after rebuff – Military delegation in CPR: arms agreement				
1966					
Mar	– Government delegation under deputy premier in USSR: arms agreement				
Apr	– CPR deputy premier in Cambodia			Apr	– Journalists in Cambodia
				May	– Cultural agreement renewed
Aug	– De Gaulle visits Cambodia	Aug	– 1957 trade agreement extended again	Aug	– Protocol extended for Soviet aides at hospital, technical institute – Cultural protocol for 1966
Sept	– Deputy foreign minister Firyubin in Cambodia			Sept	– Doctors delegation in Cambodia for medical conference
Oct	– Chinese-Cambodian agreement on arms, military technicians – Municipal delegation in USSR			Oct	– Gift of cholera vaccine
Nov	– Parliamentary delegation in USSR	Nov	– Gift of radio station		
Dec	– Supreme Soviet delegation in Cambodia – Foreign ministry official in Cambodia	Dec	– Chinese-built textile factory completed	Dec	– Gift of books to technical institute
1967					
Apr	– Further arms deliveries to Cambodia, including aircraft				
May	– Foreign minister in USSR			May	– Gift of equipment for hospital; Soviet doctors to lecture at Royal University in Phnom Penh
				June	– Cultural protocol – Buddhist delegation in USSR
Aug	– Parliamentary delegation in USSR and CPR – Foreign minister in CPR				

	Political	Economic	Cultural
1967 (cont.)			
Sept	– Sihanouk threatens rupture with CPR over cultural revolution activity in Cambodia; Chou En-lai offers new arms agreement		
Nov		– Trade protocol	– Cultural protocol
1968			
Jan	– Foreign minister in CPR		
Feb	– Military delegation in USSR: new arms agreement ($5.5m)[35]		
May			– Gift of cholera vaccine
June		– Chinese-built glass works opens	
Aug	– Government delegation in CPR		
Oct		– Chinese-built airport at Siem Reap opens	
Dec			– Delegation at film festival in Phnom Penh
1969			
Feb	– Komsomol delegation in Cambodia		
Mar		– Trade minister Patolichev in Cambodia	
Apr	– Military delegation in USSR		
May	– Foreign minister in USSR		– Education delegation in Cambodia: contracts extended for teachers at technical institute
Aug	– General Lon Nol heads new government – Cambodia resumes relations with USA		
Sept	– Lon Nol heads delegation to CPR for anniversary		
Nov	– Soviet destroyer calls at Sihanoukville		
1970			
Winter	– Mounting dispute between Phnom Penh and Hanoi over Vietnamese bases in Cambodia		

	Political	Economic	Cultural
1970 (cont.)			
Mar	– SIHANOUK IN USSR after visit to France; overthrown by Lon Nol while in Moscow; takes refuge in Peking		
Apr	– Summit conference of Indochinese leaders in south China; Chou En-lai attends		
May	– American, South Vietnamese troops drive into Cambodia to destroy Viet Cong bases		
	– Sihanouk forms government-in-exile under national united front: recognized by CPR		
June	– US troops withdraw from Cambodia		
Aug	– Arms agreement between CPR and government-in-exile	Aug – Sihanouk's finance minister in USSR	
Oct	– Delegation from Sihanouk's regime in USSR for anniversary		
	– Lon Nol proclaims Cambodia a republic		
		Dec – Finance minister again in USSR	
1971			
Sept	– National united front delegation in USSR at invitation of Afro-Asian solidarity committee		
		Oct – Trade agreement extended	

References

[1] Pravda, 19 March, 1956.

[2] A. Baturin, writing in Pravda, 18 May, 1956.

[3] P. Yur'yev, in Izvestiya, 9 November, 1958.

[4] Pravda, 9 November, 1959.

[5] See, for instance, the exchange of Notes, or telegrams, between Sihanouk and Khrushchev in Izvestiya, 29 August, 1962; Pravda, 28 March, 1964; and Trud, 29 May, 1964.

[6] Official Soviet support for a conference on Cambodia was indicated in Notes to representatives of the United Kingdom, co-sponsor (with Russia) of the 1954 conference on Indochina and therefore jointly responsible for Cambodian security: see Izvestiya, 22 January, 1964; Komsomol'skaya pravda, 27 February, 1964; and Izvestiya, 31 July, 1964.

[7] Pravda, 21 February, 1965.

[8] Pravda, 9 April, 1965.

[9] E.g. Izvestiya, 6 July, 1966; Pravda, 2 and 15 October, 1967.

[10] Trud, 20 October, 1965 and Izvestiya, 7 November, 1965.

[11] New China News Agency, 5 September, 1963.

[12] See Roger M. Smith, Cambodia's Foreign Policy (Ithaca: Cornell University Press), pp. 104-21 passim.

[13] The episode is reviewed by W.A.C. Adie in an article

in Mizan, November-December, 1967, pp. 234-35; see also Mizan, September-October 1967, Supplement B, pp. 8-9. For an account of the arms agreement following the impasse, see Marsot Alain-Gerard, "China's Aid to Cambodia", Pacific Affairs, Summer 1969, p. 192. See also Gurtov, China and Southeast Asia (full listing in Bibliography), pp. 118ff.

[14] General Lon Nol estimated in September 1969 that 35,000-40,000 Vietnamese troops were in Cambodia; Le Sangkum, October 1969, p. 95 (cited in Asian Survey, February 1970, p. 173).

[15] See, for instance, B. Sakharov's articles in International Affairs, No. 3 (March), 1968, pp. 89-90 and No. 6 (June), 1969, pp. 92-93.

[16] Radio Phnom Penh, 22 August, 1968.

[17] Radio Phnom Penh, 10 January, 1969.

[18] Pravda, 25 March, 1970; see also Peter Howard's analysis of the Mayevskiy article in Mizan, November 1970, p. 82.

[19] Pravda, 20 April, 1970.

[20] Pravda, 30 April, 1970.

[21] Pravda, 13 May, 1970.

[22] Izvestiya, 4 July, 1970.

[23] Pravda, 4 July, 1970.

[24] Prince Sihanouk received from the outset full diplomatic courtesies in Peking as a "visiting" Chief of State. He appeared frequently at receptions and reviews with the Chinese leaders, including Mao and Chou En-lai, and his activities were given generous coverage in the Chinese press.

[25] E.g. Sihanouk's interview with Wilfred Burchett, carried on Japanese television on 6 May, 1971, and Premier Penn Nouth's remarks in Sinkiang on 12 September, 1971 (reported by the New China News Agency on the same day).

[26] Interview with Alessandro Casella, Far Eastern Economic Review, No. 52, 1971, pp. 19-21.

[27] Literaturnaya gazeta, No. 2 (12 January), 1972, p. 9.

[28] E.g. M. Il'inskiy in Izvestiya, 23 March, 1972.

[29] Roger Smith, for instance, estimates nearly $50 million to the end of 1964, basing his estimate on figures provided by the Soviet embassy in Phnom Penh; op. cit., p. 123. Marshall Goldman's estimate, as of mid-1963, was only $12 million in loans and $6 million in gifts; Soviet Foreign Aid, p. 143. The cumulative total by the end of 1970 given by the U.S. Department of State is $25 million (which is close to the total shown in Table B, below); RECS-15, 22 September, 1971, p. 3. Whichever figure is accepted, Soviet economic aid was a fraction of American aid, which has been estimated at more than $350 million between 1955 and 1963, when Sihanouk renounced further US assistance; see The Far East and Australasia, 1970, p. 420.

[30] Joshua and Gibert, Arms for the Third World (full listing in Bibliography), pp. 63-64.

[31] According to Smith, op. cit., p. 105, this was the cost of the completed hospital.

[32] U.S. Department of State, RSB-43, 18 June, 1964, p. 23.

[33] Goldman, op. cit., p. 143.

[34] No credit is shown in Soviet sources announcing the protocol, but an additional Russian credit of $4 million in 1966 is reported elsewhere and may relate to this project; see U.S. Department of State, RSB-80, 21 July, 1967, p. 2.

[35] Sihanouk reported this figure in an address in February; Radio Phnom Penh, 21 February, 1968.

5. RELATIONS WITH CEYLON

The Soviet Union established diplomatic relations with Ceylon in 1956, following general elections in which the Sri Lanka Freedom Party (SLFP) defeated the incumbent United National Party (UNP). The new government of S.W.R.D. Bandaranaike, a coalition of the SLFP and a fragmentary Marxist group, promptly proclaimed its neutralist posture in international relations and took steps to affirm its "socialist" intentions. Defence pacts with Great Britain were abrogated; on the home front, there was talk of nationalization. The Russians needless to say were highly pleased with this turn of events in Ceylon and after setting up an embassy extended credits to the Bandaranaike government and negotiated trade agreements.

Soviet commentators wrote with growing enthusiasm of the new regime. They praised steps to nationalize the rubber and tea plantations; they excoriated the UNP and its allies; they deplored the "narrow party interests" of the Trotskyites (the Lanka Sama Samaj Party), who had refused to collaborate with the SLFP.[1] Although this was not a period when Russian observers as a rule accused ordinary Third World nationalists of being reactionaries, they did so in Ceylon. The struggle there, on the eve of Bandaranaike's assassination by a disillusioned Buddhist in 1959, was seen as one between irreconcilable "progressive" and "reactionary" forces.[2] For nine months after the assassination, Soviet journalists painted a dark picture of events in Ceylon. Then the formation of a new government by Bandaranaike's widow, after two general elections, was greeted warmly and called a victory for the "progressives".[3] Soviet relations with Colombo could, and did, proceed as before.

The four and three-quarter years of Mrs. Bandaranaike's first government marked the peak of Soviet-Ceylonese relations. Aid projects which had been stalled during the uncertain events of 1959 and 1960 were started again; trade grew; cultural exchange expanded. The Soviet press, meanwhile, resumed its sympathetic treatment of developments in Ceylon. The struggle with foreign oil companies, leading first to the establishment of the Ceylon Petroleum Corporation (1961) and ultimately to their nationalization (1963), was followed enthusiastically in the economic journals.[4] The development of a three-year plan for 1962–64, projecting an annual investment of 16 to 18 per cent of the GNP, also attracted sympathetic attention.[5] The opposition parties during these years were treated with disdain and their efforts to thwart the government were considered sinister - especially an alleged "plot" in December 1961.[6] As general elections approached, Soviet observers singled out the UNP for their most acid comments.

The defeat in Parliament of Mrs. Bandaranaike's government in January 1965 and the UNP's victory over the SLFP in the ensuing election were viewed as a return to "reaction" and ascribed to the "intrigues of foreign imperialists".[7] Relations cooled between Moscow and the new government in Colombo, headed by Dudley Senanayake. Political exchanges became less frequent; a new cultural agreement, signed in November 1964, was left largely unimplemented; press coverage of Ceylon, if less explicitly hostile towards the UNP than during the Bandaranaike governments, was non-committal. Trade, however, continued to grow and the economic aid projects proceeded on schedule, though without new credits (see below).

As time passed, the Russians appear to have become reconciled to the new regime. The Pravda correspondent A. Filippov, for instance, wrote in February 1967 that "despite the intrigues of international reaction, Ceylon is pursuing an independent foreign policy based on neutrality".[8] K. Perevoshchikov wrote in Izvestiya at the end of 1968 that the UNP, once pro-Western and hostile to the USSR, had learnt a lesson from its 1960 defeat and now, returned to power, had adopted a rigorously neutralist position in foreign policy.[9] Moscow, to judge from these mild commentaries on the UNP government, was willing to set aside distinctions between "progressive" and "reactionary" forces in Ceylon - at least until the next parliamentary elections in 1970.

Peking's relations with Ceylon followed a pattern similar to Moscow's: cordial ties were established with the two Bandaranaike governments - more cordial than Moscow's, to judge from the greater number of political and economic exchanges and the larger aid commitments - and there were misgivings in Peking, as in Moscow, when the SLFP was defeated in 1965. The Cultural Revolution in China aroused certain fears in Ceylon over Chinese activities there and led to incidents which strained relations between the two countries. One such incident in August 1967 - the plundering by Ceylonese citizens of a ship in Colombo harbour bearing supplies for the Chinese embassy - provoked a particularly vigorous protest by the Chinese, who insisted that the episode was "perpetrated with the connivance and on the instructions of the Ceylon government"; trade relations, the Chinese warned, could not continue under these circumstances.[10] Trade did continue, however. Commercial delegations were exchanged regularly with the UNP government during the latter part of the 1960s, and China remained Ceylon's second most important trading partner after the United Kingdom; in 1967 and 1968, at the peak of the Cultural Revolution, China's trade with Ceylon was two and a half times greater than Russia's and accounted for about 11 per cent of Ceylon's total trade, as contrasted with approximately four per cent for the USSR.[11]

Sino-Soviet rivalry in Ceylon was heightened in the 1960s by divisions within the Ceylonese Communist movement. The party, legal under all governments, had had continuous open relations with Moscow since the mid-1950s. Pieter Keuneman, undisputed leader of the CPC since its founding in 1943, visited Moscow on many occasions (undoubtedly more often than shown in the Chronology) and by the 1960s was acknowledged in Moscow as one of the senior Communists in Asia. CPC strategies meanwhile were openly discussed in the Soviet press: much was made, for instance, of Communist support for the Bandaranaikes, especially for Mrs. Bandaranaike's government in 1960;[12] in 1963 Pravda carried an article by Keuneman which proclaimed a united front of Leftist forces in Ceylon the best way to assure "a non-capitalist course".[13]

In January 1964, following steep escalation of the Sino-Soviet dispute during the preceding six months, the CPC split. A pro-Chinese faction, led by N. Sanmugathasan, formed its own party and immediately established close ties with Peking. Sanmugathasan visited Peking regularly during the next few years and the Chinese press kept up a sustained attack on Ceylonese "revisionists" and their Soviet supporters.[14] The Russians replied in kind. Pravda opened its columns to Keuneman to press his case against "anti-Party splitters".[15] V. Stepanov, an editor of Kommunist who attended the CPC congress in Colombo in April 1964, charged the break-away group with playing a wholly negative role in Ceylonese politics.[16] The increased flow of Ceylonese Communist delegations to Moscow during the following years reflected the Russians' concern over the division in the CPC.

The parliamentary elections of May 1970, viewed in the context of Sino-Soviet rivalry in Ceylon, represented a clear gain for the Russians. The victorious united front under Mrs. Bandaranaike included the pro-Russian, but not the pro-Chinese, Communists and Pieter Keuneman was appointed to the new cabinet. The Russians immediately hailed the success of Ceylon's "democratic forces" and chided Peking for remaining silent on the united front's landslide victory. The election demonstrated, a Russian broadcaster said in June, that "there is absolutely no need for the people of young countries to resort to political adventures or engage in false revolutionary war to consolidate their independence .... They certainly do not need to follow the Chinese leadership's wrong idea that 'political power grows out of the barrel of a gun', and that there is no alternative to armed guerrilla warfare".[17] If such attacks on Chinese policy were meant to sour Sino-Ceylonese relations, there is no evidence they did so. Trading between the two countries showed no decline in the months following the elections; in September a new Chinese credit was promised to Colombo, which eventually proved to be several times the size of a Soviet credit extended to Ceylon in October.

Russian as well as Chinese relations with the united front government were put to a test in April 1971 when an estimated 20,000 ultra-Leftist Ceylonese students rebelled against the regime. The students called themselves "Communists" and several leaders of the rebellion had studied formerly in Moscow or Peking.[18] Both Russians and Chinese promptly dissociated themselves from the uprising, which they could plausibly do since neither the pro-Moscow nor pro-Peking factions of the CPC were involved. There was uneasiness, however, in certain Ceylonese quarters about the role Peking might be playing in the background - especially after the government considered it necessary to expel the entire North Korean embassy staff "for security reasons". The uneasiness appears to have been unwarranted. At another time the Chinese might have shown interest in so formidable a radical element in Ceylon, but the spring of 1971 was not the moment for it: the exchange of new ambassadors in the preceding autumn had signalled a new era of Sino-Ceylonese friendship, in line with Peking's general shift to more moderate foreign policies during this period. The Chinese press accordingly ignored the student rebellion at the outset and Chinese diplomats and aid teams in Colombo went about their normal business. At the end of May, some weeks after the insurgency had been brought under control, Chou En-lai congratulated Mrs. Bandaranaike on her government's success in ending the chaos caused by a handful of self-styled "Guevarists"; China, he went on, had always opposed both "ultra-Left and Right opportunism in their respective revolutionary struggles".[19]

The Russians were prompter and more forthright in coming to the government's aid during the insurgency.

TASS releases from Colombo in early April condemned the insurgents and, quoting Pieter Keuneman, labelled the "so-called People's Liberation Front" a "Fascist and terrorist organization serving the interests of sinister forces".[20] Later in the month six MIG-17 fighters were delivered to the Colombo government to combat the insurgents and Soviet crews were made available to train Ceylonese pilots.[21] A more detailed arms agreement with Ceylon was negotiated in May (see Chronology). It is clear in hindsight that Soviet influence in Ceylon was strengthened as a result of the 1971 insurgency, though not necessarily at China's expense to judge from continued cordial relations between Peking and Colombo during the months following the crisis.

Economic and Cultural Ties

An initial Soviet credit of $30 million in 1958 was apparently not exhausted before 1970 (though a Western student of Soviet aid shows a supplementary credit of $11 million in 1965).[22] One source shows utilization of the Soviet credit, during the period 1962-66, as higher than of Chinese credits - and indeed of those of other major donors.[23] However, Peking's pledges of credit over the years total considerably more than Moscow's (see Table B). The Russian projects, most of which were launched in earnest during the first government of Mrs. Bandaranaike, included the following: an iron and steel plant (the first stage of which was opened in 1967), a tyre factory (opened at the same time); a flour mill and grain silo; a prefabricated housing plant; and, in the agricultural sector, several irrigation projects, the preparation of areas for cotton and sugar cane cultivation, and a model dairy farm. Soviet geologists discovered oil in north-western Ceylon in March 1971 and during the months following plans were made for the joint exploitation of this deposit.

Soviet trade with Ceylon, while significantly less than Ceylon's trade with China, was none the less considerable and constituted an important element in relations between the two countries during the 1960s. During the period 1965-69 Ceylon ranked in the top dozen of Russia's trading partners in the Third World.

Cultural relations fluctuated, depending upon which government was in power in Colombo; exchanges were more numerous in the early 1960s, for instance, during Mrs. Bandaranaike's first government, than later in the decade. The number of Ceylonese students in the USSR declined from more than 200 in 1965 to fewer than 75 in 1970, in large part due to the fact that Soviet certificates were not accepted in Ceylon as the equivalent of Ceylonese or English degrees.[24] A number of influential Soviet academicians visited Ceylon at one time or another - e.g. G.D. Afanas'yev (1959), E.M. Zhukov (1964), and V.V. Balabushevich (1966) - and these visits were reciprocated.[25]

The record of Soviet accomplishments in Ceylon by 1971 was on balance satisfactory, Moscow must have felt. Economic relations were on a firm footing and could be expected to survive any normal change of government in Colombo. At the moment the Russians enjoyed the good will of a moderately Leftist regime, but of no less significance was their ability to accommodate themselves to the conservative governments that periodically returned to power. During the 1970 elections the Russians saw one of their favourite current strategies succeed and through Pieter Keuneman may have had a hand in shaping it: the electoral coalition, or united front, of Leftists and pro-Moscow Communists. A pro-Moscow Communist now served in a coalition cabinet - probably the first Asian to do so. In the area of foreign relations, meanwhile, Ceylon's relationship with the Chinese, for whom the Ceylonese appear to have had stronger natural sympathies than for the Russians, was tolerable from Moscow's view;

any serious risk of Ceylon's adhering to a Western alliance had been negligible for many years. Soviet naval vessels had paid courtesy calls at Colombo and the sudden opportunity in April 1971 to assist the Ceylonese government militarily in its struggle against a domestic revolt opened up prospects of a wider role in Ceylon's defence in the future. All things considered, it was a record any of Russia's rivals might envy.

Chronology

(See explanatory note on tables, p. 6.)

	Political		Economic		Cultural
Pre-1957					
Feb 1948	Independence				
Jan 1950	Ceylon recognizes CPR				
		Oct 1952	Trade agreement with CPR		
Apr 1956	Bandaranaike becomes premier after elections				
Sept 1956	Ceylon, CPR agree on diplomatic relations				
1957					
Feb	- Diplomatic relations with USSR - Chou En-lai in Ceylon				
Apr	- Parliamentary delegation in USSR			Apr	- Education delegation in USSR
				Aug	- Dancers in USSR
		Sept	- Trade and credit agreements with CPR ($16m)		
				Nov	- Musicians in Ceylon
		Dec	- Economic delegation in Ceylon		
1958					
				Jan	- Cultural agreement
		Feb	- CREDIT AGREEMENT for steel, tyre plants; flour mill; survey ($30m) - First trade agreement		
		Sept	- Additional CPR credit ($10.5m)	Sept	- TU delegation in USSR
				Nov	- Entertainers in Ceylon

	Political		Economic		Cultural
1959					
Jan	– CP secretary Keuneman in USSR for XXI congress				
				Feb	– Arts and crafts exhibition in Moscow
		Mar	– Protocol on iron, steel plant		
				May	– TU delegation in USSR
Sept	– <u>Bandaranaike assassinated; caretaker government formed</u>			Sept	– Medical delegation in USSR
				?	– Academic delegation in Ceylon
1960					
		Feb	– Protocols on various projects under 1958 credit		
July	– <u>Mrs. Bandaranaike becomes premier</u> after elections				
				Sept	– TU delegation in USSR
		Oct	– Oil purchase agreement – Protocol on water conservation project		
Dec	– CP delegation in Moscow for world conference				
1961					
Mar	– Deputy foreign minister in Ceylon	Mar	– Finance minister in USSR		
		July	– Contract for steel plant and training of technicians	July	– Health delegation in USSR
		Sept	– Contract for tyre factory		
Oct	– Keuneman in USSR for XXII congress				
				Dec	– TU delegation in USSR
1962					
		Feb	– 3-year trade agreement		
				Mar	– Gift of polio vaccine
Apr	– Parliamentary delegation in USSR			Apr	– Lumumba university rector in Ceylon
		May	– <u>New CPR credit for 5 years ($15m)</u>		
		June	– Protocol on industrial projects under 1958 credit	June	– TU delegation in Ceylon for conference

CEYLON

	Political		Economic		Cultural
1962 (cont.)					
		Sept	– Contract on jungle clearing for cotton plantation	Sept	– Cultural protocol – Book exhibition in Colombo – Dockers delegation in USSR
		Oct	– Merchant marine delegation in Ceylon: shipping agreement – New trade agreement with CPR		
Nov	– CPR delegation in Ceylon to explain Sino-Indian dispute				
				Autumn	– Ceylonese art exhibition in Leningrad
1963					
Jan	– Mrs. Bandaranaike in CPR with peace proposals on Sino-Indian dispute				
		Apr	– US suspends aid to Ceylon	Apr	– Medical workers in Ceylon: gift of additional polio vaccine
		June	– Technical assistance agreement	June	– Buddhist delegation in USSR – Cultural centre opens in Colombo
				July	– Protocol for 1963
Aug	– Keuneman in USSR – CP youth delegation in USSR	Aug	– Contract for granary and mill – Rubber purchase agreement		
Oct	– MRS. BANDARANAIKE IN USSR for 10-day visit; also to CPR			Oct	– Dancers in USSR
		Dec	– Oil companies nationalized in Ceylon		
1964					
Jan	– CP splits; pro-CPR faction formed			Jan	– Uzbek minister of justice in Ceylon
Feb	– Chou En-lai in Ceylon	Feb	– Air service agreement		
				Mar	– TU delegation in Ceylon
Apr	– CPSU delegation in Ceylon for party congress				
		June	– Fishing experts in Ceylon for aid talks	June	– Cultural protocol

	Political		Economic		Cultural
1964 (cont.)					
Aug	– Komsomol delegation in Ceylon for congress	Aug	– Oil purchase agreement for 1965–66	Sept	– TU delegation in Ceylon
Sept	– Parliamentary leader in USSR	Sept	– Trade minister heads delegation to USSR: agreement for 1965–67		
			– Economic delegation in CPR: credit agreement ($4.2m)		
Oct	– Parliamentary delegation in CPR				
Nov	– Deputy foreign minister Firyubin in Ceylon			Nov	– New cultural and scientific agreement
1965					
		Jan	– Aid to hurricane victims		
			– Gift of cement plant		
Mar	– General elections: Senanayake replaces Mrs. Bandaranaike as premier	Mar	– Economic delegation in Ceylon: protocol on steel plant		
June	– Firyubin in Ceylon				
Nov	– Moscow city delegation in Colombo				
1966					
Mar	– Keuneman in USSR for XXIII congress	Mar	– Minister of industry in USSR for aid talks		
	– Firyubin again in Ceylon				
		Nov	– Trade protocol for 1967		
1967					
				Feb	– TU delegation in Ceylon
		Mar	– Government delegation in Ceylon for opening of steel, tyre plants		
		Apr	– Protocol on sugar sales to Ceylon		
Nov	– Keuneman heads CP delegation to USSR				
1968					
		Jan	– Oil purchase agreement		
				Feb	– TU delegation in USSR

	Political		Economic		Cultural
1968 (cont.)					
Mar	– CP delegation in USSR – Komsomol delegation in Ceylon				

		Apr	– Protocol on further
			  stages of steel plant
				Apr	– Buddhist delegation
					  in USSR

June	– Parliamentary, govern-
	  ment delegation in USSR
		June	– Planning officials in
			  USSR for talks
				June	– Buddhist delegation
					  in Ceylon

July	– Naval vessel visits Ceylon				

		Aug	– Trade delegation in
			  USSR: new agreement
			  for 1969–70
			– Chinese-built textile
			  plant opens		

		Dec	– Ministerial delegation
			  in Ceylon for opening
			  of flour mill		

1969					
Feb	– Supreme Soviet delegation in Ceylon				
Mar	– Komsomol delegation in Ceylon				

Apr	– CP delegation in USSR
	  for preparatory commis-
	  sion and world conference				

		June	– Chairman of coconut
			  council in USSR for
			  trade talks		

July	– Colombo municipal delegation in Moscow				
1970					

				Feb	– USSR and CPR
					  donate supplies
					  to flood victims

Apr	– CP delegation in USSR for Lenin centenary				

May	– United front under
	  Mrs. Bandaranaike
	  wins in Ceylonese
	  elections; Keuneman
	  appointed to cabinet				

				June	– Cultural protocol for 1970

Sept	– Parliamentary dele-
	  gation in USSR
		Sept	– Trade minister in CPR:
			  preliminary credit
			  agreement		

		Oct	– Trade minister in USSR:
			  trade agreement for
			  1971–72 and credit for
			  purchase of machinery
			  ($8.4m)		

Political	Economic	Cultural

1971

| | Jan | - Housing delegation in Ceylon: gift for projects ($3m)
- Chinese foreign trade minister in Ceylon: protocol for 1971 | |

| Apr - Insurgency in Ceylon: USSR sends aircraft, armoured cars
- CP delegation in Moscow for XXIV congress | Apr - Oil experts in Ceylon to survey new deposits | |

| May - Reported arms agreement ($7.2m)[26] | May - 12-year Chinese credit ($25m)[27] | |

| | | July - Agreement on degree equivalency |

| | Aug - Agreement on co-operation and aid in fishing industry | |

| | Sept - Agreement on Sino-Ceylon shipping service
- Minister of industry in USSR: agreement on oil prospecting | Sept - TU leaders in Moscow for international conference |

| | | Nov - Muslim delegation in Ceylon |

| Dec - Gift of Chinese patrol boats to Ceylonese navy | | |

References

[1] E.g. S. Sofieva, in International Affairs, No. 11 (November), 1957, and I. Semenov, in Mirovaya ekonomika i mezhdunarodnyye otnosheniya, No. 5 (May), 1959, pp. 109-10 (reviewed in Yuva Newsletter, April 1963, p. 10).

[2] E.g. K. Vladimirov, in International Affairs, No. 8 (August), 1959, pp. 94-95.

[3] E.g. A. Malov, in Sovremennyy Vostok, No. 8 (August), 1960, p. 58 and No. 12 (December), 1960, pp. 12-13.

[4] E.g. Vneshnyaya torgovlya, No. 3 (March), 1961, p. 22; Mirovaya ekonomika i mezhdunarodnyye otnosheniya, No. 8 (August), 1961, pp. 103-6 and No. 7 (July), 1964, pp. 95-97.

[5] G. Molchanov, Tseylon, 1964, p. 19 (reviewed in Yuva Newsletter, January 1965, pp. 8-14) and L.G. Ivanov in Kratkiye soobshcheniya Instituta narodov Azii, No. 75 (1964), pp. 138-48.

[6] Pravda, 30 January, 1962; Izvestiya, 25 February, 1962; and International Affairs, No. 3 (March), 1962, pp. 90-91.

[7] Pravda, 8 January, 1965 and Izvestiya, 30 March, 1965.

[8] Pravda, 3 February, 1967.

[9] Izvestiya, 28 November, 1968.

[10] New China News Agency, 19 August, 1967; the Chinese sent five sharply-worded protest Notes on this episode between August and October.

[11] Far East and Australasia, 1970, p. 172 and U.S. Department of State, RSE-65, 5 September, 1969, p. 23.

[12] E.g. I. Petrov, in Sovremennyy Vostok, No. 12 (December), 1960 (reviewed in Yuva Newsletter, April 1963, p. 11).

[13] Pravda, 3 July, 1963; see also his article in Kommunist, No. 11 (July), 1963, pp. 114-20. For a fuller treatment of CPC history and tactics, see Robert Kearney's chapter in Scalapino, ed., The Communist Revolution in Asia (cited in Bibliography).

[14] Sanmugathasan's visits to Peking are reported by New China News Agency, 12 June, 1965, 2 January, 1966, and 6 October, 1966; and in Peking Review, No. 25, 1967.

[15] E.g. Pravda, 6 April, 1964 and 3 October, 1964.

[16] Pravda, 31 May, 1964.

[17] Radio Moscow, 30 June, 1970 (in Chinese); see also earlier comments on the elections by A. Maslennikov in Pravda, 29 May, 1970 and V. Shurygin in Pravda, 11 June, 1970.

[18] The stated purpose of the student revolt was to hasten socialist measures promised by the united front during the 1970 elections; a more underlying cause of the rebellion, however, was unemployment – especially the inability of the students to find positions appropriate to their university educations. For a discussion of the origins of the carefully planned rebellion, see Trends and Highlights, No. 309 (1 June, 1971), pp. 45-50.

[19] The text of Chou's letter was broadcast on Radio Colombo, 26 May, 1971.

[20] Pravda, 10 April, 1971.

[21] Announcement of the MIG deliveries was made by the Ceylonese Army Commander; see the dispatch by James P. Sterba in the New York Times, 22 April, 1971, p. 2.

[22] Janos Horvath, "Economic Aid Flow from the USSR", Slavic Review, December 1970, p. 626; the credit, extended in March 1965, is said to have been for a harbour and fishing equipment. Since the credit is not confirmed in other sources, it is not shown in the Chronology.

[23] Foreign aid drawings by Ceylon during this four-year period are given as follows in Far East and Australasia, 1969, p. 156:

USSR	$14.8
West Germany	13.9
Great Britain	9.8
China	8.0
USA	5.4

The low drawings on American credits reflect the fact that US aid was suspended in 1963 because of problems arising from the nationalization of oil companies, and resumed only after the 1965 elections; see Goldman, Soviet Foreign Aid, p. 144.

[24] U.S. Department of State, RSES-35, 12 August, 1970, p. 80; the Ceylonese government reversed its position in 1971 (see Chronology).

[25] Korneyev, Nauchnyye svyazi Akademii nauk SSR so stranami Azii i Afriki, pp. 75-76.

[26] Financial Times, 17 May, 1971.

[27] This was the figure given in a Radio Colombo broadcast on 28 May, 1971. U.S. State Department sources report a Chinese credit of $12 million in September 1970 for rice purchases and a conference hall in Colombo (RECS-15, 22 September, 1971, p. 6) and an additional loan of $32 million in 1971 (RECS-3, 15 May, 1972, p. 6); it is possible that these loans were overlapping.

Of the three early targets of Soviet strategies in the Asian sub-continent in the mid-1950s - Afghanistan, India and Burma - India was incomparably the most important. Not only was its size impressive, and its influence in Asian developments thereby assured, but more than the other two states it figuratively and literally straddled the two American-sponsored alliances in South-East Asia and the Middle East that the Russians were determined to hold in check. It is doubtful, of course, that India in 1955 had any intention of joining either of these alliance systems. The Russians did not make India non-aligned; India already was. But the particular way in which Soviet observers had analysed India's "bourgeois" development since the late 1940s apparently heightened Moscow's fears of the course New Delhi might take and gave special urgency to measures designed to assure Indian neutrality. The Indians for their part were receptive to Soviet approaches in the mid-1950s because of the pro-Western orientation of their major rival, Pakistan, which by 1955 had already become heavily dependent on the United States. Soviet-Indian relations accordingly flowered in the latter half of the 1950s and were in no way inhibited by the fact that on both sides the motivation was political rather than ideological.

Relations between India and the Soviet Union had gradually improved even before 1955. The departing Indian ambassador in 1952, V.P. Radhakrishnan, and his successor, K.P.S. Menon, had both been received by Stalin - a rare occurrence in Stalin's last years.[1] In August 1953 Malenkov, in a major speech on foreign policy, made flattering reference to India.[2] The five-year trade agreement signed in December of the same year was another indication Soviet-Indian relations were improving. Cultural co-operation, which had been carried on amongst academicians since 1952,[3] was stimulated in 1954 by the highly successful exchange of Russian and Indian dancers (see Chronology). Improving relations between China and India, marked in 1954 by an exchange of visits by Chou En-lai and Nehru, undoubtedly hastened the Russian-Indian détente.

These developments were the prelude to a remarkable escalation of activity in 1955, beginning with a pledge of credits in January for India's first steel plant (eventually constructed at Bhilai) and climaxed by the state visits of Nehru in June and of Bulganin and Khrushchev in November. Nehru's visit was given more play in the Soviet press than that of any foreign leader, Communist or non-Communist, ever to visit the USSR; the Bulganin-Khrushchev visit was described both in Moscow and New Delhi as "triumphal". From 1955 on there was never a significant lag in Soviet-Indian relations.

The diplomatic gains to both countries were not inconsiderable during the early years of their relationship. India, for instance, was assured of Soviet support on the Kashmir issue, the major focus of its foreign as well as domestic policies. Russian commentaries consistently backed India's claims to Kashmir. In 1957, presumably at India's request, the Soviet Union vetoed a Security Council resolution on a plebiscite in Kashmir; a few years earlier Russia had abstained from voting on a similar resolution. New Delhi, for its part, refrained from criticizing the USSR in the Hungarian episode of 1956 - a restraint made more palatable in India by the simultaneous (and, to most Indians, far more objectionable)

assault on the Suez Canal by Great Britain, France and Israel. Meanwhile, Moscow gained an authentic Third World voice to supplement its own in opposing colonialism, imperialism and military alliances like SEATO and the Baghdad Pact.

For these advantages the Russians could afford to be casual about certain ideological considerations normally injected into their political commentaries. Notions such as proletarian hegemony, socialist transformation, and the proper role of Communist parties in colonial revolutions were rarely discussed in Soviet articles on India during the 1950s. Nehru, once the "running dog of imperialism", was by 1955 considered an "outstanding statesman";[4] Gandhi, for years excoriated by Soviet spokesmen, was referred to by Bulganin in his speech before the Indian Parliament in November 1955 as "the distinguished leader of the Indian national movement".[5] It was the "common friendship and unity" of Russia, China and India, two leading Soviet scholars wrote in 1957, which constituted the major force for peace in Asia.[6] No other non-Communist power in the Third World enjoyed so high a regard in Moscow during these years.

The Russians, meanwhile, managed to maintain outwardly normal relations with Indian Communists without upsetting the diplomatic relationship. CPI delegations came regularly and openly to Moscow for consultations and to attend international conferences; in 1960 Mikhail Suslov led a CPSU delegation to India to attend an Indian party congress. While there is no reliable evidence of what was privately discussed on these occasions, there is also no evidence that the CPI's policies during these years were at variance with Moscow's. When the CPI government in Kerala was dismissed in 1959, the Russians refrained from sharp criticism of Nehru's action.[7]

All evidence, in short, suggests an unruffled era in Soviet-Indian relations during the latter half of the 1950s. A Russian description of this relationship in 1957 as "a classic illustration of the principles of peaceful coexistence in practice"[8] appears to be essentially correct.

During the 1960s complex international rivalries in South Asia affected the course of Soviet-Indian relations. The most formidable rivalry early in the decade, that between India and China, was in some measure brought on by Soviet policies in India, especially aid policies. Credits extended to India by the end of 1960 were significantly greater than announced credits to China (nearly $800 million as compared to $450 million) and there is little doubt that this was a serious irritant to Sino-Indian relations, already strained by other factors; even if aid to China was larger than announced - as suggested, for instance, in the large trade imbalance between the two countries during the 1950s[9] - it was still greatly limited by Soviet commitments to India.

When the first Sino-Indian clashes along the Tibetan border occurred in September 1959, the Russians reacted cautiously. News coverage was initially confined to reporting, without comment, the official communiqués and statements by both parties. A TASS release on 9 September accused the Western press of exploiting the incident and expressed a hope, without seeking to attach blame, that the two nations would soon resolve their dispute.[10] Khrushchev, reporting at the end of

October on his recent visit to China (following his visit to the United States), also struck a neutral pose: negotiations, he hoped, would yield "satisfaction to both sides".[11] On an issue of some importance to Peking, then, Moscow had withheld its support in order not to jeopardize good relations with New Delhi; if the price of these good relations was to be worse relations with Peking, the Russians were evidently prepared to pay it. The Chinese were subsequently to make much of Soviet restraint on this occasion, calling it a "betrayal of proletarian internationalism" and therefore the entering wedge against the unity of the Communist bloc.[12]

Three years later, responding to a new and far more serious clash between China and India, the Russians were less restrained. Reporting of the border war of October-November 1962 in the Soviet press was as dispassionate as in 1959, but Russian behaviour could no longer be described as neutral. Arms shipments to India continued during the crisis, in accordance with an agreement concluded in August, and the Russians made no effort to conceal this.[13] Even if the Russians had been able to demonstrate their neutrality, however, this would have to be construed - in a crisis as severe as the Sino-Indian border war of 1962 - as a repudiation of the Chinese; indeed, Soviet behaviour was everywhere understood to be so.

As the Sino-Soviet dispute progressed, following bitter exchanges during 1963, the Russians of course became more outspoken in attaching blame to Peking where border clashes between India and China were concerned. By 1969 Soviet observers were charging the Chinese not only with provoking local incidents along the disputed border but with arming and training guerrilla forces for more deliberate aggression.[14]

If the logic of deteriorating Soviet relations with Peking led to greater support of New Delhi in its feud with the Chinese, a different logic led to withdrawal of Soviet support to the Indians over Kashmir. The arms Moscow had been sending in increasing volume to India since 1960 (reaching a value of about $300 million by 1964) were used not only against China but equally, and inevitably, against Pakistan. For reasons discussed elsewhere (see below, under Pakistan), an escalation of Indo-Pakistani rivalry was not in Moscow's interests and after 1962, when Moscow again, at India's request, vetoed a Security Council resolution on a plebiscite in Kashmir, the Russians adopted an increasingly neutral posture over the Kashmir issue. They were spared the necessity of deciding whether to veto yet another United Nations resolution in 1964, since the United States did not press for a vote,[15] but had somehow to respond to the serious fighting which broke out the following year, first in the Rann of Kutch and later in Kashmir itself. On both occasions the Soviet Union unambiguously asserted its neutrality; neither party was as much to blame, Soviet observers argued, as certain foreign powers - notably the United States.[16] The Russians meanwhile worked conscientiously for a resolution of the conflict and succeeded in bringing the Indians and Pakistanis together at Tashkent in early 1966. Prime Minister Shastri and President Ayub Khan, with some patient prodding by Kosygin, agreed to settle their differences "through peaceful means" and in an atmosphere of outward good will diplomatic relations were resumed; Shastri's death in Tashkent, immediately after signing the declaration, added a special dimension of significance to the settlement. The Tashkent

Declaration, though it was by no means final with respect to the Kashmir issue, was considered by many to be Russia's most impressive diplomatic victory in Asia in the post-1955 era.

If Soviet neutrality in the sub-continent was to have any meaning after Tashkent, the Russians needed to reconsider their arms policies. During the 1965 crisis, while asserting its neutrality and seeking a settlement, the Soviet Union had none the less continued to discuss arms deliveries with India[17] - in contrast to Great Britain and the United States who promptly suspended military aid to both belligerents. The Russians could not continue their one-sided policy: they must either halt arms deliveries to India or provide arms to Pakistan. They chose the latter course and in doing so provoked the first serious impasse in Soviet-Indian relations. Following the announcement of the Soviet-Pakistani arms agreement of July 1968, conservative Hindu leaders both in and outside the Congress Party were incensed by what appeared to them to be Moscow's defection from their just cause in Kashmir.[18] The Russians of course denied that the arms agreement with Pakistan signified any shift in Soviet policies towards India: Madame Furtseva, the Russian Minister of Culture, made such a denial in Madras in March 1969 and Kosygin did the same in Calcutta in September.[19] Mrs. Gandhi, who had been close to the Soviet leaders for many years, also sought to assure her Indian colleagues that "the totality of India's relations with the USSR" was unaffected by the arms agreement with Pakistan.[20] But uneasiness in India was not quieted. The mounting opposition to Mrs. Gandhi in the Congress, which was characterized by much anti-Soviet sentiment in the summer of 1969 and which led to the split in the party in November, was in no small measure due to the Soviet arms agreement with Pakistan the year before. It was a dilemma that admitted no easy solution. In the context of tangled rivalries in South Asia, closer relations with Pakistan inevitably meant a cooling of relations with India, just as warmer relations with New Delhi in the 1950s had contributed to resentment in Peking.

The 1968 arms agreement with Pakistan was not the only cause of Indian dissatisfaction with the Russians. Other reasons for discontent, as reported in the normally outspoken Indian press, included: Soviet mapping of the Sino-Indian border, which persistently ignored New Delhi's claims; inflexible Soviet trade policies, as India's import needs shifted from industrial equipment, which the Russians had provided since the mid-1950s, to raw materials which the Soviet Union could not provide as cheaply as other suppliers;[21] hostile commentary on Indian public figures in programmes of Radio Peace and Progress, a new Moscow-sponsored radio station designed for foreign listeners;[22] and - perhaps most serious of all, given the sensitivity of the Indians - the arrogance of Russian representatives in their negotiations with Indian officials. When a Soviet delegation under the Deputy Foreign Minister Firyubin visited New Delhi in September 1968 to discuss various matters, the Times of India charged that members of the delegation behaved "in the manner of representatives of an imperial power dealing with a dependency"; The Statesman said of the Russian foreign aid chief Semën Skachkov, following a visit to India in December, that he behaved "rather like a viceroy of yore on an inspection tour".[23]

It should not be imagined, of course, that

disillusion in the Soviet-Indian relationship came only from Indians. The Russians too were increasingly critical of Indian developments at the end of the 1960s - and not merely in crudely prepared broadcasts over Radio Peace and Progress. The misgivings of Soviet scholars and commentators, usually more circumspect than those of journalists in New Delhi, never exceeded the large volume of favourable reporting of Indian developments in the Russian press, but they reflected serious concern over India's course. Even before Nehru's death in 1964 Russian commentators complained of the slow progress towards socialism in India. In 1962, for instance, a Soviet scholar noted with some perplexity, in the course of praising initial steps towards a "state sector" in the Indian economy, that contrary to experience elsewhere the growth of this sector in India encouraged bourgeois tendencies and increased disparity in incomes.[24] In 1964 a Pravda correspondent observed: "Whereas in the world at large socialism is growing from day to day, the Indian monopolies and their political organizations ... keep India in a condition where capitalism may pursue its classic path."[25] In 1966 N.A. Simoniya, a persistent critic of soft views of Third World "socialism" within the Russian Orientalist community, compared India to Turkey and the Philippines, nations "where the result of national liberation has been to entrench the bourgeoisie in power".[26]

The forces in India frustrating the growth of socialism were initially identified with Rightist parties like Swatantra and Jan Sangh, whose "Fascist tendencies" were noted by Soviet commentators in the early 1960s.[27] By the end of the 1960s, however, reaction was found to be growing in the Congress itself. Economic success, R.A. Ul'yanovskiy wrote in 1970, had led to the emergence of a "compact and exploitative élite", which after Nehru's death gained increasing influence in the Congress leadership through the so-called Syndicate faction; it was this faction which brought on the mid-term crisis in Mrs. Gandhi's government in the autumn of 1969 and, in November, the split in the party.[28] The acute political instability that followed the 1969 crisis led to an extended reappraisal by Soviet observers of all aspects of Indian life. The viability of the Indian political system was questioned; religious discord and caste divisions were subjected to sharp criticism; the repeated failures of land reform were emphasized; growing disparity in India between the rich and poor was considered insoluble under existing conditions. Mrs. Gandhi was not herself held accountable for India's shortcomings, but neither was she singled out for praise in Soviet commentaries, as both she and her father had been in past years. The Russians were apparently waiting to see how her government would fare in the next General Election, which after a year or more of political turmoil was finally called for March 1971.[29]

The year 1971 brought drastic changes to the subcontinent and a decisive shift in Soviet-Indian relations. Mrs. Gandhi's spectacular success in the March elections, first of all - her supporters gained two-thirds of the seats in the Lok Sabha - prompted an immediate reappraisal of her regime in Moscow. The Russians could now proceed with their policies in India confident that the government with which they dealt was more securely in power than at any time since the death of Nehru seven years earlier. The crisis that broke out in East Pakistan soon after the election also strengthened Soviet-Indian relations. The Russian government remained officially neutral in the

mounting crisis, but there was little doubt, to judge from Soviet press commentaries and emergency relief efforts for the Bengali refugees, where Moscow's sympathies lay. It is not certain whether these sympathies for the East Bengalis and their Indian allies were strong enough during the spring and early summer of 1971 to bring about a reversal of Russia's neutralist policy in the sub-continent in the event of an open clash between India and Pakistan. The Russians knew their Tashkent policy to be unpopular in India, not only among Rightists, who were of course discredited after the March elections, but in government circles as well. Congress leaders close to Mrs. Gandhi, buoyed by the size of the recent mandate, felt less dependent on the USSR than they had in some years and during the spring pressed for a less ambiguous Soviet posture in India; there was talk, if that failed, of a wholly new orientation in Indian foreign policy. It was Sino-American détente, however, not Indian distaste for the Tashkent policy, that finally led the Russians to abandon the policy. The sudden prospect of an American-Chinese-Pakistani alliance in South Asia, following Dr. Kissinger's secret visit to Peking in July and the announcement of President Nixon's forthcoming visit to China, was acutely disturbing to the Russians and prompted them to act quickly. The Indians, no less troubled by the same prospect as the crisis over Bangladesh intensified, were responsive to Russian overtures. It was in this atmosphere that the Treaty of Peace, Friendship and Co-operation was signed during Gromyko's hastily arranged visit to New Delhi in early August.

The pact appears to have had a predominantly political rather than military object and in this sense was different from the Soviet-Egyptian Treaty of Friendship and Co-operation, signed in May, with which it was immediately compared in foreign commentaries and which it in certain respects resembled. The Soviet-Indian treaty was meant to reaffirm the diplomatic alliance of Moscow and New Delhi in South Asia, especially against any coalition including China, the United States and Pakistan. There were, however, military implications in the treaty. According to Article IX, "In the event that either side is attacked or threatened with attack, the high contracting parties shall immediately enter into mutual consultations in order to remove such a threat and to take appropriate effective measures to ensure the peace and security of their countries."[30] It is not likely that the Russians in August intended this article to be used as a device for their active participation in any Indo-Pakistani conflict. The communiqué at the end of Gromyko's visit explicitly rejected a "military solution" in East Pakistan.[31] Subsequent coverage of the East Pakistan crisis in the Soviet press reiterated this position and official documents carefully refrained from any mention of "Bangladesh". Soviet relations with Islamabad, meanwhile, were carried on as normally as possible (see below, under Pakistan). When fighting finally broke out, however - in East Pakistan in late November and along all frontiers a week later - the Russians promptly sided with the Indians. Press commentaries unambiguously supported the Indians, blamed the crisis entirely on Pakistan's policy of "cruel repression" of the Bengalis and described the conflict in East Pakistan as a "people's liberation war".[32] Delegations were exchanged to conduct "mutual consultations" in accordance with Article IX of the August treaty (see Chronology). Soviet diplomats in the United Nations vetoed three cease-fire resolutions in the Security Council that appeared to attach blame, or equal blame, to India. The extent of Soviet military support to New Delhi during the war itself is difficult to fix, but virtually all foreign observers agreed that so decisive a victory for the Indians would not have been possible without the impressive build-up of Russian arms over recent months.[33]

Soviet-Indian relations were never more cordial than during the months following the brief war between India and Pakistan. This was reflected in the increased tempo of high official exchange, the accelerated rate of co-operation in cultural and aid programmes, expanded trade, and the generally warmer press commentaries in each country with respect to the other. The Soviet government, meanwhile, recognized India's protégé Bangladesh in January 1972 and in March warmly received Prime Minister Mujibur Rahman with a large delegation of his chief aides. There were, to be sure, no tangible Soviet gains in India such as naval bases and refuelling stations, but there were not a few foreign observers who believed, despite repeated denials by Soviet and Indian spokesmen, that the acquisition of such bases was high among the Russians' next objectives in South Asia.[34]

We should return finally to Moscow's relations with the Indian Communists, for the close ties with the CPI - that is, its orthodox faction - were unique in a nation where Moscow simultaneously maintained such excellent relations with the non-Communist government in power.

The Indian Communists by 1970 were split three ways. The original CPI, headed by S.A. Dange, claimed a membership of 243,000, mainly concentrated in four states - Bihar, Andhra Pradesh, Kerala and West Bengal.[35] The so-called Parallel, or Marxist, faction which had broken off from the CPI in 1964, had a smaller total membership but was the strongest single party in West Bengal. The third faction, a Naxalite group called the Marxist-Leninists, was organized in 1969 by younger Communists in West Bengal who opposed the leadership of both major groups; it was endorsed by the Chinese Communists, but had a membership of fewer than 10,000.[36] The Russians of course supported the Dange faction - or party, since the three groups were organized into separate parties - but maintained ties with the Marxists as well; Sundarayya, for instance, Secretary-General of the Parallel CPI, spent several weeks in Moscow in 1966 undergoing a medical cure (see Chronology).

One might have expected that the growing misgivings in Moscow about the course of Indian affairs in the latter half of the 1960s would signal a greater interest in the CPI. This was not apparent. The exchange of delegations during the national and international congresses and on other formal occasions was perfunctory, so far as is known (see Chronology); even high-level talks between CPI and CPSU officials - including on several occasions Brezhnev himself - do not appear to have been designed, at least so far as the Russians were concerned, to give the CPI a special voice in Indian politics. Students of Communist affairs should not assume, of course, that conversations between Communist leaders have no political significance because the strategies agreed upon are not always apparent; Russian and Indian party leaders may indeed have discussed long-range plans to increase the CPI's stature in India. Nothing in the behaviour of the CPI, however, suggests that the Russians urged strategies

on them which might have embarrassed Moscow's allies in the Congress.

Moscow's strategy for the Indian Communists, as for Communists everywhere in the latter half of the 1960s, was to unite among themselves and form alliances, or united fronts, with other Leftist groups. In the General Election of 1967, Soviet observers noted that Communists had scored successes only in Kerala where rival Communist factions had united; elsewhere Congress losses had been gains for Swatantra and Jan Sangh, which had allied in a temporary coalition.[37] In the 1969 state elections, Communists had been able to double the number of their seats in local legislatures and won an outright victory in West Bengal by forming a United Left Front.[38] The Russians urged the same strategy in the 1971 General Election, but without success. The West Bengal coalition had by this time fallen, due to personal and other rivalries between the Communist factions, and unity had not been restored when Mrs. Gandhi dissolved Parliament. The outcome of the 1971 elections, from the Communist viewpoint, was mixed. Mrs. Gandhi's huge majority freed her from dependence on the CPI and accordingly reduced the Moscow-oriented Communists once again to the role of a minor party. On the other hand, the CPI held its 23 seats in the lower house; the Marxists gained six seats and, with a total of 25, became the second largest single party in the Lok Sabha (although 20 of these seats were from West Bengal). Mrs. Gandhi's gains, in short, came not at the expense of the two major Communist factions but rather at the expense of the Right. The Marxist-Leninists, meanwhile, lost influence throughout India and by 1972 faced extinction.[39] If the two surviving factions should reunite, as the Russians wished, the Communists could again become an important second force in India, capable of wielding a deciding vote once Mrs. Gandhi's 1971 majorities were whittled away in subsequent elections. The Soviet leadership apparently sought no more than this degree of leverage for its comrades-in-arms in India - at least in the short term.

Aid, Trade and Cultural Co-operation

The Soviet aid programme in India was by a considerable margin the largest in the Third World. The total credit extended was in excess of $1.5 billion, though sources are not in agreement on the exact amount.[40] These credits, covering both specific projects and general Five-Year Plan development, were utilized more promptly than in other developing nations - a circumstance that explains in part the prompt extension of new credits through the mid-1960s as old ones ran out. In August 1969 Mrs. Gandhi stated that the unused portion of all Soviet credits stood at approximately $400 million,[41] a figure which reflected a utilization rate of about 75 per cent over the period 1955-69; although Mrs. Gandhi was dissatisfied with this rate, it was none the less considerably higher than in the Third World as a whole.[42]

The greater part of Soviet aid was in four areas of development: steel (with the giant plants at Bhilai and Bokaro, two of India's four plants in this sector); power (with the largest plants at Neyveli, Korba, Obra and Bhakra); machine tools (with plants at Ranchi, Durgapur and Hardwar); and oil (with the largest refineries at Barauni and Koiyali). In addition to these major projects, the following lesser activities are noteworthy: pharmaceutical, antibiotics and surgical instrument plants (Hyderabad, Rishikesh and Madras); precision and mechanical instruments (Kota and Palghat); a technical college (Bombay); a mechanized farm (Suratgarh); and a compressor and pump factory. By 1972 the Russians had completed 37 of these major projects and 30 more were in progress.[43] According to Mrs. Gandhi, 55 per cent of India's oil production, 30 per cent of its steel and 20 per cent of total power production came from plants built with Soviet aid.[44]

Although the total aid extended to India by the Soviet Union up to the end of 1969 was greatly less than that extended by the United States,[45] its effectiveness, as an instrument of foreign policy, was undoubtedly greater. The Russians advertised their aid more effectively than did Americans. Meanwhile, their decision at an early date to concentrate on very visible projects, though few in number, helped to create an image of the Soviet Union as India's principal benefactor. Bhilai and Bokaro, for instance, are names known to every Indian, as Aswan is known to every Egyptian; no such identity attaches to the more numerous American projects, despite their greater impact on the Indian economy as a whole.

The Soviet aid programme appears to have run into some difficulties after the mid-1960s. Kosygin, during his visit to New Delhi in January 1968, was reported to have been disturbed by the poor performance of the Russian-built plants and to have ordered more rigorous steps to assure efficiency.[46] Russian commentators continued to complain - even after relations between the two countries had begun to improve during 1971 - of India's slow economic growth and the growing gulf between rich and poor.[47] Meanwhile, the cost of servicing its huge debt to the USSR was becoming increasingly burdensome to the Indians. By 1970 India was paying more to the USSR in the form of debt service than it was receiving in new aid. Moreover, it often proved impossible to agree on the price of manufactured goods India wished to export to the USSR in payment of the debt, since the Soviet market was already glutted with Russian-made goods that could not be sold abroad.[48] Many of the minor irritations and frustrations in the Soviet aid programme, exacerbated during the years of relatively cool relations at the end of the 1960s, were undoubtedly removed with the rapid improvement of relations in 1971. The increased tempo of visits by economic delegations after the Indo-Pakistani war suggested that lagging programmes would be accelerated and new credits extended.

The major increases in Soviet-Indian trade occurred in the 1950s - a tenfold increase, for instance, in the years 1954-58, following the agreement of 1953.[49] Trade continued to grow until the mid-1960s when it levelled off, despite projections of significant increases in the trade agreement of January 1966 (a two and a half-fold increase projected for 1966-70 over the previous five-year period). India remained the Soviet Union's leading trading partner in Asia in the latter half of the 1960s; in 1968 it was estimated trade with India constituted 40 per cent of Russia's trade with all developing nations in Asia.[50] The Soviet Union, however, ranked only third or fourth among India's trading partners, along with Japan, and well behind the United States and Britain.[51]

Soviet military aid to India followed economic aid, the reverse of the pattern in Egypt. It is likely that the Soviet Union offered arms to India in the 1950s - for instance, during the exchange of high military missions in 1957 (see Chronology) - but no agreement was announced until October 1960. That agreement, involving the purchase of various types of aircraft, was followed by further orders in 1961 and 1962. In August 1962, on the eve of the Sino-Indian border war, a major agreement was concluded for a plant in India to produce MIG-21s - apparently the first licensing for the building of Russian military aircraft outside the USSR, including the Soviet bloc. Additional arms agreements were reported in succeeding years, including the construction of a missile complex and training school (1963) and the purchase of advanced fighter-bombers and other modern weapons. The value of Soviet military aid to India by the end of 1971 probably exceeded $1 billion. This made Russia the largest supplier of arms to India, its deliveries exceeding by more than four to one those of the United States (which did not resume significant arms sales to India after suspending shipments during the Kashmir crisis of 1965).[52] On the eve of war with Pakistan in the autumn of 1971 it was reported that India had more than 200 MIG-21s and an estimated 140 SU-7 bombers; more aircraft were said to be en route to India.[53] Estimates from the year before indicated that India possessed 450 Russian tanks, 50 SAM-2 (Guideline) missiles and four submarines of Soviet make, in addition to various other naval craft, artillery of different types and assorted small arms.[54]

The emergence of the Soviet Union as the principal supplier of arms to India in the 1960s was, of course, an important factor in international developments in South Asia, but so far as Moscow's policies in India are concerned, this new undertaking must be seen in the context of continuing Soviet activity there. Russian objectives in India had from the start been to decrease New Delhi's dependence on the Western powers, especially the United States, and to increase its obligation to the USSR. The sale of arms to India - at least before the Friendship Treaty of 1971 - was merely another way of accomplishing this end, along with trade, economic aid, cultural co-operation and diplomatic exchange. Suggestions that the Russians were being allowed to build a naval base in India, in partial repayment for their arms, were vigorously denied by spokesmen for Mrs. Gandhi's government.[55]

Cultural co-operation between Russia and India (meagrely reflected in the Chronology in the interest of space) was the most extensive in the Third World between 1955 and 1970 and by the end of this period probably exceeded co-operation between the Soviet Union and its closest allies in Eastern Europe. Four information centres operated in India by 1970 (in New Delhi, Bombay, Calcutta and Madras), in addition to a large cultural centre in New Delhi. The cultural protocol for 1968-69 provided for 500 personal exchanges, exclusive of dozens of technical, trade union and official government delegations which were exchanged annually outside the protocol. Approximately 400 Indians each year followed academic or technical courses in the Soviet Union, many of them on four- to six-year scholarships provided by the Soviet government.[56]

In the area of "information exchange" (a euphemism for Soviet propaganda), Moscow was directing radio programmes to India by the end of the 1960s in eight local languages, in addition to English and Hindi.[57] A bimonthly journal entitled Soviet Land, designed specifically for Indians and published in 14 languages, had a circulation of over half a million by 1965. The Information Department of the Soviet Embassy in New Delhi was at this time releasing 16 different news serials (both daily and weekly) which covered virtually all aspects of Soviet life and Soviet foreign policy.[58] If any significant number of Indians remained ignorant of what Russian propagandists wished them to know of the USSR, it was not for want of effort on the propagandists' part.

The record of Russia's relations with India is from one perspective a classic illustration of the pre-eminence of national interest over ideology in Soviet foreign policy. India at no time during the 17 years reviewed here aroused the enthusiasm of Russian ideologues: it was never considered a "progressive" state, comparable in Soviet eyes to Ghana, Guinea, Mali, Algeria, the UAR, or even Burma; its social structure and economic policies were often criticized, sometimes sharply. Yet India received more Soviet credits for economic development than all the "progressive" states combined and nearly a quarter of Soviet credits by the end of 1970 to the entire Third World. Political and cultural exchanges were more extensive than with any other developing nation outside the Communist camp. In trade, India stood second only to the UAR among Russia's Third World trading partners. And in military aid, though a late recipient of Russian arms, India stood behind only the UAR, Indonesia and possibly Syria in total deliveries up to the end of 1970. Other nations, to be sure, stood in a stronger relationship to India in certain areas - the United States, for instance, in aid and trade - but the magnitude of Russia's total commitment is not in question. So extensive a commitment to a nation attracting only moderate ideological interest in Moscow indicates clearly that doctrine was less crucial than other considerations in fixing Soviet policies.

These "other considerations", as we have defined them here, were defensive at the outset - that is, the protection afforded by a neutralist India against American-sponsored alliances aimed at the USSR. Subsequently Russia's concern shifted to expanding Chinese interests in South Asia, and again the relationship with India was crucial. India's oil resources undoubtedly attracted the Russians, as Middle East reserves did after 1965 when the Soviet Union began to formulate petroleum policies on a global scale. Certainly Moscow eyed India's many ports and harbours as potential bases for Russia's rapidly expanding Indian Ocean squadron. At all times, meanwhile, India's massive presence in the sub-continent was a factor the Russians were obliged to consider in any strategies they devised in Asia, whether militant or benign.

Russia's multiple motives in India and the considerable investment there did not prevent the relationship from becoming strained in the late 1960s - and this impasse was as important to the profile of Asian politics as Moscow's huge commitment to India in the first place. Uneasiness, we have seen, grew on both sides for varied and complex reasons. But the grievances enumerated should be seen in a reasonable perspective. They were irritants to the Soviet-Indian relationship; they did not foreshadow its collapse. By the 1970s India and the Soviet Union relied too heavily on each other to jeopardize an alliance built up over nearly two decades. India needed Russia as an ally against Pakistan and China, as financier and contractor for a significant sector of its industry and - perhaps most important - as supplier of arms and of spare parts and replacements for those arms. Russia's reliance on India was less explicit, but no less important. Whether India's friendship served Soviet purposes in rivalry with the West, in confrontation with China, in the management of the rest of Asia, or in some other enterprise, it was central to Russian foreign policy. The coming together of Russia and India in the Treaty of Friendship was a predictable end to the impasse in their relationship. The Tashkent policy was, from the Soviet viewpoint, the preferred posture in South Asia, but it could not replace the alliance with India in a crisis.

Bibliography

Barnds, William J. "Moscow and South Asia", Problems of Communism, May-June 1972, pp. 12-31.

Bhabani, Sen Gupta. "Moscow, Peking and the Indian Political Scene After Nehru", Orbis, Summer 1968, pp. 534-62.

Bibliografiya Indii, 2nd edition, 1965, 608 pp.

Central Asian Review, No. 3, 1961, pp. 307-13: "Indian-Soviet Cultural Relations".

____. No. 4, 1961, pp. 413-16: "India's Economic Relations with the Socialist Bloc".

____. No. 3, 1968, pp. 229-43: "Recent Soviet Writing on India" (by Hubert Evans).

Donaldson, Robert Hershel. "The Soviet Approach to India: Doctrinal Assessment and Operational Strategy", Harvard University doctoral thesis, 1969 (to be published under the title Soviet Policy toward India: Ideology and Strategy).

____. "India: the Soviet Stake in Stability", Asian Survey, June 1972, pp. 425-92.

Dutt, Vidya Prakash. "India, China and the Soviet Union", chapter in Kurt London, ed., Unity and Contradiction (see Main Bibliography), pp. 248-62.

Eldridge, P.J. The Politics of Foreign Aid in India, London, 1969, 289pp. (Chapter 4 deals with the objectives of Soviet aid to India).

Gelman, Harry. "The Communist Party of India: Sino-Soviet Battleground", chapter in A. Doak Barnett, ed., Communist Strategies in Asia (see Main Bibliography), pp. 101-47.

Goldman, Marshall I. Soviet Foreign Aid (see Main Bibliography), pp. 84-114.

Graham, Ian. "The Indo-Soviet MIG Deal and Its International Repercussions", Asian Survey, May 1964, pp. 823-32.

Hasan, Zubeida. "Soviet Arms to Pakistan and India", Pakistan Horizon, Fourth Quarter, 1968, pp. 344-55.

Kapur, Harish. "The Soviet Union and Indo-Pakistan Relations", International Studies, July-October 1966, pp. 150-57.

____. "India and the Soviet Union", Survey, No. 78 (Winter 1971), pp. 189-215.

Kocharian, M.A. Druzhba i sotrudnichestvo SSSR i Indii, 1959, 46pp. (covers relations between

India and the USSR, 1947-58).

Kondrat'yev, V.A. and L.A. Fituni. Indiya: ekonomi-cheskoye razvitiye i sotrudnichestvo s SSSR, 1965, 144pp.

Menon, K.P.S. The Flying Troika, Oxford, 1963 (extracts from the diary of India's ambassador to the USSR, 1952-61).

____. "Indo-Soviet Relations", in A. Appadori, ed., India, Studies in Social and Political Development, Delhi, 1967, pp. 227-37.

Mizan, March-April 1967, pp. 75-79: "Indian Elections: Soviet Reactions".

____. September-October 1968, pp. 199-205: "Soviet Writing on India".

____. November-December 1969, pp. 315-20: "The USSR and the Indian Political Crisis".

Naik, J.A. Soviet Policy Toward India: From Stalin to Brezhnev, Vikas Publications (Delhi), 1970 (uncritical study praising Russian policies).

Nezavisimaya Indiya: 10 let nezavisimosti, 1958 (includes articles on early economic and cultural relations with the USSR).

Noonan, Norma C. "Soviet-Indian Relations, 1953-1963", Indiana University doctoral thesis, 1965.

Retzlaff, Ralph. "Revisionism and Dogmatism in the Communist Party of India", in Robert A. Scalapino, ed., The Communist Revolution in Asia (see Main Bibliography), pp. 309-42.

Rothermund, Dietmar. "India and the Soviet Union", Annals, the American Academy of Political and Social Sciences, November 1969, pp. 89-101.

Sager, Peter. Moscow's Hand in India, Berne, 1966 (a biased study, but with useful data on Soviet propaganda activity in India).

Seth, S.P. "Russia's Role in Indo-Pakistani Politics", Asian Survey, August 1969, pp. 614-24.

Siegal, Richard Lewis. "Soviet Policy Towards India, 1956-64: Causes and Effects of Sino-Soviet Divergence", Columbia University doctoral thesis, 1967.

Simon, Sheldon W. "The Kashmir Dispute in Sino-Soviet Perspective", Asian Survey, March 1967, pp. 176-87.

Stein, Arthur B. India and the Soviet Union: the Nehru Era, Chicago, 1969 (the most detailed study of Soviet-Indian relations published up to the end of 1969).

Tansky, Leo. US and USSR Aid to Developing Countries (see Main Bibliography), pp. 69-119.

Tidmarsh, Kyril. "The Soviet Re-assessment of Mahatma Gandhi", St. Antony's Papers (Oxford), No. 8, 1960, pp. 86-115.

Vaidyanath, R. "Some Recent Trends in Soviet Policies Toward India and Pakistan", International Studies, January 1966, pp. 429-47.

INDIA

Chronology

(See explanatory note on tables, p. 6; routine exchanges of commercial and trade union delegations are not shown.)

	Political		Economic		Cultural
Pre-1955					
Apr 1947	Agreement on dip- lomatic relations				
Aug 1947	Independence				
Dec 1949	Diplomatic relations with China				
July 1953	Indira Gandhi in USSR				
		Dec 1953	5-year trade agreement		
				Jan 1954	Bolshoy dancers in India
Apr 1954	Sino-Indian agreement on Tibet and on "pantsheel" concept				
June 1954	Chou En-lai in India				
				July 1954	Indian dancers in USSR
Oct 1954	Nehru in CPR				
		Nov 1954	Economic delegation in USSR for oil, trade talks		

	Political		Economic		Cultural
1955					
				Jan	– Cultural delegation in India
		Feb	– Agreement on steel plant; credits promised		
Apr	– Nehru, Chou En-lai meet at Bandung				
				?	– Academician Ostrovityanov heads delegation to India
June	– NEHRU IN USSR for 16-day visit				
Nov	– KHRUSHCHEV, BULGANIN IN INDIA for 12-day visit	Nov	– USSR represented in Delhi trade fair; pur- chase agreements on drilling rigs, tractors, etc.		
		Dec	– Indian handicraft exhibition opens in Moscow		

	Political		Economic		Cultural
1956					
Feb	– CPI secretary Ghosh in USSR for XX Congress			Feb	– Scientists in India
Mar	– Mikoyan heads delegation to India				
		Apr	– CREDIT AGREEMENT on Bhilai steel works ($125m) – Shipping agreement: creation of Bombay-Odessa line		
June	– Vice-president Radhakrishnan in USSR				
				July	– Deputy foreign minister heads cultural delegation to USSR
Aug	– Maharaja of Jaipur in USSR				
Oct	– Radhakrishnan in CPR			Oct	– Film delegation in India
Nov	– Nehru persuades Dalai Lama to return to Tibet	Nov	– CREDIT AGREEMENT for second 5-year plan: oil refineries, fertilizer plants, coal mining equipment, etc. ($125m)	Nov	– Indian film festival in USSR
Nov–Dec	– Chou En-lai twice in India				
Dec	– Nehru in USA	Dec	– Agricultural delegation in India	Dec	– Writers in India for Afro-Asian congress – Scholarly delegation in Delhi for philosophical congress
1957					
Jan	– Defence minister Zhukov in India	Jan	– Trade protocol	Jan	– Soviet film festival in Delhi – Scholars in India for scientific conference
Feb	– USSR vetoes UN resolution on Kashmir plebiscite				
Mar	– CPI wins Kerala election, forms new government				
		May	– Technical assistance agreement on oil drilling: USSR to provide experts, equipment and training – Work begins on Bhilai plant		

INDIA

	Political		Economic		Cultural
1957 (cont.)					
July	– Military delegation in USSR				
Sept	– Radhakrishnan in CPR	Sept	– Economic delegation in India		
		Oct	– Agricultural delegation in India		
Nov	– Ghosh heads CPI delegation to USSR for anniversary and world congress	Nov	– Protocol on 5 major projects under November 1956 agreement		
		Dec	– Steel minister heads delegation to USSR		
1958					
Jan	– Government delegation in USSR	Jan	– Oil survey completed in Punjab – 1953 trade agreement extended to 1959	Jan	– Formation of Soviet-Indian cultural society
Feb	– Parliamentary delegation in India	Feb	– Air officials in USSR	Feb	– Radio delegation in India
				May	– Academic delegation in USSR
		June	– Air service agreement		
Aug	– Parliamentary delegation in USSR for opening of air service				
		Sept	– Gift of steel mill equipment	Sept	– Education delegation in USSR
		Oct	– Trade delegation in USSR: new shipping agreement – Oil minister in USSR	Oct	– Film festival in Delhi
		Nov	– New expanded trade agreement for 1958–63 – First blast furnace completed at Bhilai	Nov	– Lawyers in USSR
		Dec	– Protocol on Bombay technical institute – Economic delegation in India to tour tea plantations – Gift of computer to statistical centre	Dec	– Cultural delegation in USSR
1959					
Jan	– Ghosh in USSR for XXI congress	Jan	– Gift of locomotives	Jan	– Scientists in India for conference
Feb	– High government delegation in India				
		Mar	– Mining officials in USSR		

	Political		Economic		Cultural

1959 (cont.)

	Political		Economic		Cultural
Apr	- Kashmir leader in USSR - CPR crushes Tibetan rising: <u>Dalai Lama</u> <u>flees to India</u>	Apr	- Statistics chief in USSR		
		May	- Resources minister heads delegation to USSR for oil talks - Contract for power station - Economic delegation in USSR: CREDIT AGREEMENTS for third 5-year plan ($375m); additional credit for pharma- ceutical plant (reported $20m)[59]	May	- Teachers delegation to USSR
July	- CPI government dis- <u>missed in Kerala</u>	July	- Gift of machine repair plant	July	- Cultural minister in USSR
Aug	- Delhi municipal dele- gation in Moscow	Aug	- Minister of economy in USSR: protocol on hydro-power station	Aug	- Doctors in USSR - Cultural delegation in USSR
Sept	- Ghosh in USSR - CPR-Indian border clash				
Oct	- Ghosh again in USSR <u>after Peking snub</u>	Oct	- CREDIT AGREEMENT for Barauni oil refinery (reported $25m)[60]		

1960

	Political		Economic		Cultural
Jan	- PRESIDENT VOROSHILOV IN INDIA for a fortnight			Jan	- Teleprinter service installed
Feb	- KHRUSHCHEV IN INDIA (en route to Indonesia)	Feb	- Protocols on oil extraction, engin- eering works	Feb	- Cultural agreement
		Mar	- Trade protocol		
Apr	- Suslov in India for CPI congress - Chou En-lai in India <u>for border talks</u>	Apr	- Protocol on hydro- electric generator	Apr	- Scientists in USSR
June	- PRESIDENT PRASAD IN USSR for 15-day visit	June	- Minister of mines in USSR: protocol on geological prospecting		
		July	- Finance minister in USSR: agreement on oil deliveries and survey in India		
		Aug	- SUPPLEMENTARY CREDIT AGREEMENT for third 5-year plan ($125m) - Agricultural delegation in USSR		

INDIA

	Political	Economic	Cultural

1960 (cont.)

	Political	Economic	Cultural
Oct	– Initial arms agreement (reported $31.5m)[61]		
Nov	– Ghosh in Moscow for world CP congress		

1961

	Political	Economic	Cultural
		Feb – Protocol on Neyveli power station	
Mar	– Deputy premier Kosygin in India		
		Apr – Protocol on technical, medical aid	
		May – High commercial delegation in USSR	
		July – Deputy labour minister in USSR	
		Aug – Aid to flood victims	Aug – Writers in USSR
Sept	– NEHRU IN USSR for 5-day visit – Agreement on sale of jet engines to India		Sept – Education delegation in USSR: cultural exchange protocol
Oct	– Ghosh leads CPI delegation to USSR for XXII congress	Oct – Agreement on atomic energy	Oct – Vocational educators in Tadzhikistan
Nov	– Nehru in USA		
Dec	– India occupies Goa – PRESIDENT BREZHNEV IN INDIA		

1962

	Political	Economic	Cultural
Jan	– Additional aircraft sold to India – CPI secretary Ghosh dies; succeeded by Dange		
Feb	– Parliamentary elections in India: CPI gains	Feb – Protocol on expansion of Bhilai works – Protocol on additional oil refineries	Feb – Cultural delegation in India: expanded agreement
		Mar – Contract for pharmaceutical plant	
		May – Technical delegation in USSR for talks on Ranchi, Durgapur plants	
		June – Contract for training of electrical technicians	
July	– Mikoyan and Air chief Vershinin in India (en route home from Indonesia)		

	Political		Economic		Cultural
1962 (cont.)					
Aug	– Agreement on jet aircraft factory in India and delivery of MIG-21s	Aug	– Contracts for Korba power station		
Sept	– Parliamentary delegation in USSR	Sept	– Contract for oil deliveries	Sept	– Botanists in USSR
Oct–Nov	– Sino-Indian border war: <u>USA, Britain pledge arms to India</u>	Oct	– Minister of mines in USSR – Shipping delegation in India: expanded agreement	Oct	– Tagorist delegation in USSR
Nov	– <u>CPI members arrested</u>	Nov	– Contract for drilling equipment		
1963					
		Jan	– Foreign ministry aide in USSR for trade talks		
		Feb	– Agreement to increase capacity of Neyveli power station		
		Mar	– Trade delegation in India: expanded 5-year agreement for 1964–68 (June)	Mar	– Scientific delegation in India to advise on water supply
Apr	– Defence minister Malinovskiy in India (en route from Indonesia)			Apr	– Agreement on training of engineers in USSR – Writers delegation in India
		May	– Protocols on precision instrument plant and expansion of oil refineries at Barauni and Koyali	May	– Cultural protocol for 1963
July	– Mrs. Indira Gandhi in USSR – Air chief of staff in USSR – Military delegation in USSR for arms talks – Dange in USSR	July	– Trade minister in USSR – Protocol on equipment at Bhakra power station	July	– Indian national exhibition in Moscow
		Aug	– Contract for coal mining project		
		Oct	– Bhakra dam completed – Pharmaceutical plant completed – Gift of polio vaccine – Gift of tractors		
Nov?	– Agreement on anti-aircraft missile complex and school (reported $40m)[62]	Nov	– Ranchi and Durgapur works completed – Protocol on oil survey	Nov	– Education delegation in USSR

INDIA

	Political		Economic		Cultural
1964					
		Jan	– Contract for tool plant survey	Jan	– Orientalist delegation in India for international congress
Feb	– Parliamentary delegation in India – Chou En-lai in Karachi: CPR supports Pakistan in Kashmir			Feb	– Cultural delegation in India; protocol for 1964
		Mar	– Protocols on pump plant, steel deliveries to India – Contract for Neyveli power station	Mar	– Education minister in India
				Apr	– Cultural delegation in India for conference
May	– Nehru dies; Shastri succeeds as premier – USSR supports India in UN debate on Kashmir	May	– Promise of credits for steel plant at Bokaro – Contract for electrical plant at Ranipur		
June	– MIKOYAN IN INDIA				
		July	– Trade protocol	July	– Cultural minister in USSR
Aug	– Defence minister Chavan in USSR – CPI members arrested after food riots	Aug	– Nuclear energy minister in India	Aug	– Russian language institutes open in India
Sept	– PRESIDENT RADHAKRISHNAN IN USSR for 8-day visit – Arms agreement (reported $300m)[63]			Sept	– Agreement on academic exchanges
Oct	– Foreign minister Swaran Singh in USSR				
Nov	– Mrs. Gandhi in USSR – CPI splits – Deputy foreign minister Lapin in India				
1965					
		Jan	– Economic delegation in India: CREDIT AGREEMENT for Bokaro plant ($225m) – Oil refinery completed		
Feb	– Parliamentary delegation in India – Mrs. Gandhi in USSR				
		Mar	– Protocol on oil prospecting		
Apr	– Indo-Pakistan fighting in Rann of Kutch; Shastri visit to USA postponed			Apr	– Expanded cultural agreement for 1965-66

	Political	Economic	Cultural

1965 (cont.)

May — SHASTRI IN USSR
on 8-day visit:
treaty of friendship

July — Mrs. Gandhi again
in USSR

Aug — Deputy premier
Mazurov in India
— Defence delegation in
USSR to buy submarines

Aug– — Indo-Pakistan fighting
Sept in Kashmir

Oct — State parliamentary
delegates in USSR

Nov — Finance minister
in USSR: proto-
cols for thermal
power plant and
radio station

Nov — Russian studies
institute opens
in New Delhi

Dec — Foreign minister Swaran
Singh in USSR on eve of
Tashkent conference

1966

Jan — SHASTRI DIES IN
TASHKENT after Indo-
Pakistan talks
— KOSYGIN IN INDIA
for Shastri funeral
— Mrs. Gandhi becomes
premier

Jan — New long-term trade
agreement

Feb — Left CPI secretary
Sundarayya returns
from medical cure
in USSR

Mar — Deputy foreign minister
Firyubin in India
— Dange leads CPI delega-
tion to USSR for XXIII
congress

Mar — Agreement on helicopter
deliveries
— Gift of tractors

Apr — Mrs. Gandhi in USSR
for 2 days en route
home from USA

Apr — Cultural delegation
in India: protocol

May — Contract for steel
plant equipment

June — Planning minister
in USSR

June — Education minister
in USSR

July — MRS. GANDHI IN USSR
for 5-day visit
— Congress party president
Kamaraj in USSR

Sept — Army chief of staff
in USSR
— Firyubin again in India

INDIA

	Political		Economic		Cultural

<u>1966</u> (cont.)

	Political		Economic		Cultural
		Oct	– Protocol on additional oil refineries		
		Nov	– Skachkov in India for talks on fourth 5-year plan: CREDIT AGREEMENT (reported $990m, of which $440m is carry-over)[64]		
		Dec	– Protocol on engineering school – Reported gift of wheat, farm equipment ($16m)[65]	Dec	– Academicians in India

<u>1967</u>

	Political		Economic		Cultural
				Jan	– Science delegation in India: agreement on publication of Soviet textbooks in India
Feb	– Parliamentary <u>elections: CPI loses ground</u>, except in Kerala	Feb	– Protocol on increased shipping service		
Mar	– Chief of staff Zakharov in India – Svetlana Stalin breaks <u>with USSR while in India</u>				
				May	– Cultural protocol for 1967-68
June	– President Husain stops in USSR en route to Canada				
Sept	– Defence minister Swaran Singh in USSR – Delegation in Baku for international conference			Sept	– News service agreement
Oct	– Mrs. Gandhi in USSR on unofficial trip				
Nov	– MRS. GANDHI IN USSR for anniversary				
		Dec	– Deputy trade minister Kuz'min in India: protocol for 1968		

<u>1968</u>

	Political		Economic		Cultural
Jan	– Reported delivery to India of first supersonic bombers – KOSYGIN IN INDIA for 7-day visit			Jan	– Delegations in India for Indo-Soviet cultural conference

	Political		Economic		Cultural

1968 (cont.)

	Political		Economic		Cultural
Feb	– Pel'she heads CPSU delegation to Delhi for CPI congress	Feb	– Trade minister heads delegation to Delhi for international conference		
Apr	– Kosygin stops in Delhi en route home from Pakistan – Naval vessels visit India			Apr	– Nuclear scientists in India: co-operation agreement
				May	– Cultural exchange protocol
June	– Parliamentary delegation in USSR			June	– Red Cross delegation in Tashkent for symposium
July	– HUSAIN IN USSR for 10-day state visit – Soviet arms agreement with Pakistan				
Sept	– Firyubin in India				
Oct	– Defence minister Swaran Singh in USSR				
		Dec	– Contract for tractor deliveries – Economic delegation under Skachkov in India: protocol on aid		

1969

	Political		Economic		Cultural
Jan	– Mrs. Gandhi stops in Moscow en route to London			Jan	– Cultural delegation in India: new agreement – Agreement on aid for pediatric centre
Feb	– CPI gains in West Bengal elections: joins new government – Supreme Soviet leader Spiridonov in India			Feb	– Belorussian religious delegation in Kerala – Party academician Gafurov heads delegation to India for UNESCO conference – TU delegation under CPI leader Dange in USSR
Mar	– Defence minister Grechko heads delegation to India – CPI delegation in USSR for preparatory conference on world congress	Mar	– Protocol on oil surveys off Bombay	Mar	– Cultural minister Furtseva in India – Co-operative group in India
Apr	– Uzbek delegation in India				
May	– Dange leads CPI delegation to Moscow to work on preparatory commission for world congress – Kosygin in Delhi for funeral of ex-president Husain	May	– Antibiotics plants completed	May	– Cultural delegation in Tashkent – Science delegation in India to survey research centres

INDIA

	Political		Economic		Cultural

1969 (cont.)

	Political		Economic		Cultural
June	- Mysore parliamentary leader in USSR - Delhi mayor in Moscow	June	- Minister of industry in USSR - Agricultural officials in USSR	June	- Krishna Menon heads peace delegation to USSR - Cultural protocol for 1969-70 - Scientists in India
July	- Foreign ministry official in USSR				
Aug	- Krishna Menon again in USSR for Indian anniversary - Giri elected president	Aug	- Trade delegation in USSR for talks on 1971-75 agreement - Minister of industry in USSR		
Sept	- Kosygin stops in India en route to and from Hanoi (for Ho Chi Minh's funeral) - Foreign minister Dinesh Singh in USSR - State parliamentary leaders in USSR	Sept	- Aviation delegation in India to discuss commercial aircraft sales		
Oct	- Defence minister Swaran Singh in USSR - Supreme Soviet leaders in India	Oct	- Government delegation in USSR for economic talks - Agreement on forestry co-operation - Delegation in India to conclude agreement on railway wagons	Oct	- Education minister in USSR to discuss science information centre - Agreement on translation training
Nov	- Congress party splits after prolonged crisis	Nov	- Forestry delegation in India to study resources - Agreement on co-operation in ferrous, non-ferrous industries - Air delegation in USSR: protocol on expanded service - Aircraft minister in India for talks on aircraft production	Nov	- Oil workers in USSR
		Dec	- Trade delegation in India: protocol for 1970	Dec	- Gift of additional smallpox vaccine

1970

	Political		Economic		Cultural
		Jan	- Power plant at Aligarh completed - Power engineering minister in India		
Feb	- Deputy premier Dymshits in India - Air chief Kutakhov in India	Feb	- Skachkov in India: protocols on Bhilai expansion and co-operation in oil, chemical industries - Contract for steel exports to USSR from Bhilai	Feb	- Agreement on computer centre in Bangalore

Political		Economic		Cultural	
1970 (cont.)					
		Feb	– Contract for tractor deliveries to India		
Mar	– West Bengal government resigns after break in united front	Mar	– Protocol on precision instruments plant at Kota	Mar	– Cultural, friendship delegation in India
Apr	– CPI delegation in USSR for Lenin centenary			Apr	– Krishna Menon in USSR for world peace council meeting – Journalists in India
May	– Foreign ministry officials in USSR for talks on Soviet-Indian relations – Cruiser calls at Bombay	May	– Protocol on delivery of surgical instruments to India – Shipping delegation in India: protocol	May	– Protocol on meteorological collaboration
June	– Air chief in USSR			June	– Cultural protocol for 1970-71
July	– Parliamentary speaker in USSR – Firyubin in India to discuss Vietnam peace				
Aug	– Dange arrested				
Sept	– GIRI IN USSR for 9-day state visit	Sept	– Agreement on Calcutta underground railway	Sept	– Telex service opens between Moscow, Delhi – Soviet Baptists in India
Oct	– Foreign minister Swaran Singh stops in USSR en route from Europe – First MIG-21 built in India – Mrs. Gandhi stops in Moscow en route to United Nations – Foreign ministry official in Moscow to discuss Soviet maps of Indian frontier			Oct	– Academy of sciences president in USSR – Dange leads TU delegation to Moscow for WFTU meeting
Nov	– CPI delegation in Moscow for anniversary	Nov	– Contract for additional tractor deliveries to India	Nov	– Cultural delegation in India for Indian-Soviet friendship week
Dec	– Parliament dissolved; new elections set	Dec	– Trade minister Patolichev in India: new long-term trade agreement – Contract on shoe deliveries to USSR		
1971					
		Jan	– Contract on sale of surgical instruments to USSR – Soviet experts report on feasibility of Calcutta underground railway		

	Political		Economic		Cultural

<u>1971</u> (cont.)

	Political		Economic		Cultural
Mar	- <u>Mrs. Gandhi victorious in general election</u> - <u>CPI delegation in Moscow for XXIV congress</u> - <u>Crisis erupts in East Pakistan</u>				
		Apr	- Agreements on sale of petroleum, cotton to India		
May	- Cruiser calls at Bombay	May	- Deputy minister of oil exploration in India	May	- Cultural delegation in USSR: protocol for 1971-72 - Gift of vaccine, rice for Bengali refugees - Meteorological rocket launched in India under co-operation agreement - Agreement on sale of Indian films to USSR
June	- Foreign minister Swaran Singh in USSR	June	- Agreement on agricultural co-operation for 1971-75	June	- Indo-Ukrainian agreement on oceanography research
July	- State minister for parliamentary affairs stops in Moscow	July	- Minister of steel, mines in USSR - Agreement on ship sales to India - Contract on heavy electrical equipment for India		
Aug	- Indian diplomat D.P. Dhar in Moscow - Gromyko in India: TREATY OF FRIENDSHIP AND CO-OPERATION	Aug	- State minister for company affairs in Moscow for aid talks		
Sept	- Agreement on production of MIG-21s in India - Soviet diplomat Tsarapkin in India - MRS. GANDHI IN USSR for 3-day visit: agreement on inter-governmental commission for co-operation - CPSU delegation in India for CPI congress	Sept	- Further agreement on supply of cotton to Indian textile industry - Agricultural minister in USSR: aid pledged in sugar beet production	Sept	- Co-operative delegation in USSR - Aid for flood victims in Bihar - TU delegations in Moscow for international conference
Oct	- Podgornyy stops in Delhi en route to Hanoi - Firyubin in India for annual talks on Soviet-Indian relations - Air marshal Kutakhov in India: reported agreement on delivery of planes and parts[67]			Oct	- Additional aid for Bangladesh refugees

Political	Economic	Cultural

1971 (cont.)

Nov — Parliamentary delegation in USSR for opening of Soviet-Indian friendship month
— Supreme Soviet delegation in India
— Mrs. Nehru and Chou En-lai exchange greetings on China's admission to UN

Nov-
Dec — Armed conflict between India, Pakistan: USSR supports India in UN
— Deputy foreign minister Kuznetsov in New Delhi and D.P. Dhar in Moscow, for exchange of views
— Indian forces occupy Bangladesh before cease-fire (Dec 16)

Nov — Deputy minister of merchant marine in Delhi: protocol on expanded service
— Agreement on watch factory in West Bengal

Nov — Buddhist delegation in New Delhi for international meeting
— Emergency aid for typhoon victims in Orissa

References

[1] Menon's interview was a fortnight before Stalin died; see Menon, The Flying Troika, pp. 26ff (full listing in Special Bibliography on India).

[2] See K.P.S. Menon, "Indo-Soviet Relations" in Appadori, ed., India: Studies in Social and Political Development, p. 229.

[3] Korneyev, Nauchnyye svyazi Akademii nauk SSSR so stranami Azii i Afriki, pp. 26-27.

[4] E.g. an editorial in Pravda, 26 January, 1955.

[5] See Kyril Tidmarsh, "The Soviet Reappraisal of Mahatma Gandhi", St. Antony's Papers, No. 8, 1960, p. 87.

[6] G.F. Kim and R.A. Ul'yanovskiy, in Sovetskoye Vostokovedeniye, No. 2, 1957, p. 13.

[7] See Central Asian Review, No. 1, 1962, p. 68, reviewing Soviet commentary on the Kerala episode.

[8] Editorial in Sovremennyy Vostok, No. 2 (August), 1957, p. 2.

[9] From 1949 to the end of 1955 Soviet exports to China exceeded imports by more than a billion dollars; by the end of 1960 the imbalance was still more than $400 million. See Goldman, Soviet Foreign Aid, p. 39.

[10] See the summary of Soviet press coverage of the episode in Central Asian Review, No. 1, 1960, p. 112.

[11] Pravda, 1 November, 1959.

[12] See Arthur Stein, "India and the USSR: the Post Nehru Period", Asian Survey, March 1967, p. 169, citing Peking Review, 30 August and 11 October, 1963.

[13] A TASS statement in Pravda, 24 February, 1963 denied rumours of arms shipments beyond those agreed to before October 1962 - thus acknowledging implicitly that the MIG-21s covered in the August agreement were delivered while the crisis persisted.

[14] E.g. Radio Moscow, 20 March, 1969.

[15] For an account of the Soviet Union's position in the Kashmir debates within the United Nations, see Sheldon W. Simon, "The Kashmir Dispute in Sino-Soviet Perspective", Asian Survey, March 1967, pp. 170-71.

[16] E.g. Izvestiya, 29 April, 1965; TASS, 9 May, 1965; and Pravda, 24 August, 14 and 23 September, 1965.

[17] An agreement on naval vessels, for instance, was reported in the Indian Express, 7 September, 1965, cited in Joshua and Gibert, Arms for the Third World, p. 71. It is unlikely that Soviet arms were actually delivered to India during the fighting, but there was no formal statement to this effect.

[18] See, for instance, "Disenchantment with the Soviet Union", Round Table (New Delhi), January 1969, pp. 85-90.

[19] Madame Furtseva's remarks were reported on Radio Delhi, 19 March, 1969 and Kosygin's in The Statesman (New Delhi), 13 September, 1969 (cited in Harish Kapur, "India and the Soviet Union", Survey, Winter 1971, p. 212).

[20] See her New Year's Day press conference in New Delhi, noted in Mizan, January-February 1969, Supplement B, p. 3. Mrs. Gandhi visited the Soviet Union, on official delegations and on her own, more than a dozen times from 1963 to 1970 - more often, surely, than any other Indian leader and probably more often than any Third World leader.

[21] See Harish Kapur, op. cit., p. 213.

[22] Mrs. Gandhi herself reportedly protested against the

propagandistic content of Radio Peace and Progress broadcasts, but the Russians replied that the station was "independent" and accordingly "unofficial"; see Mizan, September-October 1968, p. 203.

[23] See Marian P. Kirsch, "Soviet Security Objectives in Asia", International Organization, Summer 1970, p. 462, citing New York Times, 28 September, 1968 and 24 January, 1969.

[24] Kommunist, No. 13 (September), 1962, p. 89.

[25] Pravda, 20 August, 1964.

[26] Narody Azii i Afriki, No. 6 (November-December), 1966 (summarized in Mizan, March-April 1967, p. 47).

[27] E.g. Pravda, 24 April, 1963.

[28] Pravda, 4 September, 1970.

[29] For typical comments on the Indian scene between the 1969 crisis and the General Election of March 1971, see - in addition to Ul'yanovskiy's article cited above - articles by G.K. Shirokov in Narody Azii i Afriki, No. 6 (November-December), 1969, pp. 23-35; I. Belyayev and A. Maslennikov in Pravda, 19 February, 1970; A. Maslennikov in Pravda, 17 May, 1970; L. Pochivalov in Pravda, 30 June, 1970; and A. Maslennikov and V. Shurygin in Pravda, 24 October, 1970.

[30] Pravda, 10 August, 1971. Comment on the Soviet-Indian Treaty in the world press was, of course, voluminous. I signal here merely a few items that may be of interest to readers: Ashok Kapur, "Indo-Soviet Treaty and the Emerging Asian Balance", Asian Survey, June 1972, pp. 463-74 (a background survey of the treaty and analysis); "Symposium on the Indo-Soviet Treaty", Shakti (New Delhi), Nos. 1-2, 1971, pp. 141-79 (comments by Indian scholars and officials); USSR and Third World, No. 7, 1971, pp. 352-57 (official English text and summary of Western press comments).

[31] Pravda, 12 August, 1971.

[32] For Soviet comment on the conflict see USSR and Third World, No. 10, 1971, Special Supplement and No. 1, 1972, pp. 1-9.

[33] Pakistani officials claimed subsequently that the Russians assisted the Indians during the fighting, especially in communications, but these claims have not been proved; John Fricker in The Times, 8 February, 1972.

[34] E.g. K.K. Sharma in the Financial Times, 11 February, 1972.

[35] TASS dispatch in Pravda, 17 May, 1970; the total - undoubtedly inflated - was said to have been achieved after a membership increase of 80 per cent during the preceding two years.

[36] Details of membership, organization and policies of the various Communist factions in India may be found in the annual editions of Yearbook of International Communist Affairs and World Strength of the Communist Party Organizations (see Bibliography for full listings).

[37] See Mizan, March-April 1967, pp. 75-79; also the account of a CPI plenum in Calcutta after the elections in Pravda, 5 May, 1967.

[38] A. Maslennikov, in Pravda, 19 February, 1969.

[39] See, for instance, a dispatch by Kasturi Rangan in the New York Times, 5 August, 1972, which notes, among other factors in the Naxalites' decline, their loss of a refuge in East Pakistan after the creation of Bangladesh.

[40] Some estimates (projected through 1970 on the assumption the last credits shown in the Chronology during 1965 and 1966 are correct) are as follows:

USSR and Developing Countries, p. 47	$1,666 million
Tansky, U.S. and U.S.S.R. Aid to Developing Countries, p. 108	1,658 "
Goldman, Soviet Foreign Aid, p. 103	1,597 "
U.S. Department of State, RECS-15, 22 September, 1971, p. 4	1,593 "
Kondrat'yev, Indiya: ekonomicheskoye razvitiye ..., p. 101	1,541 "

The discrepancies arise from uncertainty over the amount of the initial Bhilai credit in 1956 and over the inclusion, or non-inclusion, of grants in 1959 in previous credits. My total is $1,586 million (see Table B, below).

[41] The Hindu (New Delhi), 8 August, 1969.

[42] While students of Soviet aid do not agree on utilization rates, the most reliable estimates to the end of 1968 appear to be about 45 per cent. See Carter, The Net Cost of Soviet Foreign Aid, p. 25 and Janos Horvath, "Economic Aid Flow from the USSR", Slavic Review, December 1970, p. 632.

[43] According to the Deputy Chairman of the Soviet Foreign Economic Relations Committee, in an interview appearing in Aziya i Afrika segodnya, No. 1, 1972, pp. 12-17.

[44] TASS, 19 September, 1971. See the Special Bibliography on India for more detailed studies of the Soviet aid programme in India.

[45] Leo Tansky estimates that the United States provided 54 per cent of India's foreign aid up to 1964, as compared to Russia's nine per cent - that is, six times more; U.S. and U.S.S.R. Aid to Developing Countries, p. 96. An Indian economist estimated in 1968 that the United States had provided 40 per cent of foreign aid for the First, Second and Third Five-Year Plans, as against 10 per cent provided by the USSR; P.S. Lokanathan, in Appadori, ed., India: Studies in Social and Political Development, p. 140. American commitments to India by the end of the 1967-68 fiscal year, according to official US government sources, totalled $7,806 million; Walters, American and Soviet Aid, p. 84.

[46] See Elizabeth Kridl Valkenier, "New Trends in Soviet Economic Relations with the Third World", World Politics, April 1970, p. 427.

[47] E.g. R.A. Ul'yanovskiy in New Times, No. 40 (October), 1971, pp. 18-19.

[48] This was the difficulty, apparently, in the break-down of negotiations concerning the export of Indian railway wagons to the USSR in 1969. For an analysis of India's debt-servicing problem, see The Economist (London), 6 November, 1971, p. 67.

[49] Kondrat'yev, Indiya: ekonomicheskoye razvitiye ..., p. 69.

[50] Radio Moscow, 13 December, 1969.

[51] The Far East and Australasia, 1970, p. 219.

[52] A total of $1 billion is estimated by Zubeida Mustafa in Pacific Community, April 1972, p. 507. Another Pakistani writer estimated $900 million as early as 1968; Zubeida Hasan, "Soviet Arms to Pakistan and India", Pakistan Horizon (Karachi), Fourth Quarter, 1968, pp. 349-51. A more modest estimate ($600-700 million up to the end of 1967) is given in Joshua and Gibert, Arms for the Third World, pp. 68-72. President Nixon's press secretary estimated Russian military aid to India from 1965 to the end of the Indo-Pakistani war in 1971 at $500 million; The Times, 16 December, 1971.

[53] International Herald Tribune (Paris), 8 and 11 November, 1971, reviewed in USSR and Third World, No. 10, 1971, p. 577.

[54] The Military Balance, 1970-1971, pp. 62-63.

[55] E.g. Radio Delhi, 3 July, 1970 and 31 May, 1971.

[56] See U.S. Department of State, RSE-25, 7 May, 1969, pp. 88-90; RSES-35, 12 August, 1970, p. 76; and RSES-44, 30 August, 1971, p. 18.

[57] See Mizan, September-October 1968, p. 203.

[58] Many details of Soviet publishing activity in India are given in Sager, Moscow's Hand in India, pp. 42ff.

[59] See reference 40.

[60] Ibid.

[61] Joshua and Gibert, op. cit., p. 58.

[62] Ibid., p. 69, citing Western news sources.

[63] Ibid.

[64] U.S. Department of State, RSB-354, 19 December, 1967, p. 36.

[65] U.S. Department of State, RSB-80, 21 July, 1967, p. 4.

[66] Washington Post, 25 January, 1968.

[67] International Herald Tribune, 11 November, 1971.

Soviet appraisals of Indonesia and Sukarno were as uncompromising during the so-called Zhdanov era after 1947 as they were of most other newly independent nations in Asia and their "bourgeois-nationalist" leaders, but these harsh views were relaxed sooner. By 1952, a year before Stalin's death and well before Indian, Burmese and other Third World leaders were accorded similar treatment, Sukarno was receiving respectful treatment in most Soviet commentaries.[1] Diplomatic relations between the two nations none the less improved slowly. Although an exchange of embassies had been discussed as early as 1950, when Moscow formally recognized Indonesia's independence, Sukarno did not agree to the exchange until the end of 1953; the first Soviet ambassador reached Djakarta only in the following September and it was another year and a half before there were contacts of any significance. The Russians were preoccupied during this period with improving relations with India and the Arab states, as well as with the Western powers, and apparently sensed no urgency in establishing a closer relationship with Djakarta. Sukarno, preoccupied with the projection of his image as a Third World leader (at Bandung and after), presumably felt likewise. China, meanwhile, whose mission had been established at Djakarta in 1951, had by 1956 established cordial relations with Sukarno's government - thanks in large measure to Chou En-lai's skilful diplomacy at Bandung and the initial agreement between the two nations on the troublesome question of the overseas Chinese in Indonesia.

Sukarno's two-week visit to the Soviet Union in 1956 opened an era of intense activity in Russian-Indonesian relations. This activity, measured in ministerial and state exchanges, military aid, cultural co-operation, and such criteria, remained relatively constant until the coup of September 1965 - that is, for nine years - but there was a particular intensity to the relationship during the period up to the early 1960s. During these years the Indonesians could do no wrong in the eyes of Soviet observers. Economic progress was hailed, especially the nationalization measures taken in 1958 and the strengthening of the "state sector" in the eight-year plan adopted in 1960. Indonesia's "positive neutrality" in foreign affairs was exemplary. Sukarno himself was eulogized as a Third World luminary and his domestic policies - such as the adoption of "guided democracy" in 1959 - were widely praised. "The correct course of the Indonesian people", Professor Guber (Russia's foremost authority on Indonesia and a frequent visitor there) wrote in 1961, "has the sympathies of all progressive forces in the world ... and is certain to succeed."[2]

The Russians meanwhile gave Sukarno full support on the West Irian issue, the central one in Indonesian foreign policy. Moscow had indeed always supported Indonesia on this issue, even in the years after Madiun,[3] but in the late 1950s, Soviet identification with the Indonesian cause became more explicit and more sustained. The Soviet press was crowded for some years with articles on West Irian (in 1961, for instance, nearly as many as on the secession of Katanga - with which the "rape of Irian" was sometimes compared);[4] official government statements were issued periodically affirming Indonesia's absolute right to West Irian and defending Sukarno's plan to seize it by force;[5] the large arms shipments between 1958 and 1962 were expressly intended for use in the Irian campaign (see below).

It is clear from the foregoing that by the early 1960s Indonesia was one of the most favoured Third World nations in Russian strategies - if not the most favoured nation. There are many reasons why this was so. In the first place, Indonesia's size (nearly equal in population to the rest of mainland South-East Asia) and growing influence among Afro-Asian nations made her a natural object of Soviet interest; this was especially the case by the end of the 1950s as the imagined menace to Soviet security from American-sponsored alliances along Russia's southern flank declined, making Moscow's preoccupation with Indians and Arabs less urgent. The staunchly anti-imperialist posture of Indonesia's leaders and their receptivity to Soviet approaches also facilitated the relationship. Another factor was the obvious rapport between Khrushchev and Sukarno: their meetings were memorable occasions in the diplomacy of each nation. Euphoria at the summit filtered down to the ranks below, including Russian correspondents and scholars who filled the pages of the daily and periodical press. Still another circumstance at the end of the 1950s and in the early 1960s that favoured close Soviet-Indonesian relations was the temporary absence of serious competitors on both sides. Russia's preoccupation with the Arab world had diminished, as relations with Egypt and Iraq grew strained for several years; interest in Africa did not fully emerge until after 1960 and in the Northern tier states (Iran and Turkey in particular) only in the mid-1960s; the relationship with India, to be sure, was vigorous, but it did not have the zest of an ideological partnership. As for Indonesia, relations continued to be tense with Washington - despite some improvement in the early months of the Kennedy administration - because of suspected American involvement in the Sumatran rising of 1958; relations with Peking were all but suspended from 1959 until the spring of 1961 because of new difficulties over the perennial problem of the overseas Chinese.[6]

One should meanwhile not overlook the importance in Soviet eyes of the Indonesian Communist Party (PKI) in shaping Moscow's strategies in Indonesia. The extraordinary recovery of the Indonesian Communists, following their débâcle at Madiun in 1948, had been much noted in the Soviet press during the latter half of the 1950s. D.N. Aidit, the architect of this recovery, was often in Moscow and his writings were widely circulated; indeed, Soviet observers frequently relied on his judgment of Indonesian developments and quoted him to give more bite to their remarks than they felt it prudent to put in their own words.[7] There was clearly satisfaction in pointing out that the PKI, which by 1960 numbered over two million members, was "the strongest party in Indonesia".[8] The growing strength of the PKI and its increasing collaboration with Sukarno must be considered a further reason for Moscow's satisfaction in the course of events in Indonesia in the early 1960s - and therefore a stimulation to ever greater intimacy with Djakarta.

Russia's favourable attitude towards Indonesia gradually shifted after 1961. It was not a dramatic shift and indeed is seen more clearly in hindsight than it was at the time. Outwardly relations appeared to remain constant. Political and cultural exchanges were as frequent as before; military exchanges were even more numerous (see Chronology). Articles appearing in Soviet journals at least throughout 1962 were as uncritical of Indonesia as those which had appeared a few years earlier.[9] Meanwhile, Moscow in no way lessened its support of Sukarno's policies in West Irian. "The Soviet Union is prepared to provide the necessary aid for the liberation of West Irian", Air Marshal Vershinin told his hosts during a visit to Djakarta in June 1962.[10] When Sukarno, after the settlement of the Irian issue in May 1963, shifted his focus to Malaysia and launched his "Crush Malaysia" campaign, or konfrontasi, Moscow continued to promise support. In September 1964 the Soviet Union vetoed a resolution in the Security Council condemning Indonesia for its activity against Malaysia.[11] And in January 1965, when Indonesia withdrew from the United Nations over the seating of Malaysia in the Security Council, Soviet writers criticized, not so much Djakarta, but imperialists who deliberately forced Indonesia's action by "manoeuvring" to seat Malaysia. Pravda's "Observer", in commenting on the episode, took occasion to reaffirm the official Soviet position on the Malaysian question: "The people of Indonesia are carrying on a just struggle against Malaysia as a weapon of imperialism.... The support and sympathy of the Soviet people are on their side."[12]

Despite these outward manifestations of continued cordiality, however, two circumstances were beginning to trouble Soviet-Indonesian relations. One was the growing crisis in the Indonesian economy – a crisis which had been widely discussed in Western commentaries for some years but which Soviet writers, until mid-1963, had regarded lightly. Now Russian economists expressed concern. The state sector was doing badly, it was argued in Narody Azii i Afriki, because of "anti-popular" elements directing it; the food problem was growing more acute, despite a good harvest in 1962, because of purchasing policies which were "unprofitable to peasants" and, in consequence, increased peasant alienation; despite the high costs of the Irian campaign (said to account for over three-quarters of Indonesia's expenditure in 1962), the nation's economy must be put in order. "The national problem of utmost importance at the present time is the stabilization of the economy and restoring the finances to health."[13] A year later another article in the same journal noted that the Indonesian economy "continues to deteriorate". The 1963 budget still showed an "enormous deficit", despite cuts in military expenditures; inflation and living costs were rising; food production was down, forcing the government to import rice "in conditions of a severe currency crisis".[14] A similar review the following year, on the eve of the 30 September crisis, found that "inflation is worsening ... reserves of foreign currency have decreased ... and the debts on foreign loans have risen excessively".[15] These judgments, needless to say, reflected concern not so much over the Indonesian economy per se as over Djakarta's ability to repay its huge debt to the Soviet Union; meanwhile, the debt continued to rise, since Moscow found it impolitic to reject Indonesia's request for more arms in the cause of "anti-imperialism".

The second circumstance affecting Moscow's attitude towards Indonesia was the gradual radicalization of Sukarno's foreign policy under the influence of the PKI. The Indonesian Communists dropped their posture of neutrality in the Sino-Soviet dispute during 1963 and turned increasingly to Peking, drawing Sukarno with them. Much of the popular support in Indonesia for konfrontasi was mobilized by the PKI at Peking's urging; Indonesia's withdrawal from the United Nations in 1964 and its project to forge a "new forces" (NEFO) alliance with other radical states were also prompted by the Chinese. For the Russians, Indonesia's failure to endorse Soviet participation in the second "Bandung" conference, scheduled for June 1965 in Algiers, was the crowning irony to their efforts during the preceding decade to cultivate Djakarta's good will.

Under these circumstances Moscow had little leverage in Indonesian politics. Though official contacts continued until the eve of the 1965 coup – with PKI leaders as well as government and military officials – the intensity of Soviet interest declined. Sukarno's final visit to Moscow in September 1964, to judge from the treatment given it in the Russian press, was a pale imitation of his earlier pilgrimages. The object of Mikoyan's mission to Djakarta earlier in the year was not good will, but to breathe life into lagging Soviet aid programmes. There were meanwhile fewer commentaries on Indonesian affairs than formerly and those that appeared in Soviet journals were increasingly critical – either of the economy (see above) or of other aspects of Indonesian policy: Sukarno's NASAKOM policy, for instance, praised for some years by the Russians as a proper merging of nationalist, Islamic and Communist forces, was attacked in 1964 for its "eclecticism and friability", which left the country vulnerable to reactionary elements.[16] Soviet-Indonesian relations, it is clear from this evidence, were in a state of suspension during the last year or so of Sukarno's rule.

The relationship came virtually to a halt after the dramatic events of 30 September, 1965, when an abortive coup by Leftist officers supported by the PKI led to the establishment of a military regime under General Suharto and the end of Sukarno's absolute rule in Indonesia. Aid projects were suspended, despite occasional indications that the Russians for their part were prepared to continue them.[17] Cultural co-operation all but ceased for several years. It was more than a year after the crisis before official exchanges were resumed, allowing representatives of the two countries an opportunity to consider the major issue carried over from the pre-coup relationship – Indonesia's debt. Negotiations on this matter were carried on intermittently from 1966 to mid-1970, when the issue was finally resolved (see below).

The debt issue was no less damaging to Soviet-Indonesian relations than Suharto's treatment of former members of the PKI. The Russians had every reason, of course, to welcome the check on PKI power implicit in Sukarno's fall and the Army's rise; they could not, however, look on silently while Suharto methodically liquidated Indonesian Communists. "Even if we assume that individual members of Left organizations succumbed to provocations and were in one way or another involved in the events of September 30", a New Times correspondent wrote in November, "that is no justification for the present repressive measures against the three million-strong Communist Party."[18] This issue was a main theme in Soviet commentaries on Indonesia for the next few years and the subject of numerous official and semi-official protests. Brezhnev said at the Twenty-third

Congress in March 1966 that the Russian people regarded the "anti-Communist terror in Indonesia ... with profound indignation".[19] Podgornyy appealed to Suharto for clemency in the death sentence awarded Njono, the highest ranking PKI leader to survive the initial roundup and summary execution of Communists.[20] As the time approached for carrying out the sentence, two years later, the CPSU issued a bitter statement condemning the government's anti-Communist pogrom. "History has not previously witnessed such mass extermination of people in time of peace for ideological reasons"; the refusal of Indonesian leaders to heed world opinion demonstrated that it was catering to the forces of "blackest reaction".[21] Podgornyy again appealed to Suharto for clemency for Njono and his colleagues, but without success. After the sentences were carried out, on 19 October, 1968, it was stated in Pravda that the Communists had been executed "because reactionaries, imperialist agents, landlords, usurers and embezzlers tried to take vengeance on leaders of the party which was always a threat to them".[22] Thereafter Soviet attention to Communist persecution declined somewhat, though support for the PKI – at least those portions of it loyal to Moscow – persisted. "Indonesian Communists", a Russian broadcaster asserted in the summer of 1970, "have been fighting gallantly to defend national independence, in the face of imperialist suppression manifested in the anti-popular, anti-nationalist policy adopted by Indonesia's rulers."[23] Some students of Soviet policies in Indonesia have seen in Moscow's continued attention to the PKI a serious effort to wean the exiled leaders away from Peking and to reconstruct a new party oriented to the USSR.[24]

Soviet commentary on Indonesia after 1965 was not confined to the debt and anti-Communist issues; in fact, the Soviet press appears to have devoted more attention to Indonesia in the years after the 30 September episode than during the year or two preceding it. The commentary was ambivalent. Some of it was moderately favourable to the new regime. V.L. Kudryavtsev, for instance, took the position in 1967 that in spite of many shortcomings in its foreign policy, Indonesia was still neutralist;[25] a broadcast marking the 20th anniversary of Soviet-Indonesian diplomatic relations also praised Djakarta's neutralist policies despite the efforts of Rightists out of power to sabotage them.[26] Most commentary, however, was critical of developments in Indonesia. The arrest of military officers in January 1970 demonstrated the inability of the regime to keep its house in order, especially the Indonesian Army;[27] the measures taken to improve the economy were "superficial" and provided few benefits for the poor;[28] Indonesia's sponsorship of an Asian conference on Cambodia in June 1970 showed the extent of Djakarta's willingness to enter into "the Pentagon's and CIA's schemes";[29] ASEAN, under the influence of Indonesian generals, was being turned into "a military bloc under the Pentagon's protection";[30] the elections of July 1971 were judged a "farce", designed to assure military rule and to conceal the unemployment, corruption and incompetence that was rampant in the country.[31] Russian diplomats from time to time sought to soften the impact of this sharp criticism – the Russian ambassador in Djakarta, for instance, complimented Indonesian leaders on the outcome of the 1971 elections – but the persistent hostility towards Indonesia in the Soviet press inevitably prolonged the impasse in relations between the two

nations. Spokesmen in Djakarta complained frequently about Soviet press and radio coverage of Indonesian affairs and from time to time suspended Russian periodicals (such as New Times) that were too critical of the Suharto regime. Objection was also made to broadcasts over Radio Moscow by Indonesian Communists, whose views the Soviet government sought to publicize in its effort to combat pro-Chinese Indonesians in Peking.[32] It was no wonder, under these circumstances, that Soviet-Indonesian relations failed to improve, even after the debt question had been resolved.

Aid, Arms and Cultural Co-operation

Indonesia by the mid-1960s had received more credit from Russia than any other Third World nation, except perhaps Egypt – more than $1.5 billion in credits of all types.[33] Loans for economic projects amounted to about $370 million of this total, but had been poorly utilized. The Soviet Union encountered difficulties in its aid programme from the outset. The initial loan of $100 million in September 1956 was not ratified in Djakarta until nearly a year and a half later, due to opposition to the loan from conservative elements then in the government; meanwhile, about one-fifth of the credit was diverted to military purchases even before ratification.[34] When negotiations began for implementation of the credit, they were plagued by unexpected technical problems, shifting priorities in Djakarta and the lack of competent Indonesian administrators. When Khrushchev pledged an additional $250 million during his visit to Indonesia in 1960, none of the initial projects had been completed and it is doubtful if many were even started. The new credit, which was to have been used for a variety of industrial projects (including a steel mill in Kalimantan, various hydro-electric facilities, and similar ambitious undertakings) apparently fared no better than the first. By September 1965 the only Soviet aid projects completed in Indonesia were a hospital in Djakarta, several technical institutes, a portion of the scheduled road construction, some monuments and a sports stadium (which the Russians had not wanted to build but finally did after a personal appeal by Sukarno to Khrushchev).[35]

Military aid was more successful, for the simple reason that arms did not have to be constructed in Indonesia; they had merely to be delivered. Deliveries began as early as 1957 (counting the February agreement on jeep deliveries as a military agreement) and escalated rapidly in 1958 as Moscow gave its full support to the West Irian campaign. No very exact figure has been fixed for Soviet arms transfers to Indonesia, but it is probable that they ran as high as $1.2 billion before they dwindled off in 1964 or 1965.[36] Soviet deliveries included a heavy cruiser, seven destroyers, six submarines and several dozen torpedo and coastal craft; more than 150 fighters and bombers, including approximately two dozen MIG-21s; and miscellaneous artillery and anti-aircraft weapons, including SA-2 missiles at three known sites.[37] By 1971 it was reported that because of lack of spare parts only a third of the Soviet-built naval vessels, which constituted 80 per cent of the Indonesian Navy, were in operation; 90 per cent of the Indonesian Air Force was grounded for the same reason.[38] Periodic discussion of this problem between Soviet and Indonesian military officials after 1965 (see Chronology) led to no solution. When the Russians finally offered spare parts in 1971, on what Adam Malik called "easy terms", Indonesian defence leaders are reported to have refused them on the grounds that the equipment to be repaired was already obsolete.[39]

Repayment of the enormous debt to the USSR constituted one of the principal difficulties in Soviet-Indonesian relations, especially (as noted above) after the 1965 crisis. The credits for economic projects presented no urgent problem for some years, since the schedule for repayment - as with most Soviet foreign aid - was to commence only after the projects were completed. The arms transfers, however, were a different matter. Subandrio insisted in 1964 that the arms transfers to Indonesia from the Soviet Union were sales, not aid,[40] but the parlous state of the Indonesian economy at the time makes his claim hardly creditable. It is more likely that the greatest part of arms transfers was covered by special credits, probably bearing the usual two and a half per cent interest with payments due after a specified period of time. Moratoria on such payments were occasionally reported in the Western press.[41]

A year after the change of government in Indonesia in 1965, discussions were held in Moscow on Djakarta's debt, which was set by the Intergovernmental Group for Indonesia (a body of creditor nations) at $864,100,000. An agreement in November 1966 specified that payment of interest should begin in July 1967 and payments on capital in April 1969. As the first date approached, however, Suharto first requested a postponement, then unilaterally put off payments. Negotiations were resumed during 1969 and in due course led to the agreement of August 1970: a 30-year debt term was agreed to and the debt fixed at $750 million; according to Malik, certain aid projects were to be resumed, among them the nuclear reactor, a superphosphate plant and the iron works at Tjilegon.[42] It was another year before the first Soviet aid team, expected in Indonesia for many months, finally arrived to conduct a two-month feasibility study of the steel and superphosphate projects; Russian assistance for the nuclear reactor, it was announced in due course, had been abandoned.[43] The feasibility study was completed on schedule, but its results were not immediately announced and no work on the stalled projects had been announced by the end of July 1972.

Trade statistics reflect the uncertain nature of Soviet-Indonesian economic relations (see Table C, below). Even during the years of greatest intimacy, from 1958 to 1963, Soviet exports to Indonesia were modest, given the size of aid commitments. After 1965, the substantially larger Indonesian exports to the USSR over imports (nearly $100 million over about $18,500,000 for the three-year period 1966-1968) indicate that Djakarta was making some effort to repay its debt, despite the apparent impasse in formal negotiations. After 1969 the large quantities of rubber and coffee bought by the Russians in Indonesia brought the total volume of trade back to pre-1965 levels.

Cultural co-operation between Russia and Indonesia paced political and economic links into the early 1960s.

Thereafter, until September 1965, China's cultural programme in Indonesia was apparently more active than Moscow's. However, the number of Indonesian students in the USSR continued to exceed those of any other Third World nation: there were reportedly about 800 at the time of the 1965 crisis and as late as 1970 there were still a small number left in Russia, all of them Communist sympathizers stranded in exile after Sukarno's fall.[44] The majority of student Communists stranded abroad after 1965 eventually found their way to China where, despite Moscow's efforts (see above), a more congenial climate existed for the rebuilding of the PKI during the years of the Cultural Revolution. It is in fact likely that the Russians sped a number of these students on their way - as they did militant PKI correspondents in 1967, arguing that Soviet hospitality was "not extended to the lunatic fringe".[45] Other than this residual "student exchange", cultural relations between the Soviet Union and Indonesia were trivial after September 1965.

Such has been the uneven course of Soviet relations with Indonesia, judged by some Western observers to reflect Russia's greatest failure in dealing with nations of the Third World. Whether or not the judgment is valid depends upon how one views the Russian objective in Indonesia. If one assumes this to have been the substitution of Russian influence for Western, then the spectacular Soviet successes before 1965 must indeed be considered to have been more than cancelled out in later years, since Western influence - and especially American - became stronger during the Suharto regime than it had ever been under Sukarno. If, on the other hand, Russia's main object after 1960 was to destroy Peking's influence, then the course of events in Indonesia does not represent a catastrophe for Soviet policy. It is unlikely, as some observers have speculated, that the Russians were intentionally instrumental in checking Chinese ambitions in Indonesia - by providing arms to military leaders which allowed them to seize power[46] - but it is a fact that the basis of Chinese policy in Indonesia was totally destroyed by the events of 30 September, 1965 and their sequel. Relations with Peking were suspended in October 1967 and had not been normalized by the end of 1972 (despite Adam Malik's periodic assertions that Indonesia desired a resumption of economic and even diplomatic ties).

Whatever Moscow's earlier objectives in Indonesia, they were surely modified after Gestapu. The experience in Indonesia had been too tumultuous and costly to repeat. Russia's strategic interest in Indonesia was considerably less than, say, in India or Egypt. Indonesia was too distant and too complex to cultivate as a reliable Third World ally. The Russians accordingly appeared to be resigning themselves to a lesser role in Indonesia by the early 1970s. Economic and cultural co-operation would presumably be resumed in due course, along with trade, but Moscow's political goals were not likely to extend beyond a normalization of relations with Djakarta and Indonesian neutrality in world affairs. The Russians would meanwhile watch over the fortunes of the PKI for whatever contingencies that might arise.

Bibliography

Aleshin, Yuriy. Sovetsko-indoneziyskiye otnosheniya v 1945-1962 godakh, 1963, 176pp. (includes documents and many details of aid agreements).

Belen'kiy, A.B. "Sovetskiye nauchnyye trudy po Indonezii", Narody Azii i Afriki, No. 4, 1961 (useful bibliographic notes on Soviet sources to the end of 1961).

Derkach, Nadia. "The Soviet Policy towards Indonesia in the West Irian and Malaysian Disputes", Asian Survey, November 1965, pp. 566-71.

Farizov, I.O. Sovetsko-indoneziyskoye ekonomicheskoye sotrudnichestvo, 1964, 94 pp. (lists major economic agreements and protocols).

Goldman, Marshall I. Soviet Foreign Aid (see Main Bibliography), pp. 124-34.

Horn, Robert C. "Soviet-Indonesian Relations since 1965", Survey, Winter 1971, pp. 216-33.

McVey, Ruth T. "Indonesian Communism and the Transition to Guided Democracy", chapter in A. Doak Barnett, Communist Strategies in Asia (see Main Bibliography), pp. 148-98.

Mizan, January-February 1966, pp. 14-22: "The USSR and Indonesia."

____. May-June 1967, pp. 109-17: "USSR and Indonesia."

____. March-April 1968, pp. 60-63: "Collapse of the Indonesian Communist Party."

____. March-April 1969, pp. 105-17: "Moscow, Jakarta and the PKI."

Note. The above articles, like those in Yuva Newsletter, were written by Peter Howard.

Pauker, Guy J. "Indonesia: The PKI's Road to Power", chapter in Robert A. Scalapino, ed., The Communist Revolution in Asia (see Main Bibliography), pp. 256-89 (mainly on PKI developments, but includes material on Soviet policies towards the Indonesian Communists).

Ra'anan, Uri. The USSR Arms the Third World (see Main Bibliography; military aid to Indonesia is one of the two case studies in this volume).

Respublika Indonezii, 1961 (articles by various scholars include coverage of Soviet-Indonesian relations to the end of 1960).

Shakow, Alexander. "Foreign Economic Assistance to Indonesia, 1950-1961", 1962 (a doctoral thesis at London School of Economics, with much material on Soviet activity; based on research in Indonesia).

Trudy 25ogo Kongressa Vostokovedov, 1963, pp. 382-89 (a review of Soviet-Indonesian relations to 1962).

Yuva Newsletter, July 1962, pp. 1-23: "Soviet Writing on Indonesia."

____. January 1963, pp. 16-24: "Review of Periodicals: Indonesia and West New Guinea."

____. January 1964, pp. 1-7: "Indonesia's Economic Difficulties."

Chronology

(See explanatory note on tables, p. 6.)

	Political		Economic	Cultural

Pre-1955

Aug 1945	Republic of Indonesia proclaimed by Sukarno			
May 1948	Consular treaty between USSR and Indonesia (not implemented)			
Sept 1948	PKI rising at Madiun suppressed; PKI leaders executed			
Nov 1949	Hague talks: Dutch recognize Indonesian independence			
Jan 1950	USSR recognizes Indonesia			
Apr 1950	Delegation in USSR to discuss diplomatic relations			
June 1950	CPR, Indonesia establish diplomatic relations; (missions exchanged July 1951)			
		Apr 1952	Delegation in USSR for Moscow economic conference	
		Nov 1953	Trade agreement with CPR	
Dec 1953	Sukarno agrees to diplomatic relations with USSR (missions exchanged September 1954)			
		Sept 1954	Economic delegation in USSR and CPR	

1955

Apr	- Chou En-lai, Chen Yi in Indonesia for Bandung conference; CPR, Indonesia conclude dual nationality treaty			
May	- Premier Sastroamidjojo in CPR			
Sept	- National elections: PKI emerges as a major party			

1956

Feb	- Naval delegation in CPR			

	Political		Economic		Cultural

1956 (cont.)

	Political		Economic		Cultural
Feb	– PKI secretary Aidit in USSR for XX CPSU congress; stops in CPR en route home				
May	– Parliamentary delegation under Sartono in USSR – Aidit again in CPR				
Aug	– SUKARNO IN USSR for 15-day visit	Aug	– Trade delegation in USSR: first trade agreement		
Sept	– Sukarno in CPR – PKI delegation in CPR for CP congress	Sept	– CREDIT AGREEMENT for mining, power and other projects ($100m; ratified by Indonesia February 1958)		
				Oct	– Muslim delegation in USSR
Nov	– Sumatran rising against Sukarno	Nov	– CPR credit ($16.2m)	Nov	– Information minister in USSR

1957

	Political		Economic		Cultural
		Feb	– Interim credit for jeeps ($8.4m of the 1956 credit)		
				Apr	– TU delegation in USSR
May	– Military mission in CPR – PRESIDENT VOROSHILOV IN INDONESIA for 2-week state visit				
June	– Parliamentary delegation in CPR				
July	– Sastroamidjojo leads government delegation to USSR				
		Aug	– Djakarta-Black Sea shipping line established		
Sept	– Former vice president Hatta in CPR: Chinese offer arms				
				Oct	– Artists in USSR
Nov	– PKI delegation in USSR for world CP congress; stops in CPR en route home			Nov	– Cultural delegation in USSR

1958

	Political		Economic		Cultural
Feb	– Indonesian military mission in Czechoslovakia: arms agreement (estim $250m)[47]				
		Mar	– Ships delivered to Indonesia		

	Political		Economic		Cultural

1958 (cont.)

		Apr	– CPR credit for cotton, rice purchases ($11m)		
May	– PKI leaders in CPR				
June	– PKI delegation in USSR – Parliamentary leader in USSR				
				July	– TU delegation in USSR
		Aug	– Industrial delegation in USSR for trade talks		
				Oct	– TU delegation in USSR
Nov	– Foreign minister Subandrio in USSR				

1959

Jan	– Aidit in USSR for XXI congress	Jan	– Protocols on metallurgical works, experimental farms, roads in Kalimantan, surveys, etc.		
Mar	– Aidit in CPR				
Apr	– CPR military mission in Indonesia	Apr	– CPR credit for textile mills ($30m)		
				May	– TU delegation in USSR for May Day
				June	– Education minister in USSR
July	– Constitutional assembly dissolved; Sukarno proclaims "guided democracy" (Aug)	July	– Trade delegation in USSR: protocol for 1960 – SUPPLEMENTARY CREDIT for stadium, oceanographic institute ($17.5m)		
Sept	– PKI congress adopts united front policy – PKI delegation under Njoto in CPR for 5-week tour			Sept	– TU delegation in USSR – Cultural delegation in USSR
Oct	– Soviet warships visit Indonesia – Mukhitdinov heads parliamentary delegation to Indonesia – Subandrio in CPR for talks on overseas Chinese issue				
Nov	– Government delegation in USSR			Nov	– TU delegation in USSR
		Dec	– Geologists in Indonesia for surveys – Indonesia nationalizes Dutch companies		

INDONESIA

	Political		Economic		Cultural
1960					
Feb	– KHRUSHCHEV IN INDONESIA for 12–day visit	Feb	– CREDIT AGREEMENT for industrial and agricultural projects, textile works, atomic reactors ($250m)	Feb	– Cultural agreement
		Mar	– Trade delegation in USSR		
May	– Sukarno awarded Lenin peace prize			May	– Cultural delegation in USSR: protocol
July	– Ministerial delegation in USSR	July	– Protocol on nuclear reactors – Trade agreement for 1961–63		
Aug	– Military delegation in USSR			Aug	– Cultural delegation in USSR
		Oct	– Promise of 200–bed hospital as a gift – Soviet trade fair opens in Djakarta		
Nov	– PKI delegation in Moscow for world conference	Nov	– Foreign trade minister in Indonesia	Nov	– Artists in Indonesia
		Dec	– Protocol on super-phosphate plant		
				?	– Academic delegation in Indonesia: agreement on scholarly exchanges
1961					
Jan	– Nasution heads military delegation to USSR: agreement on sale of bombers and patrol boats	Jan	– Further protocol on 2 nuclear reactors		
		Feb	– Planning chief in USSR: protocol on power station and chemical works		
Mar	– Chen Yi in Indonesia: friendship treaty			Mar	– Scientists in Indonesia: protocol
Apr	– Abdulgani, a Sukarno aide, in USSR				
May	– PKI delegation in USSR			May	– TU delegation in Indonesia – Cultural protocol
June	– SUKARNO IN USSR for 8–day visit; then in CPR – Nasution in USSR on separate visit: arms agreement – Aidit leads PKI delegation to USSR and CPR				
		July	– Gift of helicopters – Jet bombers delivered to Indonesia	July	– Botanists in Indonesia

	Political		Economic		Cultural
1961 (cont.)					
Sept	– Warships call in USSR			Sept	– Health minister in USSR
Oct	– Navy chief Gorshkov in Indonesia: gift of gunboats	Oct	– Additional CPR loan (reported $30.2m)[48]	Oct	– Academicians in USSR
Nov	– Aidit in USSR for XXII congress; stops in CPR en route home				
		Dec	– Trade protocol for 1962 – Communication and air service agreement		
1962					
		Jan	– Air service opens between Moscow and Djakarta – Agreement on training oil technicians in USSR		
Feb	– Air chief Dhani in USSR			Feb	– Academician Guber heads cultural delegation to Indonesia: protocol – TU delegation in Indonesia
		Mar	– Economic official in Indonesia to review Soviet projects: contracts for steel, superphosphate plants and geological surveys		
				Apr	– University delegation in USSR
May	– Subandrio heads parliamentary delegation to USSR: arms agreement	May	– Planning delegation in USSR	May	– Cultural protocol – Gift of research vessel to Indonesia scientists
June	– Mme. Sukarno in USSR, later CPR (Sept) – Air chief Vershinin in Indonesia				
July	– MIKOYAN IN INDONESIA for stadium opening	July	– CPR delegation in Indonesia for aid talks	July	– Uzbek film group in Indonesia
		Aug	– Gift of floating docks – Engineers in Indonesia for surveys in Sumatra	Aug	– Botanists in USSR
Oct	– Military leader in CPR	Oct	– Bankers delegation in USSR for trade talks	Oct	– Deputy radio chief in USSR
Nov	– PKI delegation in USSR and CPR				
Dec	– CPR delegation in Indonesia to give views on Sino-Soviet dispute				

	Political		Economic		Cultural
1963					
Jan	– PKI delegation under Njoto in USSR and CPR				
Feb	– Another PKI delegation in USSR				
Mar	– Defence minister Malinovskiy in Indonesia	Mar	– Supplementary protocol on road construction in Kalimantan		
Apr	– Air chief Dhani in USSR and CPR – Liu Shao-chi, Chen Yi in Indonesia	Apr	– Trade delegation in Indonesia: 1960 agreement extended to end of 1965	Apr	– Academician Zhukov in Indonesia at PKI invitation
May	– Agreement on West Irian: end of emergency in Indonesia	May	– Economic delegation in USSR: new technical assistance agreement	May	– Cultural protocol for 1963
June	– Navy chief in USSR				
July	– Navy chief in Indonesia – Aidit leads PKI delegation to USSR and CPR – Police chief in USSR			July	– Economic scholars in Indonesia for conference
Sept	– Parliamentary delegation under Sastroamidjojo in USSR – Air force delegation in USSR and CPR – Indonesia implements "Crush Malaysia" policy (konfrontasi) after formation of Federation; US aid cut				
Nov	– Nasution in USSR: further arms credit reported and moratorium on existing debt[49]	Nov	– Health minister in Indonesia for handing over of hospital – Economic delegation in USSR: protocol on rubber purchases	Nov	– Academician Guber heads delegation to Indonesia for friendship week – Soviet delegation in Indonesia for Asian games (GANEFO)
Dec	– Marine chief in USSR	Dec	– Gift of floating docks	Dec	– Information minister in USSR
1964					
		Jan	– Supplementary contracts for steel and phosphate plants, power station, oceanographic institute, nuclear reactors and Kalimantan roads	Jan	– Academy of Science delegation in Indonesia
		Mar	– Trade protocol for 1964 – Air service protocol – Promise of aid for mechanized rice growing	Mar	– Gift of meteorological equipment
Apr	– Chen Yi in Indonesia for talks on 2nd Afro-Asian (Bandung) conference			Apr	– Cultural protocol – Muslim TU delegation in USSR

	Political		Economic		Cultural
1964 (cont.)					
May	– PKI delegation in USSR and CPR	May	– Fishing experts in Indonesia: agreement on surveys – Gift of floating cranes		
June	– MIKOYAN IN INDONESIA for aid talks: arms agreement	June	– Gift of monument		
July	– Subandrio, army chief Yani in USSR	July	– Trade protocol	July	– Writers in USSR
Sept	– SUKARNO IN USSR for 3-day visit – Nasution in USSR on separate visit: new arms agreement (Oct)			Sept	– TU delegation in Indonesia – Co-operative delegation in USSR
Oct	– Air chief Dhani in CPR			Oct	– Journalists in USSR
Nov	– Sukarno in CPR – Chen Yi in Indonesia – Deputy foreign minister Firyubin in Indonesia			Nov	– Artists in Indonesia
Dec	– Subandrio in USSR: arms agreement				
1965					
Jan	– Subandrio in CPR – Indonesia withdraws from UN	Jan	– Protocol on ship construction – Cornerstone laid for nuclear reactor	Jan	– Deputy health minister leads women's delegation to USSR – SOBSI delegation in USSR for WFTU congress
		Mar	– CPR economic delegation in Indonesia: protocol on textile works (reported credit of $16m)[50]		
Apr	– Chou En-lai, Chen Yi in Indonesia for Bandung anniversary				
May	– CPSU and Chinese CP delegations in Indonesia for PKI anniversary – Nasution heads military delegation to USSR – Subandrio in CPR again	May	– Agreement on truck purchases (reported $3m credit)[51]	May	– Guber heads academicians to Indonesia – Film exchange agreement
				June	– Communication and sports ministers in USSR
July	– Aidit heads PKI delegation to USSR and CPR – Another PKI delegation in CPR – Parliamentary speaker in USSR and CPR			July	– TU delegation in Indonesia
Aug	– Deputy premier Mazurov in Indonesia for anniversary – Chen Yi in Indonesia			Aug	– Trade minister leads TU delegation to USSR – Gift of additional meteorological equipment to Indonesian scientists

INDONESIA

	Political		Economic		Cultural
1965 (cont.)					
Sept	– Abortive coup (Gestapu); military leadership under Suharto takes power; widespread arrests of Communists			Sept	– Academic delegation in Indonesia
1966					
Mar	– PKI formally proscribed				
		May	– Aid to flood victims		
		June	– Gift of 2 dredgers		
Oct	– Foreign minister Malik in USSR for debt talks			Oct	– Journalists in Indonesia
		Nov	– Economic delegation in USSR: agreement on rescheduling of debt (ratified July 1968)		
		Dec	– Electric power station completed for navy		
1967					
Aug	– Navy chief in USSR to discuss debt and spare parts				
Oct	– Indonesia suspends relations with CPR – Defence official in USSR for debt talks			Oct	– Journalists in USSR
1968					
				Jan	– Youth delegation in Indonesia
				Mar	– TU delegation in USSR
Oct	– PKI leaders executed				
1969					
				Apr	– TU delegation in USSR for May Day – Library delegation in Indonesia for conference
		May	– Aviation officials in Indonesia		
				July	– Religious delegation in USSR for conference
		Aug	– Economic delegation in Indonesia to review debt question and uncompleted projects		
				Sept	– Soviet film week in Djakarta

	Political		Economic		Cultural

1970

Jan – Air cadets defect to USSR

Feb – Malik in USSR for political, economic talks

Feb – Soviet-built dredgers launched in Djakarta

Mar – TU delegation in Indonesia

June – <u>Djakarta conference of Asian leaders on Cambodia</u>
– Malik again in USSR to report on Djakarta conference
– <u>Sukarno dies</u>

July – Gift of technical literature to Bandung institute

Aug – Malik returns to USSR: agreement on 30-year debt term

Aug – Journalists in USSR

1971

Mar – Intelligence chief in USSR

Apr – Nasution in USSR

July – <u>General election in Indonesia: government party wins</u>

July – Agreement on survey for resumption of work at steel and superphosphate plants

Aug – Technicians in Indonesia for 2-month survey

Aug – Journalists in USSR

Sept – Ban on certain Soviet publications in Indonesia

References

[1] For Soviet views of Indonesia during this period see my earlier study, <u>Soviet Strategies in Southeast Asia</u>, pp. 455-57.

[2] <u>Respublika Indoneziya</u>, p. 25. A sampling of Soviet commentaries on Indonesia from 1956 to the end of 1961 – drawn from many hundreds of articles and monographs – is in <u>Yuva Newsletter</u>, July 1962, pp. 1-23.

[3] See, for instance, articles in <u>Izvestiya</u>, 7 January and 2 February, 1951, where West Irian is called "an inalienable part of Indonesian territory". The Madiun rising of 1948, during which Indonesian Communists rebelled openly against the Sukarno regime, virtually ended all contacts between Moscow and Djakarta until the early 1950s.

[4] E.g. <u>Trud</u>, 12 November, 1961.

[5] E.g. <u>Pravda</u>, 15 May, 1958 and 9 February, 1962.

[6] Implementation of the 1955 Dual Nationality Treaty broke down in 1959, leading to bitter recriminations on both sides and a virtual suspension of diplomatic contacts; the issue was resolved during Chen Yi's visit in March 1961 – an occasion marked by much official rejoicing in Djakarta (where the author happened to be visiting at the time).

[7] A typical example of this, for instance, is A. Lavrent'yev's article in <u>Aziya i Afrika segodnya</u>, No. 3 (March), 1961, pp. 3-5. Aidit's works most frequently quoted were <u>Aidit Accuses Madiun Affair</u> (1955), <u>Indonesian Society and the Indonesian Revolution</u> (1957), and <u>The Birth and Growth of the Communist Party of Indonesia</u> (1958); all were translated into Russian and other foreign languages and distributed from Moscow.

[8] M. Model', in <u>Problemy vostokovedeniya</u>, No. 4, 1960, p. 27.

[9] See Yuva Newsletter, January 1963, pp. 16-24 for a summary of Soviet writing on Indonesia in 1962.

[10] Krasnaya zvezda, 29 June, 1962.

[11] Pravda, 20 September, 1964.

[12] Pravda, 22 January, 1965.

[13] Narody Azii i Afriki, No. 4, 1963, p. 64; also Mirovaya ekonomika i mezhdunarodnyye otnosheniya, No. 8 (August), 1963, p. 75. See Yuva Newsletter, January 1964, pp. 1-7 for a review of other articles on the Indonesian economy in 1963.

[14] Narody Azii i Afriki, No. 4 (1964), pp. 53-55.

[15] Mirovaya ekonomika i mezhdunarodnyye otnosheniya, No. 9 (September), 1965, Supplement, p. 147.

[16] Mirovaya ekonomika i mezhdunarodnyye otnosheniya, No. 6 (June), 1964, pp. 85-86 (cited in Mizan, January-February 1966, p. 17).

[17] Deputy Premier Polyansky, for instance, said in November that Russia intended to increase its economic co-operation with Indonesia; Pravda, 7 November, 1965. A Soviet official in Indonesia asserted in 1967, to scotch rumours that no further aid would be forthcoming, that Moscow had every intention of implementing its $1 billion credit; see Mizan, May-June 1967, pp. 111-12.

[18] New Times, No. 44 (2 November), 1965, p. 6.

[19] Pravda, 30 March, 1966.

[20] See Mizan, March-April 1966, p. 94.

[21] Izvestiya, 11 October, 1968.

[22] Pravda, 1 November, 1968. Estimates of the number of executions have varied greatly, some claiming over a million. A Soviet source claimed in 1968 that 80 per cent of the Central Committee had "disappeared"; Literaturnaya gazeta, 14 August, 1968.

[23] Radio Moscow, 5 July, 1970 (in Indonesian); see also a broadcast by G. Avrin on 20 March, 1971 (reviewed in USSR and Third World, No. 4, 1971, p. 166).

[24] E.g. Robert C. Horn, "Soviet-Indonesian Relations since 1965", Survey, Winter 1971, pp. 224ff.

[25] Izvestiya, 1 February, 1967.

[26] Radio Moscow, 3 February, 1970.

[27] R. Voznesenskiy, broadcasting on Radio Moscow, 24 January and 18 February, 1970.

[28] Radio Moscow, 13 April, 1970.

[29] For coverage of Soviet commentary on the Djakarta conference, both before and after it took place, see Mizan, May-June 1970, Supplement B, pp. 17-18.

[30] Radio Moscow, 2 February, 1971.

[31] New Times, No. 22 (28 May), 1971, p. 20; Aziya i Afrika segodnya, No. 6, 1971, p. 36; New Times, No. 29 (16 July), 1971, p. 13.

[32] See, for instance, Radio Djakarta, 2 June and 6 June, 1971.

[33] This is the approximate total of credits reported for economic aid and the estimated value of arms transfers to the end of 1964 (see above). Soviet estimates, made after the 1965 crisis, show credits of $1.2 billion; Radio Moscow, 14 May, 1969. This is a lower estimate if military credits are included – the Soviet sources do not make this clear – but of course is greatly higher than the $1.5 billion total estimate if they are not.

[34] Ra'anan, The USSR Arms the Third World, pp. 192, 195.

[35] For a critical but largely accurate account of Soviet economic aid to Indonesia, see Goldman, Soviet Foreign Aid, pp. 125-34; also Alexander Shakow, "Foreign Economic Assistance in Indonesia" (see Bibliography on Indonesia for full listing), pp. 449ff.

[36] Joshua and Gibert, Arms for the Third World, p. 73.

[37] The Military Balance, 1970-1971, pp. 63-64.

[38] See USSR and Third World, No. 3, 1971, p. 102, citing Singapore and London newspapers. The percentage of unusable planes given by the Chief of Staff of the Indonesian Air Force in a broadcast over Radio Djakarta on 7 March, 1970 was 80 to 85 – also because of lack of spare parts from the USSR.

[39] See Adam Malik's statements on Radio Djakarta, 22 March and 15 June, 1971; rejection of the Soviet offer by Indonesian naval and military spokesmen was reported on Radio Djakarta, 27 March, 1971 and in Far Eastern Economic Review, No. 14 (3 April), 1971.

[40] See Yuva Newsletter, March 1965, p. 5, citing a Radio Djakarta broadcast.

[41] E.g. Washington Post, 13 December, 1963 and 3 October, 1964, cited in Joshua and Gibert, op. cit., p. 67.

[42] Statement in the official Indonesian news outlet Antara, 31 August, 1970; the official Soviet announcement of the agreement did not give details. Some sources continued to give the debt as $800 million: e.g. Radio Djakarta, 12 May, 1971 (announcing payment of the first instalment) and New York Times, 25 August, 1971, p. 8.

[43] Antara, 29 September, 1971.

[44] See U.S. Department of State, RSES-34, 30 August, 1971, p. 100.

[45] Pravda, 27 January, 1967, reporting the expulsion of a PKI correspondent formerly accredited to Moscow. The PKI appears to have split into three centres of power after 1965: a home based force in Java, about which little is known; the so-called "Delegation of the PKI Central Committee" in Peking, which issued frequent pronouncements through Chinese news services; and the "Marxist-Leninist Group of the PKI" in Moscow, which made similar use of Soviet media. It was not clear in 1970 which of the three exercised greater influence over the ruptured movement; see Yearbook on International Communist Affairs, 1971, pp. 584-93.

[46] This hypothesis is advanced, for instance, by Stephen P. Gibert, "Wars of Liberation and Soviet Military Aid Policy", Orbis, Fall 1966, p. 857.

[47] Joshua and Gibert, op. cit., p. 57.

[48] Goldman, op. cit., p. 46.

[49] Joshua and Gibert, op. cit., p. 67, citing Western news sources.

[50] U.S. Department of State, RSB-50, 17 June, 1966, p. 5.

[51] Ibid., p. 4.

The turbulent politics of Laos engaged Soviet attention during the years 1955–1971 as much as those of any other Third World nation (except perhaps the Congo early in the 1960s), yet Russian concern for Laos itself was minimal. It was an arena of international diplomacy in which Moscow had an active stake; it was a vacuum which must not be filled by forces hostile to Soviet interests elsewhere. But Laos was rarely an object of Soviet strategies in its own right, as most other Third World nations were.

During the years following the 1954 Geneva agreements on Indochina, the Russians adopted a relatively inflexible position on Laos. Governments in Vientiane which delayed unification with the Pathet Lao were vilified; those which brought unification nearer were approved.[1] Thus the Katay government, which replaced Souvanna Phouma's government in 1954, was compared to the regime in Saigon and criticized for failing to respond to Prince Souphanouvong's efforts to hasten a coalition; unilateral elections held by Katay in December 1955 without the participation of the Pathet Lao were repudiated.[2] The return of Souvanna Phouma to power in March 1956 and subsequent negotiations between the Royal half-brothers which led to a preliminary agreement on unification and Laotian neutrality were warmly approved.[3] When a coalition government was eventually formed in November 1957, Soviet commentators welcomed it.[4] Moscow failed to establish diplomatic relations with Laos during this first eight-month coalition – for reasons that are not clear – but Soviet observers unambiguously continued to support it and to express satisfaction in the neutralist premier, Souvanna Phouma; he was seen as the Laotian leader most likely to bring stability to the country.

The Russians grew increasingly concerned with developments in Laos during the two years of Rightist governments following Souvanna Phouma's fall in July 1958. Calls were made periodically for the return of the International Control Commission, which had suspended its work on assurances from Vientiane that with the formation of a national government the obligation of the Geneva protocol had been met.[5] In August 1959, after the detention by the Sananikone government of Prince Souphanouvong and other Neo Lao Hak Xat (NLHX) leaders in the coalition, the Soviet Foreign Office released an official statement on Laos, expressing "grave uneasiness" over the course of events there, deploring the recent arrests, charging the Americans with "intervention" and again demanding the recall of the ICC.[6] To the Russians, the principal danger in Laos in 1959 was that the Sananikone government, which no longer considered itself bound by the Geneva agreements, apparently felt it had "the option of joining SEATO".[7] It was this situation which led to Moscow's initial call, in September 1959, for an international conference on Laos. The call came during a debate in the Security Council on Sananikone's complaint of North Vietnamese "intervention" in Laos, which led to the dispatch of a special commission to investigate – an action which Russia vigorously condemned and considered "illegal"; the full-scale international conference was to serve as a substitute for the piece-meal investigation.[8] The "illegal" investigation, as it turned out, discovered no Vietnamese intervention – and so "knocked the ground out from under the feet of the authors of the

'Laotian question'", as an Izvestiya correspondent put it.[9] The Soviet Union, however, continued to call for an international conference on Laos during the latter part of 1959 and more urgently during the first half of 1960 when the Vientiane government moved even closer to the SEATO powers under Sananikone's successor, General Phoumi Nosavan.

The overthrow of the Rightists by Kong Le in August 1960 and the return of Souvanna Phouma at the head of a Left-centrist coalition in Vientiane gave the Russians a fresh point of leverage in Laos. They were quick to make use of it. The first Soviet ambassador to Laos was named in October and a month later the Russians agreed to provide military assistance to the new regime, already pressed by Rightist forces assembling in the south under Phoumi Nosavan and Boun Oum. The first arms reportedly reached Vientiane, via Hanoi, at the end of November.[10] The Russians were therefore able to pose as the defenders of neutralism in Laos when the Rightists, with strong American and Thai support, re-entered Vientiane in mid-December. Souvanna Phouma was compelled to retire to Phnom Penh and Kong Le to the Plaine des Jarres, where he joined forces with the Pathet Lao. On 22 December the Soviet government once again – and more forcefully than heretofore – called for a full-fledged conference to regularize the Laotian problem and, in the meantime, the restoration of the full authority of the ICC.[11] During the complex negotiations of the next 18 months, in Geneva, Zurich, Vientiane and elsewhere, the Russians did not diminish their support of Souvanna Phouma and his allies: they recognized only his government, wherever it might be located; a regular supply of Soviet arms continued to reach Kong Le's forces in the Plaine des Jarres, via Hanoi (see below).

There was an inclination among the foreign powers involved in Laos in early 1961 to freeze the situation there for the time being. Washington, at the outset of the Kennedy administration, appeared to seek a disengagement in Laos in favour of a firmer posture in South Vietnam. The Chinese and North Vietnamese, on the eve of a greater commitment in South Vietnam (indicated, for instance, in the resolutions of the third Lao Dong Congress in Hanoi in September 1960), were agreeable to a formal neutralization of Laos, so long as the Pathet Lao stronghold in Phong Saly and Sam Neua was not jeopardized and the Ho Chi Minh trail kept open. The French, who had expressed little interest in Laos for some years, and the English, who never had, were also prepared to negotiate a settlement there. There was accordingly a favourable response to Soviet calls for an international conference, even though few of the parties concerned imagined that any settlement would be permanent. As the 14-power conference at Geneva inched forward (from May 1961 to July 1962), it was indeed apparent that the problem of bringing the three warring Laotian factions together was more complex than discovering agreement among the three major powers taking part in the negotiations. Russia, China and the United States shared at least one common goal: each sought to check the influence in Laos of any other.

Soviet interest in the Laotian settlement during the 1961–62 negotiations was reflected in massive press coverage of the proceedings (nearly as extensive as of the

Congo crisis and considerably more extensive than of events at the time in Vietnam). The Russians meanwhile played host to a procession of Laotian leaders passing through Moscow en route to and from Geneva. Souvanna Phouma and Kong Le are each reported to have visited Moscow twice during this period; Prince Souphanouvong visited Moscow on at least five occasions. The Soviet press played endless variations on the theme put forth by Foreign Minister Gromyko in his opening remarks at Geneva in May 1961: settlement in Laos could come about only through "respect for and maintenance of Laotian neutrality".[12] The final agreement and establishment of a coalition government including the three princes was greeted with enthusiasm. It was called a "black Monday" for Western diplomats, who were pictured – quite erroneously – as having opposed the final composition of the coalition.[13]

Russia's attitude towards the new Laotian government, as befitted a sponsor of the Geneva conference, was sympathetic and relations were outwardly cordial. The Russians continued to play host to visiting Laotians, including even the Rightist Phoumi Nosavan (in November 1962 and again in September 1964). Aid was discussed and a modest supply of arms continued to reach Vientiane until 1964 (see below). The numerous difficulties which plagued the coalition – a wave of assassinations in the spring of 1963, culminating in the murder of the Left-centrist Foreign Minister Pholsena; the internal rivalries that led to the withdrawal of NLHX members of the coalition later in the year; the persistent scheming of Phoumi Nosavan to return to power – were blamed on "American provocation". The Soviet government made repeated statements on these developments, expressing its concern and calling on all parties to abide by the Geneva agreements.[14]

It seems clear, however, that Soviet interest in Laos declined during Khrushchev's last years in power. The periodic calls for a new conference to resolve the Laotian question grew increasingly perfunctory, much like similar calls for a conference on Cambodia (see above, under Cambodia). The numerous visits by Laotian leaders to Moscow during 1963 and 1964 were rarely reciprocated, as such visits were with nearly all other Third World nations in which Moscow was interested. Laos, like the rest of South-East Asia, was relegated to a position of secondary importance in Khrushchev's foreign policies during these years. In July 1964 the Soviet government stated that if a new conference on Laos were not convened to resolve the endless political crises in the country, Russia would be "forced to review" the question of its continuing to serve as co-chairman of the Geneva conferences, since this role "loses whatever significance it had and becomes fictitious"; Khrushchev underscored this position in remarks made a month later.[15]

Khrushchev's fall in October appears to have had little effect on Soviet policies in Laos. Some interest was expressed in a new round of talks between the Laotian leaders in Paris at the end of 1964 and official statements on Laos continued to appear periodically during 1965, protesting against abuses of Laotian neutrality and repeating old allegations of American "provocation".[16] No evidence, however, suggests either a shift in Moscow's view of Laos or a revival of significant interest in Laotian affairs. Meanwhile, Russia's preoccupation with Vietnam following Kosygin's visit to Hanoi in early 1965 had the effect of driving the Laotian question still further into the background for the next few years.

The growing polarization of political forces in Laos in the years after the Geneva conference destroyed Russia's position there. There is little reason to doubt Moscow's desire for a neutralized Laos early in the 1960s – not because Russia was necessarily a champion of neutrality per se (as it professed to be), but because more than any other foreign power involved in Laos Russia's interests lay in preserving a balance between Communist forces in the North, supported by the Chinese and Vietnamese, and Rightists in the South, supported by Americans and Thai: a victory by either, or even the gaining of a significant advantage, would reduce Soviet influence to the vanishing point. The Chinese, meanwhile, who had never committed themselves to Souvanna Phouma to the extent the Russians had, were unperturbed by the break-up of the 1962 coalition – and perhaps hastened it; their communication with the Pathet Lao was excellent, not only over the highway completed from Yunnan province to Phong Saly in 1963 but through numerous exchanges reported during the 1960s (Prince Souphanouvong, for instance, is known to have visited Peking far more frequently than he did Moscow). The Americans, for their part, were also not averse to the break-up of the coalition, since it isolated many influential neutralists and drove them in due course into collaboration with the Right, where American influence continued to be strong. The Russians, of course, were aware of this process. A Soviet visitor to Vientiane in 1967, for instance, remarked that the defection of Kong Le to the Right, at American urging, had the effect of splitting the neutralist centre beyond recovery.[17] But the Russians could do nothing to halt the polarization. They were caught in the middle in Laos, committed to a faction that was gradually disappearing.

The collapse of the Laotian centre led the Russians to increase their contacts with the Pathet Lao. From 1967 on missions were periodically exchanged with the "liberated areas", said to cover approximately two-thirds of the country,[18] and reports on Pathet Lao activities thereafter appeared irregularly in the Soviet press. In January 1969 the Soviet ambassador himself reportedly visited Sam Neua (see Chronology), despite the nearly total impasse at this time between the Laotian government and the NLHX. The Russians did not, like the Chinese and North Vietnamese, maintain a permanent mission in the "liberated areas",[19] but the tempo of their relations with the Pathet Lao increased significantly as the years passed. Some economic aid was probably made available to the NLHX – though surely far less than the NLHX received from China[20] – and Soviet arms undoubtedly found their way into the "liberated areas" from North Vietnam. Prince Souphanouvong, in an interview with Radio Moscow in October 1970, specifically mentioned both economic and military aid from the USSR as a factor in the successes of the Pathet Lao.[21]

The position of the Russians, Chinese and North Vietnamese in Laos was, to say the least, anomalous: that is, maintaining formal, or quasi-formal, relations both with the legally-constituted government in Vientiane and with a sizeable segment of the population which was in open revolt against Vientiane and even denied the legality of the Souvanna Phouma regime.[22] The anomaly was most striking in the case of the USSR since the

Russians had for some years dealt only with properly-established regimes in the Third World and maintained overt relations with local Communists only where they were legalized and not in rebellion. The dual policies followed by the Communist powers were tolerated in Vientiane only because of Souvanna Phouma's persistent view of himself as the sole catalyst of a unified nation. He accepted the Chinese and North Vietnamese missions in the Laotian capital and dutifully attended their receptions in the apparent belief that so long as there was no open break, time worked in favour of an eventual settlement.[23] So far as Soviet relations with the Pathet Lao were concerned, Souvanna probably welcomed them as the best guarantee that Chinese and North Vietnamese activity in the "liberated areas" would not get out of hand. The Russians, meanwhile, continued to maintain correct official relations with Souvanna Phouma, exchanging friendly greetings with him on state occasions and reporting his periodic complaints of violations of Laotian neutrality. Unofficially, occasional doubts were sounded concerning Souvanna Phouma's motives: Ivan Shchedrov, a Soviet correspondent who visited both Vientiane and the "liberated areas" in mid-1970, reported rumours of a Rightist coup against Souvanna if he undertook negotiations to enter an anti-Communist bloc, as the Americans were urging him to do.[24] To believe Shchedrov, it was Souvanna Phouma, once Moscow's model neutralist in Laos, who was the possible evil genius in Vientiane, while Rightists were defenders of the status quo.

American policies in Laos came under sharp attack at the end of the 1960s. They had, of course, been condemned intermittently in Soviet publications since the first US bombing of Laotian sections of the Ho Chi Minh trail was reported in 1964, but the steep pace of American intervention in Laos after the bombing halt in North Vietnam in 1968 gave special zest to the protests. Gromyko, in a strongly-worded statement issued in November 1969, complained not only of the bombing but of the operational use of American military personnel in Laos.[25] In February 1970 it was estimated that 12,000 US "advisers" were in Laos, creating a virtual "second front" in Indochina.[26] An official TASS statement on 1 March stated that American combat sorties over Laos had reached 400 a day and called the operation "barbarous".[27] In the middle of March Kosygin called President Nixon's recent appeal for a new conference on Laos "unrealistic" so long as the United States was "continuing its war in Vietnam and expanding armed intervention in Laos"; the proper way to restore peace in Laos, once American intervention ceased, was through consultation between the Laotian leaders themselves, and Kosygin warmly supported – as Soviet spokesmen had for many years – contacts between Souvanna Phouma and Souphanouvong.[28] Reports of an impending meeting between the two Royal princes appeared in Soviet publications throughout the year, but no meeting took place and in November Souphanouvong indicated that no meeting was likely in the immediate future.[29] Events in Cambodia, meanwhile, overshadowed Laotian affairs in the spring of 1970 and the Laotian question receded from the forefront of international politics until the South Vietnamese invasion, with American logistical and air support, in early 1971.

The Russians' response to the brief invasion of Laos in February 1971 was, as might have been expected, bitter and shrill, but without serious suggestion of Soviet intervention. The Russians discounted American claims that the invasion was a South Vietnamese operation, on the argument that no American ground troops allegedly crossed the border, and called it "an unjustifiable criminal and dangerous adventure"; among other objectives, the Russians said, the invasion sought the overthrow of Souvanna Phouma in favour of "reactionary Laotian generals supported by the CIA and the Pentagon".[30] Soviet commentaries reported with some satisfaction the early rout of South Vietnamese forces, but official hostility towards American strategies persisted. The Laos intervention, the Soviet government stated after the worst of the fighting was over, "is another crime by the USA, in flagrant violation of the generally accepted standards and principles of international law and contrary to the commitments assumed under the UN Charter"; the American leadership, it was clear, "is not ready for serious and constructive discussions for a peaceful settlement in Indochina".[31] Peking, meanwhile, made similar protests against the invasion of Laos and sent Chinese work brigades back into Laos to repair and defend road networks, but gave no indication of intervening directly.[32]

After the Laos invasion, Soviet relations with the Laotians continued as before – that is, desultory ties with both the Vientiane government and the regime in the north, accompanied by infrequent commentaries in the Soviet press concerning the evil designs of the United States. From the Russians' viewpoint, the situation in Laos had reached a total impasse by mid-1971. Although their tenuous contacts with the Pathet Lao allowed them to keep abreast of developments in the "liberated areas", they had little chance of replacing Chinese influence there – let alone North Vietnamese influence which had long been dominant. In Vientiane, the Russians' chances of displacing American influence were equally remote. The Soviet Union could progress in no direction in Laos until an end to the war in Vietnam brought about a realignment of forces throughout Indochina. Indeed, even the end of the war in Vietnam, according to some Russian observers, would not necessarily clarify matters in Laos. The "true intention" of the Americans in Laos, Kudryavtsev wrote in July 1971, was "continued aggression under the guise of 'Vietnamization' and utilization of Laotian territory as a base for subversive activities against neighbouring states, even if a real pullout of American forces from South Vietnam eventually becomes necessary".[33]

The precise amount of Soviet economic aid to Laos is obscure. An aid agreement was apparently concluded at the end of 1962, following the visit to Moscow of the Laotian delegation headed by Phoumi Nosavan, and is said to have provided for a hospital, a power plant and dam, and a radio station. A non-Russian source estimates the projected cost of the three projects at more than $7 million;[34] one Soviet source shows a credit of $4 million for the power plant and dam;[35] another Soviet source (which appears to be reliable in most estimates of economic aid) shows no credits at all by the end of 1964 – and indeed no aid of any sort.[36] There is meanwhile no indication in any source, Russian or Western, that the projects reportedly discussed in 1962 were completed and there is some evidence that work on them was never even begun.[37]

Military aid was extended principally at the end of 1960 – according to American sources, nearly 200 sorties were flown from Hanoi during the last fortnight of December[38] – and in early 1961, after Kong Le's para-troopers had joined Pathet Lao forces in the Plaine des Jarres. These early shipments reportedly included artillery, anti-aircraft pieces, armoured cars and small arms, as well as food and other non-military supplies.[39] Deliveries slackened as time passed and ceased entirely in the spring of 1964. The total value of arms transferred to Laos from 1960 to 1964 is estimated at only $3 to $5 million.[40]

Cultural exchange began modestly in 1963, after the Geneva agreement, without benefit of a formal cultural agreement. By the end of the 1960s it had been to all intents and purposes suspended, except with the "liberated areas" (see Chronology).

Chronology

(See explanatory note on tables, p. 6.)

	Political	Economic	Cultural

Pre-1960

		Political
Oct	1953	Independence within French Union
July	1954	Geneva conference: Pathet Lao hold northern provinces pending unification
Aug	1956	Agreement on national union government Souvanna Phouma in CPR
Nov	1957	Coalition government under Souvanna Phouma
July	1958	ICC suspends activity in Laos Coalition falls; Sananikone becomes premier (Aug)
July	1959	Souphanouvong, NLHX leaders arrested
Sept	1959	Security council sends committee to investigate charges of North Vietnamese "invasion"
Oct	1959	Diplomatic relations established with USSR
Dec	1959	Sananikone government falls; General Phoumi Nosavan emerges as strong man

1960

		Political
May	–	Souphanouvong escapes, returns to Sam Neua
Aug	–	Kong Le seizes power in Vientiane; Souvanna Phouma returns as premier
Oct	–	First Soviet ambassador appointed
	–	Air-lift to Kong Le begins
Dec	–	Vientiane falls to Rightists; Souvanna Phouma goes into self-exile in Cambodia; Kong Le withdraws to Plaine des Jarres;

97

LAOS

	Political	Economic	Cultural

1960 (cont.)

Dec — USSR continues to
recognize Souvanna
Phouma

___

1961

Apr — Souvanna Phouma in CPR:
agreement on diplomatic
relations
— Pathet Lao delegation
in CPR
— Cease-fire in Laos

May — ICC returns; Geneva
conference opens;
Souvanna Phouma, Sou-
phanouvong stop in
Moscow and Peking
en route to Geneva

June — President Kennedy,
Khrushchev agree in
Vienna on Laos
neutrality

July — Souphanouvong again in
Moscow and Peking en
route home

___

1962

July — Geneva agreement on
Laos is signed; coali-
tion government under
Souvanna Phouma formed
in Vientiane

Sept — Souphanouvong in USSR
for medical care
— China, Laos exchange
missions

Oct — Foreign minister in USSR

Nov — Phoumi Nosavan in USSR,
also CPR and Hanoi:
gift of military aircraft
by USSR
— Souphanouvong in CPR
for 2 month visit

Dec — Trade agreement;
reported aid agree-
ment for hospital,
radio station and
power plant[41]
— Aid agreement
with CPR

___

1963

Jan — Teachers' delegation
in USSR

Political	Economic	Cultural

1963 (cont.)

	Political		Economic		Cultural
Feb	– KING SAVANG, SOUVANNA PHOUMA IN USSR for 8-day visit; delegation also visits USA, CPR (Mar)				
Mar	– Kong Le in USSR, also CPR and North Vietnam			Mar	– Radio delegation in Laos
		Apr	– Protocol on dam, power station – Chinese complete road to Phong Saly		
May	– NLHX withdraws from coalition				
Oct	– SOUVANNA PHOUMA IN USSR for 3-day visit				
				Nov	– Health minister in USSR

1964

	Political		Economic
Apr	– Souvanna Phouma in CPR – Coup in Vientiane; Souvanna Phouma remains premier		
June	– Prince Sisavang in USSR for 3-month study		
Aug	– Souphanouvong in CPR		
Sept	– Phoumi Nosavan in USSR	Sept	– Protocol on hospital
Oct	– Souvanna Phouma, Souphanouvong stop in Moscow en route home from Paris conference of Laotian factions – Government delegation, Souphanouvong in CPR for anniversary		

1965

	Political
Feb	– Foreign minister in USSR

1966

	Political		Economic
Feb	– NLHX secretary Vongvichit in CPR		
May	– KING, QUEEN, SOUVANNA PHOUMA IN USSR for official talks and holiday – Government workers in CPR for 3-month tour		
		Oct	– Aid to flood victims

LAOS

	Political	Economic	Cultural

1967

	Political		Cultural
Jan	– NLHX delegation in CPR		
			Aug – Radio, press officials in USSR
			Sept – Actors tour "Liberated areas" (Sam Neua)
Oct	– NLHX delegation in USSR		

1968

	Political
Oct	– Komsomol delegation visits Sam Neua

1969

	Political		Cultural
Jan	– Soviet ambassador reportedly visits Souphanouvong in Sam Neua[42]		Jan – Red Cross delegation from "liberated areas" in USSR
May	– Foreign office aide Kapitsa visits Vientiane – Armenian CP Secretary leads delegation to Sam Neua		May – Journalists visit Sam Neua
			June – Artists visit Sam Neua
July	– NLHX delegation in USSR to discuss co-operation		
Sept	– Kosygin confers with Souphanouvong at Ho Chi Minh funeral in Hanoi		
Oct	– Komsomol delegation in Sam Neua – NLHX delegation in CPR		
Dec	– Another NLHX delegation in USSR		

1970

	Political		Cultural
			Jan – Buddhist delegation in Laos
Feb	– Pathet Lao recaptures Plaine des Jarres		
Apr	– NLHX delegation in Moscow for Lenin centenary – Souphanouvong attends Indochina "summit" conference in south China		Apr – NLHX delegate in Moscow for world peace council meeting

Political	Economic	Cultural
<u>1970</u> (cont.)		
		May – Vongvichit leads delegation to Moscow en route to Cairo conference on Laos – TU delegation in Sam Neua
		July – Journalists in Sam Neua
Oct – NLHX leader in Moscow for 25th anniversary of Laos independence – Komsomol delegation in Sam Neua		
Dec – NLHX general stops in Moscow en route from Stockholm conference on Indochina		
<u>1971</u>		
Feb – <u>South Vietnamese forces invade Laos with US support</u>: USSR protests vigorously; Chinese resume road-building in north Laos		
Mar – NLHX delegation in Moscow for XXIV congress; <u>stops in CPR en route</u>		
May – NLHX envoy in <u>Vientiane for peace talks with Souvanna Phouma</u>		
		Sept – Buddhist delegation from Sam Neua in USSR

References

[1] The Geneva agreement allowed Communist Pathet Lao forces to remain in the two northern provinces, Phong Saly and Sam Neua, for "regrouping"; in due course, it was anticipated, they would be integrated into the Royal Laotian Army and the nation would be reunified.

[2] E.g. A. Karpikhin, in <u>International Affairs</u>, No. 1 (January), 1956, pp. 56-57.

[3] The agreement was signed on 8 August, 1956 and provided for a cease-fire in the north, new federal elections, the inclusion of the Neo Lao Hak Xat (NLHX) in a national union government, and – most important from Moscow's viewpoint – explicit rejection of all military alliances and foreign bases. See International Affairs, No. 9 (September), 1956, pp. 122-24 for a commentary on the agreement; the full text was carried in the same journal, No. 11 (November), 1956, pp. 169-70. The NLHX, or Lao Patriotic Front, founded in 1956, was the political organization in the Communist-ruled sectors; the Pathet Lao, founded in 1950 and subsequently renamed the People's Liberation Army, was the military arm. In normal usage, however, the term Pathet Lao continued to apply to the Laotian Communist movement as a whole.

[4] E.g. New Times, No. 48 (29 November), 1957, pp. 17-18 and International Affairs, No. 12 (December), 1957, p. 88.

[5] See Pravda, 7 August, 1959, p. 6, reporting such a call

by the Russians in May. International Control Commissions, composed of representatives from Poland, Canada and India (which provided the Chairmen), were established in 1954 to supervise the carrying out of the Geneva agreements in each of the three former French territories – Vietnam, Cambodia and Laos.

[6] Pravda, 18 August, 1959.

[7] International Affairs, No. 7 (July), 1959, p. 63; see also Sovremennyy Vostok, No. 7 (July), 1959, pp. 34–35.

[8] Izvestiya, 24 September, 1959, p. 3; also International Affairs, No. 10 (October), 1959, pp. 108–10.

[9] N. Karev, Izvestiya, 11 November, 1959, p. 5.

[10] See Joshua and Gibert, Arms for the Third World, p. 60, citing New York Times, 23 November, 1960. Bernard Fall has written that non-military supplies reached Vientiane as early as 27 October; Scalapino, ed., The Communist Revolution in Asia, p. 189. Donald Nuechterlein writes that Souvanna's initial request to Moscow was for rice and fuel, when Thailand refused transit rights; arms followed in December. See Donald E. Nuechterlein, Thailand and the Struggle for Southeast Asia (Ithaca: Cornell University Press, 1965), p. 173.

[11] The request, like its predecessors, was made to Great Britain, co-chairman of the 1954 Geneva conference and therefore responsible, together with Russia, for peace in Laos; see V. Pavlovskiy, Laos i bor'ba za svobodu (Moscow, 1963), p. 105.

[12] Pravda, 18 May, 1961.

[13] E.g. Aziya i Afrika segodnya, No. 9 (September), 1962 (reviewed in Yuva Newsletter, April 1963, pp. 23–24); see also M. Yegorov in International Affairs, No. 9 (September), 1962, pp. 49–55. The composition of the new cabinet was, in addition to Premier Souvanna Phouma, four Leftists, four Rightists and seven ministers acknowledged as neutral.

[14] The following official statements are representative of Soviet views on Laos during the last 18 months of Khrushchev's rule:

28 May, 1963	– Draft letter from the Geneva co-chairmen (USSR and Britain) on the issue of majority voting on the ICC, which left the Polish delegate in a perpetual minority of one (Pravda, 1 June, 1963).
3 June, 1963	– Soviet Note to Britain alleging American interference in Laos (Pravda, 8 June, 1963).
3 April, 1964	– Draft Note from the Geneva co-chairmen to Souvanna Phouma, expressing concern over the deterioration of the political-military situation in Laos and requesting talks between the different factions (Turkmenskaya iskra, 3 April, 1964).
12 April, 1964	– TASS statement in support of Souvanna Phouma following attempted Rightist coup against him (Pravda, 12 April, 1964).

26 May, 1964	– Draft Note from the Geneva co-chairmen protesting against American reconnaissance flights over Laotian territory (Pravda, 28 May, 1964).
6 June, 1964	– Draft Note from the Geneva co-chairmen approving Poland's call for talks on Laos by the Foreign Ministers of the USSR, Britain and members of the ICC (Pravda, 6 June, 1964).
21 June, 1964	– Draft Note from the Geneva co-chairmen asking for a resumption of tripartite talks among Laotian leaders (Pravda, 21 June, 1964).
3 July, 1964	– Draft Note from the Geneva co-chairmen protesting against American bombing of Khang Khay (Pravda, 3 July, 1964).
27 July, 1964	– Soviet statement on Laos calling for reconvening of 14 nation conference on Laos (Pravda, 27 July, 1964 – reviewed below).

[15] Pravda, 27 July and 28 August, 1964.

[16] For instance, the following:

23 December, 1964	– Soviet message to Souvanna Phouma, expressing hopes for success at forthcoming Paris talks of Laotian leaders (Pravda, 23 December, 1964).
19 January, 1965	– Draft Note from the Geneva co-chairmen to the United States, protesting against recent American bombing in Laos (Pravda, 22 January, 1965).
2 February, 1965	– Draft Note from the Geneva co-chairmen noting Prince Souphanouvong's complaint of American air violations in Laos and supporting his call for a new conference (Pravda, 5 February, 1965).
18 November, 1965	– Soviet Note to Britain with new proposals for the regulation of the Laotian question (Pravda, 22 November, 1965).

[17] Izvestiya, 20 July, 1967.

[18] See G. Fyodorova in International Affairs, No. 4 (April), 1969, p. 118 and Aleksandr Serbin in Pravda, 6 January, 1971.

[19] Peking and Hanoi each maintained an Economic and Cultural Mission in Khang Khay and Peking kept its consulate in Phong Saly; see Paul F. Langer and Joseph J. Zasloff, North Vietnam and the Pathet Lao: Partners in the Struggle for Laos (Cambridge: Harvard University Press, 1970), p. 101 and Chae-Jin Lee, Communist China's Policy toward Laos: a Case Study, 1954–67 (Lawrence, Kansas: University of Kansas, 1970), p. 135.

[20] A US intelligence report, made public in August 1971, estimated the number of Chinese in Laos in April at between 14,000 and 20,000, most of them occupied in the construction and defence of a road network; New York Times, 3 August, 1971.

[21] Radio Moscow, 12 October, 1970.

[22] The Pathet Lao position on Souvanna Phouma's government was that it had been "illegal" since a military coup in April 1964 which, while allowing Souvanna to remain as premier, destroyed the legitimacy of the 1962 coalition.

[23] According to Chae-Jin Lee, who was in Vientiane during the early stages of the Cultural Revolution, Chinese diplomats were less radical at this time in Laos than in neighbouring Burma and Cambodia – a circumstance that of course made it easier for Souvanna Phouma to sustain the awkward relationship; op. cit., p. 140.

[24] Pravda, 24 July, 1970.

[25] Pravda, 3 November, 1969.

[26] M. Il'inskiy in Izvestiya, 24 February, 1970. The US intelligence report cited above notes an "irregular" force of as many as 38,000 supported by the CIA in 1968-69 but indicates that these were mainly Laotian and Thai; see New York Times, 3 August, 1971.

[27] Pravda, 1 March, 1970; the CIA report acknowledges as many as 440 sorties a day in early 1969, but gives the daily figure for April 1970 as 340.

[28] Pravda, 17 March, 1970.

[29] Interview with Komsomol'skaya pravda, 27 November, 1970.

[30] Radio Moscow, 6 and 11 February, 1971; see also an official TASS statement dated 3 February, 1971.

[31] Official government statement released by TASS, 25 February, 1971.

[32] There were none the less many rumours at the time that the Chinese might intervene; see USSR and Third World, No. 3, 1971, pp. 105-6.

[33] Izvestiya, 17 July, 1971 (underlining added).

[34] Trends and Highlights, No. 154 (16 January, 1963), p. D2.

[35] Vedomosti Verkhovnogo Soveta SSSR, 10 April, 1963 (cited in Goldman, Soviet Foreign Aid, p. 146).

[36] The USSR and Developing Countries (1965).

[37] Chae-Jin Lee, op. cit., p. 143 (note 99), reporting conversations with US and Laotian officials in Vientiane in 1967.

[38] See Neuchterlein, op. cit., p. 183.

[39] Joshua and Gibert, Arms for the Third World, p. 60 and Scalapino, ed., The Communist Revolution in Asia, pp. 189ff.

[40] Joshua and Gibert, op. cit., p. 130.

[41] See discussion of economic aid at the end of the section on Laos.

[42] Radio Delhi, 1 February, 1969.

9. RELATIONS WITH MALDIVE ISLANDS

These islands gained their independence from Britain in July 1965 and became a republic in November 1968.

The Soviet Union recognized the republic and established diplomatic relations with it through the Russian embassy in Colombo, but so far as is known had no significant diplomatic intercourse with the fledgling republic up to the end of 1971.

10. RELATIONS WITH MALAYSIA

Russian interest in Malaya during the years before independence, in 1957, was confined largely to the activities of the trade unions and the Malayan Communist Party, neither of which played a significant part in the nationalist movement per se. The insurrection launched by Malayan Communists in 1948, leading to the Emergency, was followed in Soviet journals for a few years but coverage declined in the early 1950s and for a time there was virtually no interest in Malayan affairs.[1] When a rare commentary on the dwindling civil war appeared, it was usually to ridicule British efforts - "pitting one hundred thousand soldiers", as one writer put it, "against a few hundred armed patriots".[2] When Communist representatives (including the MCP leader, Chen Peng) negotiated unsuccessfully with Malayan officials at Baling in December 1955, the failure was laid to the intransigence of David Marshall's government.[3] After Baling, there continued to be occasional reference in the Soviet press to the civil war in Malaya - as there was to civil strife in Burma, but with the significant difference that Moscow had no kind words for the Malayan leaders as it had for the Burmese. Britain, it was argued in Izvestiya in early 1957, prolonged the Emergency unnecessarily in order to postpone independence; for independence would deprive England of its "chief dollar source", Malayan rubber.[4]

When independence finally came, in August 1957, Russian writers asserted it was due to the MCP's "nine years of hard and costly war", but they argued there was little change in Malaya's status since England had exacted from the new nation "a military agreement providing for the continued stay of British occupation troops".[5] Commentaries on Malaya continued for some years to be unyielding and critical. Though Malaya did not become a member of SEATO, Soviet journalists considered it none the less a "partner" and therefore as much identified with the organization as Thailand and the Philippines.[6]

Given this negative attitude towards Malaya, Russian writers of course opposed any suggestion of a Greater Malaysia long before this idea took final shape. A simple union of Malaya and Singapore, with Singapore playing a dominant role, was a different matter: this had occasionally been urged by Soviet spokesmen throughout the 1950s (see below under Singapore). But Prime Minister Rahman's proposal in the spring of 1961 for a federation in which Malays in Kuala Lumpur would play the key part was sharply attacked. Such a plan, Vladimir Kudryavtsev wrote, "was only the beginning of a more extensive manoeuvre by British colonialists", a manoeuvre, that is, to assure continued British predominance in Singapore by submerging the city in a Malay-dominated federation including the North Borneo territories.[7] As Rahman's plan gained momentum, he was criticized with increasing vigour - in one account, for instance, as "the representative of the feudal compradore élite in Malaya" - and any project which had his backing must be judged suspect.[8] After the Federation of Malaysia had been proclaimed in mid-September 1963, Khrushchev denounced it as "a new form of the old colonizing policy.... The people are doing the right thing when they resist this."[9]

It is apparent, then, that Soviet opposition to a Greater Malaysia preceded by some years Sukarno's decision to oppose the federation with arms. The Russians, long determined to curb "imperialist" expansion in South-East Asia (such as that threatened in the emergence of a strong, conservative Malaysia), needed no prompting from Djakarta to support konfrontasi; indeed, in 1963, they may have encouraged it. As Soviet-Indonesian relations grew strained, however, Russia's interest in Sukarno's venture declined. Official Soviet support of konfrontasi continued until Sukarno's fall, in September 1965, but there were indications that Moscow was shifting its attitude towards Malaysia long before this. As early as February 1964, according to a subsequent report, the Russians approached Malaysia concerning the establishment of diplomatic relations;[10] in August 1965 Moscow asked for permission to establish a TASS office in Kuala Lumpur.[11] Both requests were rejected, but if reliably reported they reflect a quite natural concern in Moscow over the course of events in Indonesia: to the Russians, Indonesian hegemony in the Malaysian archipelago, strongly influenced by Peking, was a great deal more damaging to Soviet interests than a modest growth of British influence exercised through a prosperous Greater Malaysia. When the end of konfrontasi was announced in June 1966, nine months after the coup in Indonesia, the Russians greeted the announcement as "good news"[12] and set about immediately to improve relations with Kuala Lumpur.

The rapid development of Soviet-Malaysian relations after June 1966 may be explained, at least in part, by the fact that trade relations between the two countries had been active for some years. By the mid-1960s Russia purchased annually about 20 per cent of Malaysia's rubber crop and Malaysia ranked third among the Soviet Union's trading partners in Asia and Africa (despite negligible imports from the USSR; see Table C). Russia was less important in Malaysia's total trade - accounting for less than three per cent of it, for instance, in 1968[13] - but Kuala Lumpur was none the less desirous of preserving and expanding the relationship; this was the object of extensive economic contacts after mid-1966. Political exchanges soon paralleled economic, especially after the exchange of embassies in 1968 (a Soviet Embassy opened in Kuala Lumpur in March and the Malaysian, in Moscow, in October). Cultural co-operation developed more slowly but by 1968 included periodic exchanges of trade union delegations, visits by Soviet entertainers, the establishment of a TASS office in Kuala Lumpur, and the beginning of a student exchange programme.[14] In 1970 there was preliminary discussion of a Russian aid programme in Malaysia, including assistance in the construction of a nuclear power station, cement factories and various consumer-producing enterprises.[15] Soviet commentaries on Malaysia's social and political order, meanwhile, became less critical. A series of articles in Pravda in the spring of 1967, for instance, concentrated largely on descriptive material without attempting to suggest remedies for Malaysia's problems, especially rural poverty.[16] Russian observers apparently felt that it would have been irrelevant to Soviet purposes in Malaysia to persist in criticism of the country's well-known conservative orientation in domestic and especially foreign affairs. In due course, however, even Malaysian foreign policies were considered acceptable: in an article marking the 12th anniversary of the nation's independence, an Izvestiya commentator complimented the Malaysians for their "realistic position on a whole range of important international problems".[17]

The Russians were unquestionably helped in their policies in Malaysia by China's long intransigence towards the federation and persistent support of the Malayan Communists. The MCP, which maintained a permanent mission in Peking,[18] was in more or less perpetual rebellion against the Kuala Lumpur government, especially along the Thai-Malaysian border and in Sarawak. On the 40th anniversary of the MCP's founding, the Chinese Communists professed themselves "elated and inspired by the protracted, persistent revolutionary armed struggle" of the Malayan Communists; in consequence, the "revolutionary situation" in South-East Asia continued to be excellent.[19] The Malayan Communists reciprocated by using their clandestine radio, "Voice of the Malayan Revolution", to attack Soviet policies in Malaysia as "expansionist" and "revisionist social-imperialism".[20] The continuing ties between Peking and the Malayan Communists, in a country where more than a third of the population were overseas Chinese, gave a special object from Kuala Lumpur's perspective to the friendship of a moderate Communist power like Russia. The Russians played their part without prompting. The severe racial tension in Malaysia in the spring of 1969, for instance, was blamed by Soviet commentators on "the Great Power chauvinism of the Mao Tse-tung clique", which was "closely tied up with the policy of the colonialists and imperialists".[21] The activities of the Malayan Communists, meanwhile, were ignored in Soviet publications.

By 1970 trade talks between Malaysia and China, leading to several preliminary agreements (see Chronology), signalled a normalization of relations between the two countries and eventually, in all likelihood, diplomatic ties. Russia could no longer count on Peking's intransigence to pave the way to improved relations with Kuala Lumpur. Trade, however, not threat from China, was always the dominant motivation of Soviet strategies in Malaysia. The recent surge of Soviet-Malaysian cultural, scientific and diplomatic exchanges, two Russian correspondents wrote in September 1970, "testifies to the opportunities in the future for the development of business connexions between the two countries".[22] It was the "business connexions", one imagines, that were foremost in Moscow's calculations.

MALAYSIA

<u>Chronology</u>

    (See explanatory note on tables, p. 6.)

Political	Economic	Cultural

<u>Pre-1966</u>

1948-57	<u>Emergency: Communist rebellion</u>		
Aug 1957	<u>Independence</u>		
Jan 1959	CP delegation in USSR for XXI congress		
Sept 1963	<u>Creation of Malaysian Federation; Indonesia launches "Crush Malaysia" policy</u>		

<u>1966</u>

June	– <u>Settlement of Malaysian-Indonesian confrontation</u>				
		Sept	– Commerce minister heads delegation to USSR for exploratory talks		

<u>1967</u>

Mar	– USSR, Malaysia agree on diplomatic relations in principle	Mar	– Trade delegation in Malaysia: first agreement		
				Apr	– Journalist official in USSR
Nov	– Diplomatic relations confirmed	Nov	– Trade mission establishes office in Kuala Lumpur		

<u>1968</u>

		Jan	– Rubber experts in Malaysia for trade talks		
Feb	– Rahman aide in USSR				
				Mar	– TU delegation in USSR
				Apr	– TU delegation in Malaysia
May	– Deputy premier Razak in USSR				
June	– Deputy foreign minister in USSR				
		July	– Trade delegation in Malaysia: agreement on training of mechanics in USSR		
Aug	– Good will delegation in USSR				

	Political		Economic		Cultural
1968 (cont.)					
		Sept	– Soviet commercial exhibition opens in Kuala Lumpur		
		Oct	– Deputy planning minister in USSR for aid talks	Oct	– TU delegation in USSR for Komsomol anniversary
				Nov	– TU delegation in Malaysia
1969					
		Jan	– Foreign trade minister Patolichev in Malaysia (first ministerial visit)		
May	– Racial riots in Kuala Lumpur				
		Aug	– Commerce minister in USSR for trade talks		
		Sept	– Air service agreement – Deputy trade minister heads delegation to Malaysia for trade fair	?	– TU delegation in Malaysia
		Dec	– Trade delegation in Sarawak, Sabah		
1970					
				Feb	– Soviet art exhibition in Kuala Lumpur
		Apr	– Air service inaugurated	Apr	– TU delegation in Malaysia
July	– Rahman stops briefly in Moscow en route from London	July	– Trade office opened in Kuala Lumpur		
Aug	– Labour minister in USSR			?	– Russian dancers in Malaysia
Sept	– Rahman retires as premier; succeeded by Razak				
		Oct	– Trade minister in USSR	Oct	– First tourists in Malaysia
				Dec	– TU delegation in USSR
1971					
		Feb	– Exhibition of Soviet mining equipment in Ipoh	Feb	– Buddhist delegation in Malaysia – Chinese aid to flood victims
				Mar	– Soviet solidarity delegation in Malaysia for co-operation talks: agreement on scholarships

Political	Economic	Cultural

<u>1971</u> (cont.)

Apr - Shipping delegation in Malaysia for talks on increased co-operation: contracts on timber shipments to Europe

May - <u>Commercial delegation in CPR for trade talks</u>

June - Malaysian trade commissioner posted to Moscow

Aug - <u>Chinese trade delegation in Malaysia: agreement on rubber sales to CPR</u>

Sept - Return visit of Malaysian solidarity delegation to USSR
- TU leader in Moscow for international conference
- Muslim delegation in USSR

Nov - <u>Malaysian delegation in CPR for Canton fair: banking and trade agreements</u>

Dec - Aid officials in Malaysia for talks

References

[1] This period is dealt with in my earlier study, <u>Soviet Strategies in Southeast Asia</u>, pp. 385-401.

[2] Col. A. Leont'yev, in <u>Krasnaya zvezda</u>, 12 June, 1955.

[3] For a Lasting Peace, for a People's Democracy!, 6 January, 1956, p. 4. Marshall, a Singapore Eurasian, headed the government in Kuala Lumpur at this time.

[4] <u>Izvestiya</u>, 11 January, 1957.

[5] <u>New Times</u>, No. 36 (5 September), 1957, p. 18.

[6] E.g. <u>Sovremennyy Vostok</u>, No. 4 (April), 1959, p. 34.

[7] <u>Izvestiya</u>, 26 November, 1961, p. 3.

[8] S. Zhzha, in <u>Mirovaya ekonomika i mezhdunarodnyye otnosheniya</u>, No. 7 (July), 1962, pp. 122-24; see also N.A. Simoniya's article in <u>Narody Azii i Afriki</u>, No. 2 (March-April), 1963, pp. 49-59.

[9] <u>Pravda</u>, 30 October, 1963.

[10] Radio Liberty (Munich), Research Memorandum, 29 November, 1967.

[11] Radio Kuala Lumpur, 9 August, 1965.

[12] Radio Moscow, 3 June, 1966.

[13] The Far East and Australasia, 1970, p. 505.

[14] See U.S. Department of State, RSE-25, 7 May, 1969, pp. 98-99. In 1970 four Russian students were studying at the University of Malaysia in Kuala Lumpur and one Malaysian student was in the USSR; see RSES-34, 30 August, 1971, p. 94.

[15] Radio Kuala Lumpur, 7 November, 1970, citing a statement by the Soviet ambassador to Malaysia.

[16] Yu. Yasnev, in <u>Pravda</u>, 15, 24 and 29 March and 7 April, 1967 (noted in <u>Mizan</u>, May-June 1967, Supplement B, p. 4).

[17] V. Kondrashov, in <u>Izvestiya</u>, 30 August, 1970.

[18] See New China News Agency, 12 January, 1966, announcing the establishment of the mission.

[19] New China News Agency, 29 April, 1970.

[20] See <u>Mizan</u>, July-August 1970, Supplement B, p. 11.

[21] Radio Peace and Progress, 20 May, 1969.

[22] L. Demin and A. Maslennikov, <u>Pravda</u>, 1 September, 1970.

Soviet policies in Nepal were in large measure prescribed by the geographic location of this remote Himalayan kingdom between India and China. Russia could compete with neither for dominant influence in Kathmandu and accordingly did not seek to. The Russians encouraged Nepalese nationalism under King Mahendra, but they took care not to offend India, which considered Nepal something of a protectorate; they maintained their embassy in Kathmandu more as a listening post than as an instrument for special interests.

Soviet commentators reacted cautiously to developments in Nepal during the unsettled period following the overthrow of the Rana dynasty in 1951. All accounts spoke favourably of the 1951 revolution itself, but little enthusiasm was shown for the regimes that succeeded it - including King Mahendra's during its early years. The so-called economic reforms of 1956 were "superficial", Russia's leading authority on Nepal, I.B. Red'ko, wrote in a book published in 1958; the political structure of the kingdom was little changed from that under the Ranas.[1] The Soviet Union none the less established diplomatic relations with Nepal in 1956, a year after Peking had, and withdrew its annual veto of Nepal's admission to the United Nations.

King Mahendra's state visit to the USSR in June 1958 marked a watershed in Soviet-Nepalese relations and in the character of commentaries on Nepal. Embassies were exchanged (diplomatic relations having previously been conducted through missions in New Delhi and London) and aid and scholarship programmes were initiated. Articles favourable to King Mahendra's domestic and foreign policies now appeared periodically in the Soviet press, especially after the King dissolved Parliament and assumed full power at the end of 1960.

The Russians had not until this time indicated concern over Chinese activity in Nepal, which had preceded Soviet activity by several years. The authoritative commentator V.L. Kudryavtsev, for instance, in an article in mid-1958 on the occasion of King Mahendra's visit to the USSR, applauded close Sino-Nepalese relations and argued that they "added to Nepal's international prestige".[2] Red'ko, in a new volume on Nepal published in 1960, was also sanguine about the Sino-Nepalese relationship, to which he devoted more attention than he did to Soviet-Nepalese relations; he also indicated that Nepal's support of Chinese sovereignty in Tibet, implied in the 1956 Sino-Nepalese border agreement during King Mahendra's first visit to Peking, was praiseworthy.[3] By the end of 1960, however, Chinese activity in Tibet, which threatened India, was a cause of growing concern to the Russians. Moscow accordingly looked with uneasiness at the King's second visit to Peking in September 1961, when he signed a new border agreement and received additional Chinese aid for a highway linking Kathmandu with Lhasa. The Russians recognized in Nepal's growing friendship with China, as in Mahendra's seizure of power in 1960, an assertion of Nepalese independence from India - perhaps long overdue. Still there was grave danger, the Russians felt, in Nepal's linking its fortunes too closely with Peking's. Russian spokesmen continued throughout the 1960s to express confidence in Nepal's "adherence to the principles of peaceful coexistence and positive neutrality",[4] but criticism of Chinese motives in Nepal grew increasingly acid as the Sino-Soviet dispute intensified. The two major highways constructed by the Chinese in Nepal were singled out for special attack. These served "Mao Tse-tung's policy of Great Power chauvinism", a Russian broadcast asserted in 1969. "Although Nepal certainly needs these two roads, China needs them more.... China can thus attack India by moving her troops from Tibet along these two highways."[5] (The Chinese, of course, might have made a similar argument regarding Russian-built highways in Afghanistan).

Chinese-Nepalese relations, it may be noted, were unaffected by Russian criticism of Peking's policies. Diplomatic exchanges were invariably cordial between the two countries, especially on the occasion of national holidays and celebrations. King Mahendra, for instance, received flattering praise by Chinese commentators on his 50th birthday in June 1969[6]; Chou En-lai, at the embassy ceremonies in Peking marking the wedding of Nepal's crown prince in February 1970, noted the "profound, traditional friendship" that existed between the Chinese and Nepalese peoples.[7] If there was more to Peking's designs in Nepal than met the casual eye, the Chinese concealed it behind a bland exterior. The Cultural Revolution had relatively little effect on China's policies in Nepal; outwardly, relations with Kathmandu were at all times more sustained and more cordial than Moscow's during Mahendra's rule (he died in February 1972).

Economic aid was the Russians' principal lever in Nepal and it was not, all things considered, a formidable one. The total amount of Soviet aid pledged to Nepal was less than a quarter of Chinese aid pledged, and both programmes were small compared to Indian and American.[8] The initial Russian loan, negotiated in 1959, ran into numerous difficulties. First, its signing in the interval between a general election and the formation of a new government caused much dissatisfaction among the leaders of the victorious Congress Party; secondly, all projects under the credit were slow in starting due to mismanagement and incompetence on the part of Nepalese officials - as subsequently acknowledged by the Nepalese themselves; thirdly, the East-West highway, which the Russians committed themselves to survey, was a controversial issue in Nepalese politics, having been previously rejected by both Indians and Americans.[9] In due course most projects set forth in the 1959 agreement, as well as in a supplementary agreement in 1964 (which included the controversial highway), were completed.[10] No new programmes were announced, however, in the latter half of the 1960s.

Trade between the USSR and Nepal was negligible, the lowest for any Asian country whose trade with Russia was regularly reported in Soviet sources during the 1960s. A trade agreement in 1970, which appears to have been the second ever concluded between the two countries, pledged higher goals, but it was unlikely any increase would alter Nepal's dependence on India, with which an estimated 90 per cent of its total trade was conducted.[11]

Soviet cultural relations with Nepal were also modest. They were frustrated in 1960 by intense irritation in Kathmandu over the Soviet embassy's attempt, without clearance from the Nepalese government, to screen candidates for scholarships at Lumumba University.[12] The cultural programme survived this indiscretion, but apart from student exchange[13] was never of great consequence. Young Nepalese who through their Marxist-oriented organizations had been attracted to the USSR in the 1950s, when Moscow still remained somewhat aloof from King Mahendra, became disenchanted with moderate Soviet policies in Nepal during the next decade and inclined increasingly to Peking.[14]

Chronology

(See explanatory note on tables, p. 6.)

	Political	Economic	Cultural
Pre-1956			
Nov 1951	Rana dynasty overthrown after prolonged disorders; parliamentary regime begins		
Mar 1955	King Mahendra begins rule		
Aug 1955	Diplomatic relations with CPR		
1956			
Apr	– CP legalized in Nepal		
July	– Diplomatic relations with USSR: to be conducted through Delhi		
Sept	– Mahendra in CPR: frontier agreement		
Oct	– Premier in CPR	Oct – CPR credit for power station ($12.6m)	
			Nov – Buddhist delegation in Nepal for world conference
1957			
Jan	– Chou En-lai in Nepal		
			July – Journalists in USSR
1958			
June	– MAHENDRA IN USSR on state visit	June – Aid promised; gift of plane to Mahendra	June – Scholarships offered to Nepalese students
1959			
Apr	– Agreement on embassies	Apr – CREDIT AGREEMENT for power station; road survey; sugar and cigarette factories ($7.4m); gift of hospital	
1960			
Feb	– VOROSHILOV IN NEPAL on 3-day state visit		

	Political		Economic		Cultural
1960 (cont.)					
Mar	– Premier in CPR: border treaty	Mar	– Supplementary CPR credit for industrial projects ($21.1m)		
Apr	– Mahendra in USA	Apr	– US grant to Nepal ($15m)		
		Aug	– Protocol on power station		
Sept	– Parliamentary delegation in USSR				
Dec	– CP secretary in USSR for world congress – Mahendra dismisses government, assumes full powers; all parties banned				
1961					
Feb	– Queen Elizabeth in Nepal			May	– Cultural plan for 1961–62
Sept	– Mahendra in CPR: new border agreement				
		Oct	– CPR credit for Lhasa highway ($9.8m)		
1962					
		Feb	– Protocol on 1959 credit		
				May	– Journalist delegation in USSR
				July	– More journalists in USSR
				Aug	– Doctors in Nepal to work in hospitals for 2 years
Oct–Nov	– Sino-Indian border war				
1963					
Jan	– Foreign minister in CPR for signing of border treaty	Jan	– Hospital completed – CPR, Nepal agree on road site, air link with Lhasa	Jan	– Education delegation in Uzbekistan
		May	– Industrial exhibition in Kathmandu		
Oct	– PREMIER TILSI GIRI IN USSR on 4-day visit				

NEPAL

	Political		Economic		Cultural
1964					
		Apr	CREDIT AGREEMENT for roads, agricultural tool plant (estim. $8m)[15]		
June	Foreign minister in USSR			June	First cultural agreement
1965					
		Feb	Sugar, cigarette factories completed		
				May	Cultural exchange chief Romanovskiy in Nepal: expanded protocol
					Cultural delegation in Tadzhikistan
		June	Chinese-built shoe factory completed		
		Oct	Power minister in Nepal for opening of power station		
				Nov	Buddhists in Nepal
					Cultural delegation in Nepal
					Art exhibition opens in Moscow
1966					
				Jan	Cultural delegation in Central Asia and Caucasus
May	Deputy foreign minister Firyubin in Nepal			May	Information exchange agreement
		July	CPR credit (reported $20m)[16]		
Sept	Parliamentary delegation in USSR				
1967					
				May	Cultural protocol
				Aug	Tadzhik cultural group in Nepal
					Nepal cultural group in Ashkhabad
Dec	First Supreme Soviet delegation in Nepal				
1968					
May	Foreign minister in CPR	?	Supplementary CPR credit for road-building ($2m)	May	Book exhibition in Nepal

	Political		Economic		Cultural
1969					
				Feb	– Azerbaydzhan health minister in Nepal for medical conference
May	– Kosygin meets Nepalese premier in Delhi			May	– Red Cross delegation in USSR
Aug	– Foreign minister in USSR			Aug	– Cultural protocol for 1969
Sept	– Ministerial delegation in CPR for anniversary				
Nov	– CPR ministerial delegation in Nepal				
				Dec	– Cultural delegation in Tashkent
1970					
Feb	– CPR delegation in Nepal for marriage of crown prince				
Mar	– Parliamentary delegation in USSR			?	– Buddhist delegation in Nepal
Apr	– Komsomol delegation in Nepal				
		Aug	– New two-year trade agreement	Aug	– Cultural protocol for 1970: agreement on degree equivalency
		Oct	– Section of Russian-built highway completed		
		Dec	– Agreement with CPR on power lines		
1971					
Mar	– Parliamentary delegation in CPR	Mar	– Agreement with CPR on repair of Kathmandu-Kodari highway		
May	– Princess in CPR with sports delegation				
June	– MAHENDRA IN USSR for 10-day state visit				
Aug	– Commander in chief in USSR on holiday			Aug	– Cultural exchange plan for 1971
		Oct	– Protocol on Chinese surveys of mineral deposits		

References

[1] I.B. Red'ko, Nepal, Tashkent, 1958 (reviewed in Central Asian Review, No. 1, 1960, pp. 106-7).

[2] International Affairs, June 1958, p. 79.

[3] I.B. Red'ko, Nepal posle vtoroy mirovoy voyny, 1960 (reviewed in Central Asian Review, No. 4, 1961, pp. 390-401).

[4] E.g. V. Borovoy, writing in Pravda, 18 February, 1969.

[5] Radio Moscow, 27 May, 1969. The north-south highways which despite Russian charges were intended primarily to stimulate trade with Tibet, were not in fact heavily used; they continued, however, to have political and psychological value in Nepal's effort to free itself from economic dependence on India. See Rama Kant, "Nepal's Foreign Policy and China", India Quarterly (New Delhi), July-September 1971, pp. 208-10.

[6] New China News Agency, 11 June, 1969.

[7] New China News Agency, 27 February, 1970.

[8] Marshall Goldman, who visited Nepal in 1964, cites Nepalese sources for the following estimates of foreign credit as of February 1964: United States - $71.6 million; India - $60.6 million; China - $43.4 million (with the possibility of an additional $28 million); and USSR - $14 million (Goldman, Soviet Foreign Aid, pp. 135-36 and 139). Subsequent Chinese credits raise Peking's total to at least $66 million up to the end of 1969 (the amount shown in Table B below). A Soviet source, however, shows Russian credits as slightly higher than Chinese up to the end of 1965, though both are markedly lower than American and Indian: United States - $58 million; Indian - $36 million; USSR - $8.8 million; and China - $7.2 million (Sovremennyy Nepal: spravochnik, p. 197). Another source, meanwhile, shows Nepalese draw-downs for the period 1966-69 approximately as follows: India - $24.2 million; United States - $9.6 million; China - $9.0 million; USSR - $8 million (The Far East and Australasia, 1970, p. 356).

[9] American reasons for turning down the highway project were mainly economic - that is, the usefulness of the highway in financial terms - but the Indians' reasons were apparently political as well: they wished to keep the Nepalese dependent on India by discouraging East-West travel within Nepal. For a discussion of the Russians' early difficulties with their aid programme in Nepal, see Mihaly, Foreign Aid and Politics in Nepal (Oxford: Oxford University Press, 1965), pp. 98 and 159-61.

[10] For a review of Soviet aid to Nepal, see Novoye vremya, No. 24 (11 June), 1971, pp. 26-28.

[11] The Far East and Australasia, 1970, p. 356; also Rama Kant, op. cit., p. 209.

[12] Mihaly, op. cit., p. 159.

[13] There were 300 Nepalese students in the USSR in 1971, according to Soviet sources; Izvestiya, 20 July, 1971.

[14] See Leo Rosen in Scalapino, ed., The Communist Revolution in Asia, pp. 379-80.

[15] Sovremennyy Nepal: spravochnik, 1967, p. 197.

[16] U.S. Department of State, RSB-80, 21 July, 1967, p. 2. Another source puts the size of this credit at approximately $15 million; Rama Kant, op. cit., p. 210.

Soviet policies in Pakistan from 1955 to the crisis over Bangladesh in 1971 fall into two more or less distinct eras: a period up to the early 1960s when the Russians viewed Pakistan with deep suspicion because of its ties with the West; and the subsequent years when Russia increasingly befriended the Pakistanis in what came to be called "the spirit of Tashkent". The change in Moscow's attitude is best seen against the background of international alignments in South Asia, for politics in this area during the years in question is a classic example of chess-board diplomacy. Russia's relations with Pakistan cannot be separated from Pakistan's with China, China's with India, India's with the United States – and so on in a continuous kaleidoscope.

Ambivalence marked the first period of Russian-Pakistani relations, as Soviet strategies alternated between efforts to persuade Pakistan to renounce membership in SEATO and the Baghdad Pact and warnings of the consequences if it did not. Thus, V.L. Kudryavtsev, writing in August 1955, considered that "healthy forces are forging ahead" in Pakistan and cited as evidence of this Karachi's role in calling the Bandung conference.[1] Mikoyan visited Karachi en route to India and Burma in March 1956 and reportedly offered aid; Molotov, who had not yet been replaced as Foreign Minister, also offered aid at about the same time.[2] Further offers of aid were made during the visit of a Supreme Soviet delegation to Pakistan in February 1958.[3] The number of official exchanges during these years was no fewer than with many Third World nations Moscow counted as reliable allies. On the other hand, the tone of Soviet commentaries on Pakistan grew increasingly severe as Pakistani determination to retain membership in the South-East Asia and Central Treaty Organizations (SEATO and CENTO) became clear. Periodic sharp warnings were given to Karachi over suspected American missile sites and bases in Pakistan.[4] Russian support for Afghanistan over the Pashtun issue and for India in Kashmir (see above under Afghanistan and India, respectively) now became more outspoken, and, of course, served as a further obstacle to any improvement in Soviet-Pakistani relations. Following Ayub Khan's seizure of power in October 1958, relations deteriorated even further. Indeed, for nearly two years they were virtually suspended as Ayub's government grew closer still to the Western powers and relied more and more on American arms. In May 1960 the U-2 flight of Gary Powers, which originated in Pakistan, prompted the sharpest warning yet delivered to Karachi: any nation, Khrushchev said, which authorized such flights from its territory risked immediate retaliation from the USSR – not excluding nuclear retaliation.[5] This was the nadir in Russian-Pakistani relations.

The conclusion of an aid agreement in early 1961, carrying with it a $30 million credit for oil development,[6] marked a distinct improvement in economic relations, but negative judgments of Pakistan persisted in Moscow. A new crisis over Pashtunistan in the spring of 1961, occurring about the same time as the oil agreement, once again prompted Soviet support of Afghanistan's claims. Pakistan's continued association with SEATO and CENTO was attacked as bluntly as ever in articles appearing in the Soviet press in the autumn.[7] Khrushchev, addressing the Twenty-second Party Congress in October, cited the "sad fate of Pakistan", because of its "compromise with

imperialism", as a warning to other Third World nations.[8] Meanwhile, fresh attention was given to the need for a more vigorous role in Pakistani affairs by workers and Communists[9] – despite the fact that the latter had been banned since 1954.

The international situation in South Asia, however, was changing in the early 1960s. Circumstances which had made it logical for Moscow to favour non-aligned countries like India and Afghanistan, at Pakistan's expense, no longer applied, or applied with less force than in the 1950s. For one, the new administration in Washington, whether because of the changing nature of weaponry which made fixed bases, like those in Pakistan, less essential than formerly, or because of a natural preference for democratic India over conservative Pakistan, appeared to rely less on Karachi than the Eisenhower administration had. Despite Ayub's visit to Washington in July 1961, American aid to Pakistan fell off, especially military aid. When fighting broke out between China and India in the autumn of 1962, the United States, together with England, promptly offered arms to Nehru – arms which of course could (and Karachi felt would) be directed against Pakistan as well as China. The Chinese, meanwhile, who had been careful to nurture friendly relations with Pakistan after the Bandung conference and who by the early 1960s had abandoned all pretence of friendliness with India, were ready allies for the Pakistanis. Preliminary talks between China and Pakistan in 1961 led to an agreement in May 1962 to negotiate their common border in Kashmir (that is, in the sector controlled by Pakistan) and to a frontier agreement the following year. Economic aid followed in due course – an interest-free loan of $30 million in 1964 – and the two nations collaborated in the construction of a highway linking Sinkiang and Pakistan across Kashmir. Peking, needless to say, gave Karachi its full support on the Kashmir issue.[10]

The Russians responded to this new situation by altering their attitude towards Pakistan, but they did so gradually. During 1963 and early 1964 Soviet observers rarely went beyond noting that "some circles" in Karachi had begun to question the wisdom of the CENTO and SEATO alliances.[11] By mid-1964 it was suggested that the government too "has come to recognize that isolation from the USSR and the socialist camp is not in the interests of the country".[12] Otherwise, there was no marked change in the tone of Soviet commentaries. In the autumn of 1964, for instance – at a time when national versions of socialism in many Third World countries were regarded tolerantly – "socialism" in Karachi was viewed by the leading Soviet scholar on Pakistan as "reactionary" and a weapon against Communism.[13] The pace of economic and cultural relations, meanwhile, continued about as it had been since 1961.

Ayub's visit to Moscow in April 1965, preceded by the visit of Foreign Minister Bhutto in January, was the catalyst needed to produce a definitive change in Soviet-Pakistani relations. The visit was given wide coverage in the Soviet press (though less, to be sure, than Shastri's a month later) and culminated in new trade, aid and cultural agreements, as well as a cordial communiqué. For the Pakistanis, however, the chief gain in improved relations with Moscow was not kind words and more economic and cultural co-operation, but assurances, at long last, of Soviet neutrality in the chronic struggle with India.

When fighting broke out in the Rann of Kutch a few weeks after Ayub's visit, Moscow scrupulously avoided attaching blame - other than to "imperialist provocation".[14] During the Kashmir crisis of August and September, the Russians were again neutral. The Soviet government stated officially at the outset of the crisis that it had no intention of "adjudicating" the rival claims of Pakistan and India, both of whom were "victims of an imperialist plot".[15] In mid-September, Kosygin, after having sent personal messages to Ayub and Shastri urging a cease-fire, proposed a meeting of the two leaders at Tashkent; the Soviet premier would himself be willing to participate in the talks, "if both sides so wished".[16] Kosygin's posture during the months preceding the Tashkent conference, as well as during the conference itself, was the culminating proof to the Pakistanis that Moscow had abandoned its support for India in Kashmir.

Russia's role as peacemaker at Tashkent was not, of course, disinterested. Peking's prompt offer of arms to Pakistan during the Kashmir fighting raised the threat of direct Chinese intervention in the most explosive issue in South Asia - an intervention that would have been intolerable to Moscow. It was undoubtedly this consideration, rather than any fresh judgment of Pakistani claims to Kashmir or a growing preference for Pakistan over India, which led the Russians to take the course they did. Improved relations with Pakistan, meanwhile, and the gradual shift to a neutral posture on the Kashmir issue during the preceding two years gave credibility to this course.

Soviet-Pakistani relations continued to improve after Tashkent. Trade grew and economic co-operation flourished as Pakistan became one of the major recipients of Soviet aid (see below). Russian arms began to reach Pakistan by 1967, with important consequences in Soviet-Indian relations (see above under India). State exchanges took place annually after 1965, including two by Kosygin in successive years - a rare occurrence.

Russian commentators remained neutral, of course, on the Kashmir question and were generally circumspect in discussing domestic issues. The unrest in East Pakistan in early 1969, for instance, was called "an internal problem" which the Pakistanis were quite capable of handling themselves.[17] During the crisis that followed, leading to the replacement of Ayub Khan by General Yahya Khan in March, Soviet specialists on Pakistani affairs - such as Pravda's A. Filippov and Izvestiya's V. Nakaryakov - confined themselves to reporting current developments without attempting to interpret them. (If the Russians seemed sanguine during this crisis, it was perhaps because Ayub's successor was already known in Moscow; indeed, Yahya Khan's Russian equivalent, Marshal Grechko, was in Islamabad at the general's invitation only a few days before the crisis came to a head). Russian observers were again restrained in reporting the heated campaign preceding Pakistan's first General Election in December 1970: hopes were expressed, predictably, for a Leftist coalition against the Rightist parties, but there were no dire forecasts when the coalition failed to materialize "because the leaders of the Leftist parties were afraid of playing a secondary role in the bloc".[18] The results of the election were received with some satisfaction, largely because of the gains made by the Awami League of East Pakistan, the party most favoured in Moscow; Soviet commentators also noted the "great success" of the Pakistan People's Party (PPP), but enthusiasm in this case was somewhat tempered by recent disenchantment with its leader, the former

Foreign Minister Zulfikar Bhutto.[19] During the weeks of domestic turmoil that followed the elections, before the outbreak of civil war in East Pakistan in March 1971 (see below), Soviet commentators were again noncommittal, waiting to see how matters would develop.

The Soviet effort in Pakistan after the Tashkent conference, it should be noted, did not eliminate Chinese influence there. So long as the Chinese supported the Pakistanis on the Kashmir issue, they were guaranteed a cordial reception in Islamabad. Peking accordingly gave repeated assurances of its support: Chou En-lai did so in May 1969, shortly after Yahya Khan had come to power;[20] the joint communiqué at the end of Yahya Khan's state visit to Peking in November 1970 reaffirmed China's support in Kashmir - a commitment that gave more substance to the Sino-Pakistani communiqué than to the Soviet-Pakistani communiqué five months earlier after Yahya's state visit to Moscow.[21] China's assurances meant that economic, cultural and political ties between the two nations continued to flourish (see Chronology), though Peking's influence in Islamabad was perhaps less exclusive than it had been before Soviet policies toward Pakistan shifted in the mid-1960s.

Moscow's "Tashkent policy" in the sub-continent was brought to a sharp test during the crisis in East Pakistan that erupted in civil war in the spring of 1971. The Russians had frequently expressed sympathy for the East Pakistanis. The rare criticism of domestic policies in Pakistan after Tashkent, for instance, had usually been over Islamabad's inability to cope with economic and social problems in the eastern sector of the nation: in East Pakistan, V. Nakaryakov wrote in 1970, nothing had changed in 22 years of independence.[22] Soviet sympathies were perhaps also stimulated by pro-Moscow Communists among the Bengalis of East Pakistan, who had close ties with the pro-Moscow Communists of India's West Bengal. When the Pakistani government decided in March 1971 to use military force to suppress Bengal's dissenters, the Soviet Union promptly expressed its concern. In a letter to Yahya Khan on 2 April Podgornyy said that the use of force in East Pakistan was viewed with "great alarm" in the USSR and he urged a prompt end to the "bloodshed and repression".[23] The Islamabad government, not surprisingly, considered the Podgornyy Note an intrusion in the internal affairs of Pakistan and expressed doubts of Moscow's neutrality in the issue. The Russians, however, did not go beyond the posture adopted in the 2 April Note. Coverage of developments in East Pakistan in the Soviet press was restrained during the following months; official statements were careful to avoid any reference to Bangladesh, the separatist state proclaimed by the rebels; Kosygin explicitly reaffirmed the Tashkent policy in June and indicated that the Soviet government viewed the East Pakistan crisis as a domestic problem.[24] Economic co-operation meanwhile continued, as evidenced in numerous agreements and protocols concluded during the spring and early summer (see Chronology). Even the signing of the Indo-Soviet Treaty of Friendship in mid-summer did not immediately change the facade of Soviet-Pakistani relations. This treaty, although it ultimately destroyed the Tashkent policy by altering the nature of Russia's commitment to India, was not inspired by events in East Pakistan but by the sense of isolation felt in both Moscow and New Delhi following Sino-American détente (see above, under India). The Russians were at pains to assure Islamabad that the treaty implied no change in Moscow's policy towards Pakistan. The communiqué signed in New Delhi at the end of Gromyko's historic visit in August clearly indicated that the two parties felt no "military solution" was possible in East Pakistan.[25] The Pakistani Foreign Minister was assured by Soviet officials in Moscow in September that Russia still sought the "unity and integrity" of Pakistan.[26]

When fighting broke out between India and Pakistan in November, however, the Russians could no longer preserve even the appearance of neutrality. The Tashkent policy, under severe strain for some months, had to be jettisoned altogether. An official TASS statement on 5 December laid the blame for hostilities squarely on the Pakistani government – before this, blame for the crisis had been placed more ambiguously on "the Army" or on "the military administration" in Dacca – and called for a settlement in East Pakistan "based on respect for the legitimate rights and interests of the people". In short, the Russians, along with the Indians, now openly took up the cause of the East Bengali rebels. Although Russia did not formally recognize Bangladesh until early in 1972, Soviet delegates in the United Nations demanded that Bengali representatives be given a hearing during the debate on the crisis and on three occasions the Russians vetoed cease-fire resolutions as Indian forces assisted the rebels in consolidating their control over the fledgling state.

Pakistan did not sever relations with the USSR, despite official charges – which the Russians promptly denied – that Soviet personnel were manning Indian war planes and gunboats.[27] The Pakistanis, acutely conscious of their isolation as it became clear that American and Chinese sympathies would not extend to active intervention on their behalf, could not afford the satisfaction of rebuffing the Russians. Zulfikar Bhutto, representing Pakistan during the debates in the Security Council, was bitter over Russia's cynical policies during the crisis – as bitter as the spokesman of a weak nation usually allows himself to be face to face with the spokesman of a major power – but Pakistan did not break ties. The Russians, meanwhile, had no reason to break ties with Islamabad and during the weeks following the war sought to improve relations. Podgornyy sent congratulations to Bhutto on his formal assumption of the Presidency in mid-January 1972. In March President Bhutto paid a state visit to the USSR and the aid and cultural programmes, suspended since December, were resumed. Outwardly Soviet-Pakistani relations had returned to ante-bellum status, with the significant difference that the "spirit of Tashkent" no longer prevailed in Moscow's strategies.

Economic Aid and Arms

Soviet credits extended to Pakistan to the end of 1971 totalled approximately $461 million,[28] a sum exceeded in Russian loans to only five other Third World States (India, Egypt, Afghanistan, Iran and Iraq). All of this aid was extended after 1960. Before 1970 most of it went to the oil and fishing industries, in both East and West Pakistan; smaller projects included electrical and nuclear power stations and various agricultural enterprises. Negotiations for the giant iron and steel complex in Karachi, which was to be financed by Russia's largest loan to Pakistan (announced in 1971), were suspended during the Indo-Pakistani war but were resumed when Bhutto was in Moscow the following March. According to Pakistani sources at this time, $168 million of all Russian credits had been used – that is, less than one third.[29]

Chinese credits, which were extended over a shorter period of time, were smaller than the Russian but appear to have been utilized more fully. In January 1972, during Bhutto's visit to Peking, the Chinese transferred $110 million in early credits to outright loans; payment on the large 1970 loan ($200 million) was meanwhile deferred for 20 years and additional loans were promised on the same terms when this was exhausted.[30]

Soviet-Pakistani trade grew rapidly in the mid-1960s – 1966 totals, for instance, were said to have been five times greater than 1964 totals[31] – and thereafter expanded steadily. By 1970 Pakistan ranked among Russia's 10 principal trading partners in the Third World. Russia, however, stood behind half a dozen other nations among Pakistan's trading partners, including the United States and China. The road network completed in Afghanistan in the 1960s, Moscow felt, would lead to expanded trade with Pakistan during the following decade.[32] The Indo-Pakistani war at the end of 1971 interrupted trade for several months, but it was resumed when relations were normalized.

Russian arms were reportedly delivered to Pakistan in modest quantities in the latter part of 1967,[33] before the conclusion of a major arms agreement in July 1968. This agreement, an extension of Moscow's Tashkent policy (see above), covered aircraft, tanks and artillery; subsequent reports indicated Russia might in due course provide Pakistan with submarines and other naval equipment.[34] As Soviet relations with India soured, however, over the issue of arms to Pakistan, the Russians appear to have had second thoughts about their programme and reportedly suspended deliveries in the spring of 1970.[35] The Chinese thereafter became the major supplier of arms to Pakistan, though little is known of the volume or type of arms they supplied. American deliveries, suspended during the Kashmir crisis of 1965, were resumed in due course and were reportedly increased during the East Pakistan crisis in 1971 – a quid pro quo, it was said, for Pakistan's good offices in arranging Henry A. Kissinger's visit to Peking.[36]

The second period in Soviet policy in Pakistan, as defined at the outset of this essay, was clearly the crucial one and bears further analysis. Russia's friendship towards Pakistan in the latter half of the 1960s changed the profile of international relations in the sub-continent. If improved Soviet-Pakistani relations were themselves the consequence of shifting alignments in South Asia, as argued above, it is also true that this new relationship altered political alignments still further.

The Russians appear to have had two objectives in their strategies in Pakistan during this period: first, to check Chinese no less than American influence in South Asia; second, to secure an alternative ally in the event the Soviet-Indian alliance should go awry – through a turn to the Right in India or other developments beyond Moscow's control. Soviet strategies in some measure succeeded in the first objective. Chinese influence was surely checked by 1971, if not appreciably reduced: Peking could no longer, through a monopoly of influence in Islamabad, apply significant leverage in South Asian affairs. American influence, meanwhile, already waning when Soviet policies shifted, waned still further. Although one needs to treat with a certain respect an overall commitment as formidable as the American in Pakistan,[37] the leverage once held by the United States as chief provider of arms and economic assistance to the Pakistanis was destroyed by the 1970s – as much by Russian as by Chinese policies.

The Russians' second goal in Pakistan was unachieved, and perhaps unachievable. There was no way Moscow could develop Pakistan as an alternative ally in South Asia without offending Russia's primary ally, India; no diplomacy, however adroit, could favour one of these embattled nations without antagonizing the other. The Russians may genuinely have wished regional peace and co-operation in the sub-continent, as Kosygin insisted during his visit to Islamabad in 1969,[38] but they were unable to press the "spirit of Tashkent" this far. When obliged to choose, in mid-1971, they chose India.

Chronology

(See explanatory note on tables, p. 6.)

	Political		Economic		Cultural
Pre-1956					
Aug 1947	Independence				
May 1948	Agreement on diplomatic relations (embassies exchanged in 1950)				
		July 1949	Trade delegation in Pakistan		
Jan 1950	Pakistan recognizes CPR; embassies exchanged				
Sept 1954	Pakistan joins SEATO				
		Oct 1954	Economic delegation in USSR		
Sept 1955	Pakistan adheres to Baghdad Pact			? 1955	Academicians in USSR
1956					
Mar	– Mikoyan in Pakistan for ceremony on adoption of new constitution				
				May	– Preliminary agreement on tourist exchange
		June	– Trade delegation in Pakistan: first agreement		
July	– Parliamentary delegation in USSR	July	– Gift of food to famine victims		
Oct	– Premier Suhrawardy in CPR				
Dec	– Chou En-lai in Pakistan				
1957					
Jan	– USSR supports India in UN discussion of Kashmir				
June	– Parliamentary delegation in CPR				

Political	Economic	Cultural
1957 (cont.)		
		July – Muslim delegation in USSR
	Sept – Agricultural minister in USSR	
	Oct – Trade delegation in USSR	
Nov – Government delegation in USSR for 40th anniversary		
		? – Academic delegation in USSR
1958		
Jan – Parliamentary delegation in Pakistan		
		May – Gift of cholera vaccine; Soviet doctors arrive to help in epidemic
Aug – Parliamentary delegation in USSR		
Oct – Ayub Khan seizes power in Pakistan		
1959		
Mar – Pakistan signs defence agreement with USA		
Dec – President Eisenhower in Pakistan		
1960		
	Jan – Gift of 3 tractors	
May – U–2 episode: Khrushchev threatens retaliation on countries authorizing such flights		
	Aug – Aid promised and accepted for oil prospecting	
		Nov – Aid to typhoon victims
	Dec – Minister of national reconstruction heads mission to USSR: CREDIT AGREEMENT on oil prospecting (March 1961; $30m)	

PAKISTAN

	Political		Economic		Cultural
1961					
Apr	– Afghan-Pakistani crisis over Pashtunistan				
July	– Ayub in USA	July	– Contract for oil prospecting		
1962					
				Jan	– Orientalist Gafurov heads delegation to Pakistan
May	– Tashkent municipal delegation in Karachi – Pakistan, CPR agree to negotiate border			May	– Muslim delegation in Pakistan
Oct	– USA pledges arms to India during Sino-Indian border war				
1963					
Feb	– Foreign minister in CPR: frontier agreement signed				
		May	– Oil delegation in USSR – Agricultural delegation in Azerbaydzhan to study land reclamation		
June	– UN president Mohammed Khan in USSR				
				July	– Gift of medical supplies to typhoon victims
		Aug	– Trade protocol – Air service agreement with CPR		
		Oct	– Air service agreement with USSR	Oct	– Artists in USSR
1964					
Feb	– Chou En-lai in Pakistan				
				Mar	– Delegation in Pakistan for scientific conference
		Apr	– Forestry delegation in Kazakhstan for conference		
May	– Exchange of government delegations at opening of Moscow-Karachi air service			May	– TU delegation in Kazakhstan for May Day

Political		Economic		Cultural	
1964 (cont.)					
				June	– Cultural agreement
		July	– Gift of agricultural machinery		
			– CPR credit ($60m)		
Aug	– <u>CPR deputy defence minister in Pakistan</u>				
Sept	– Parliamentary delegation in USSR				
Nov	– Deputy foreign minister Lapin in Pakistan			Nov	– Artists in Pakistan
1965					
Jan	– Foreign minister Bhutto in USSR			Jan	– Information exchange agreement
Mar	– <u>Ayub in CPR</u>			Mar	– Scholars in Pakistan for academic conference
Apr	– <u>Ayub's visit to USA postponed by President Johnson</u>	Apr	– Trade agreement for 1965–68: CREDIT ($51.7m)	Apr	– Cultural protocol for 1965–66
	– <u>AYUB IN USSR</u> on 8-day visit				
Apr–May	– <u>India, Pakistan fighting in Rann of Kutch</u>				
				May	– Aid to typhoon victims
June	– <u>Chou En-lai stops in Karachi en route home from Middle East</u>			June	– Further agreement on cultural co-operation
Aug–Sept	– <u>Fighting in Kashmir: USA suspends arms to both India, Pakistan; Pakistan receives aircraft, tanks from CPR (reported $35m);</u>[39] <u>USSR remains neutral</u>				
Nov	– <u>Bhutto in USSR</u>	Nov	– Aid promised for oil drilling		
Dec	– <u>Ayub in USA</u>				
1966					
Jan	– <u>AYUB IN TASHKENT</u> for conference on Kashmir			Jan	– More aid for typhoon victims
Apr	– <u>Liu Shao-chi, Chen Yi in Pakistan</u>			Apr	– Cultural protocol
May	– Parliamentary delegation in Pakistan				
June	– Air force chief heads military delegation to USSR	June	– Contract for power station in East Pakistan		

	Political		Economic		Cultural

1966 (cont.)

	Political		Economic		Cultural
Sept	– Deputy foreign minister Firyubin in Pakistan – Reported arms agreement with CPR[40]	Sept	– CREDIT AGREEMENT for industrial projects ($84m)		
Oct	– Foreign minister in CPR				
				Autumn	– Journalists in Kirgiziya

1967

	Political		Economic		Cultural
		Jan	– Geology minister in Pakistan		
		Feb	– Trade delegation in USSR; new agreement for 1968-70	Feb	– Uzbek dancers in Pakistan – Academic delegation in Pakistan
May	– Foreign minister in USSR			May	– Cultural protocol
Aug	– Parliamentary delegation in USSR – Reported arms agreement ($10m)[41]				
		?	– CPR credit for commodity imports (reported $7m)[42]		
Sept	– AYUB IN USSR for 10-day visit				
Oct	– CPR–Pakistani border agreement			Oct	– University exchange agreement
				Nov	– Cultural minister heads Tadzhik delegation to Pakistan for Tadzhik festival

1968

	Political		Economic		Cultural
				Jan	– Writers' delegation in Pakistan
				Feb	– Muslim delegation in Pakistan – TU delegation in USSR
				Mar	– Tadzhik cultural group in Pakistan
Apr	– KOSYGIN IN PAKISTAN for 4-day visit	Apr	– Promise of additional aid for steel mill, nuclear power station	Apr	– New cultural agreement
May	– Navy vessels visit Pakistan	May	– Trade exhibition in Karachi		
July	– Chief of staff Yahya Khan heads military delegation to USSR: arms agreement	July	– Commerce minister in USSR: CREDIT AGREEMENT for purchase of industrial equipment ($66m)	July	– Scientists in USSR to study vocational training

Political	Economic	Cultural
1968 (cont.)		
	July – Agricultural minister in USSR	
	Summer – Agreement on cooperation in fishing industry	
Aug – West Pakistan governor in USSR	Aug – <u>Chinese caravan opens old silk route to Pakistan</u>	
		Oct – Dance group in Pakistan
Dec – Komsomol official in East Pakistan to attend student conference	Dec – Oil delegation in Pakistan for talks – <u>CPR economic delegation in Pakistan: credits for industrial equipment ($43m)</u>	
1969		
	Jan – Fishing experts, vessels in Pakistan for 2-year study – Trade delegation in Pakistan	
Mar – Defence minister Grechko in Pakistan – <u>Ayub resigns after five months of rioting; Yahya Khan heads military government</u>		
	Apr – Steel delegation in USSR to complete plans for Kalabagh steel mill – Economic delegation in USSR	
May – KOSYGIN IN PAKISTAN for 2-day visit – East Pakistan CP delegation in Moscow for preparatory conference	May – Agricultural delegation in USSR to buy harvesters, parts	May – Doctors in Pakistan to aid in cholera epidemic
	June – Specialists in Pakistan for talks on electrical installations – Trade protocol	
July – Islamabad city delegation in Moscow – <u>Good will delegation in CPR</u>		July – Film delegation in USSR for festival
Aug – <u>President Nixon in Pakistan</u>	Aug – Contract on machinery for electrical plant	
Sept – <u>Chief of Staff in CPR for anniversary</u>	Sept – Geology minister in Pakistan for oil talks: CREDIT AGREEMENT on oil exploration ($20m)	

	Political		Economic		Cultural

	Political		Economic		Cultural
		Oct	– Trade delegation in USSR – Automobile delegation in Pakistan		
		Nov	– Deputy gas minister in Pakistan – Steel delegation in USSR		
Dec	– Deputy foreign minister in USSR	Dec	– Trade delegation in Pakistan: protocol for 1970	Dec	– TU delegation in Pakistan to study technical education

1970

	Political		Economic		Cultural
Jan	– Submarine stops at Karachi				
Feb	– CPR good will delegation in Pakistan				
		Apr	– CPR economic delegation in Pakistan for opening of ordnance factory; agreement on additional industrial projects – Salesroom for Moskvich cars opens in Karachi		
May	– Air force commander in Peking – Submarine again stops at Karachi	May	– Agreement on electrical complex at Taxila	May	– Scientists in Pakistan: agreement on nuclear co-operation for peaceful purposes – Technical training centre opens in Lahore
June	– PRESIDENT YAHYA KHAN IN USSR for 5-day visit	June	– Promise of credits for steel mill in Karachi – Gift of equipment to railway training centre at Lahore – Protocol on logging equipment for East Pakistan	June	– New cultural agreement
		July	– East Pakistan industrial delegation in Moscow to sign protocol on Taxila plant		
				Aug	– Radio delegation in USSR
Sept	– Naval chief in CPR – Punjab governor in CPR	Sept	– Agreement on geological exploration in Baluchistan – 1968 fishing agreement extended 2 years	Sept	– Aid to typhoon victims in East Pakistan

	Political		Economic		Cultural
1970 (cont.)					
Oct	– Ayub Khan in CPR for anniversary				
Nov	– Yahya Khan in CPR	Nov	– Credit agreement with CPR ($200m) – Trade delegation in Pakistan: agreement for 1971–75	Nov	– TV director in USSR to discuss programme exchanges
Dec	– Awami League wins in Pakistani parliamentary elections	Dec	– Chinese-built engineering complex completed	Dec	– Health officials in East Pakistan: additional aid to typhoon victims
1971					
		Jan	– Delegation in USSR for talks on steel complex: CREDIT AGREEMENT ($209m) – Trade delegation in Pakistan: agreement on sale of cotton textiles to USSR		
		Feb	– Chinese-built highway opens linking Pakistan and CPR – Soviet experts in Pakistan for project survey on Karachi steel works – Contract on sale of generators to Pakistan		
Mar	– Yahya Khan postpones opening of Parliament; East Pakistan under military administration – East Pakistan rebels proclaim government of Bangladesh	Mar	– Agreement on rice sales to USSR – Exhibition of Soviet trucks in Pakistan – Agreement on shoe sales to USSR – Protocol on Taxila electrical works		
Apr	– Podgornyy appeals to Yahya Khan for restraint in East Pakistan – CPR offers equipment, training for 2 counter-insurgency brigades – East Pakistan CP delegation in Moscow for XXIV congress – Air Force chief in Peking – Presidential aide in Moscow to confer with Kosygin	Apr	– Protocol on power station at Guddu – Protocol with CPR on sugar mill		
		May	– Border trade agreement with CPR		
		June	– Protocol on Russian chief consultant to Karachi steel works	June	– Cultural protocol

	Political		Economic		Cultural

1971 (cont.)

			Economic			Cultural

June – Additional Chinese credit (reported $107m)[43]

July – Soviet fruit buyers in Pakistan
     – New trade agreement with CPR

Aug – Soviet-Indian treaty of friendship signed

Sept – Deputy foreign minister in USSR for talks on crisis

Sept – TU delegation in Moscow for international conference

Oct – Yahya Khan meets with Podgornyy in Iran

Oct – CPR agrees to aid various projects in East Pakistan

Nov – Bhutto leads high delegation to Peking for talks on East Pakistan crisis

Nov – Chinese machine building minister in Pakistan for opening of engineering plant

Nov– Indo-Pakistani war over
Dec   Bangladesh: USSR supports India in UN

Dec – Bhutto replaces Yahya Khan as president

References

[1] Izvestiya, 14 August, 1955.

[2] See Mohammed Ahsen Chaudhri, "Pakistan's Relations with the Soviet Union", Asian Survey, September 1966, p. 495.

[3] Central Asian Review, No. 2, 1958, p. 241; a 1959 offer of aid is noted in Central Asian Review, No. 4, 1959, p. 412.

[4] Official protests were made, for instance, on 14 April, 1958, 26 December, 1958, and 18 February, 1959 – all before the U-2 episode; see Pakistan: spravochnik (Moscow, 1966), p. 238.

[5] Pravda, 14 May, 1960 and 24 June, 1960.

[6] According to Goldman, Soviet Foreign Aid, p. 145, Pakistan agreed to this credit because of difficulties it was having at the time with Western oil companies.

[7] E.g. A. Dol'gov and L. Vasil'yev, writing respectively in Aziya i Afrika segodnya, No. 8 (August), 1961, and No. 9 (September), 1961 (reviewed in Central Asian Review, No. 1, 1962, pp. 90–94).

[8] Pravda, 18 October, 1961, p. 2.

[9] Kratkiye soobshcheniye Instituta narodov Azii, No. 42, 1961 (reviewed in Central Asian Review, No. 2, 1962, pp. 178ff.).

[10] For a review of Sino-Pakistani relations during this period, see Harold C. Hinton, Communist China in World Politics (Boston: Houghton Mifflin, 1966), pp. 452–57; Klaus H. Pringsheim, "China's Role in the Indo-Pakistani Conflict", China Quarterly, October–December 1965, pp. 170ff; and S.M. Burke, "Sino-Pakistani Relations", Orbis, Summer 1964, pp. 392ff.

[11] E.g. Pravda, 23 February, 1963 and Izvestiya, 24 March, 1964.

[12] Izvestiya, 24 July, 1964, citing the Karachi newspaper Dawn.

[13] M.T. Stepanyants, in Voprosy filosofii, No. 9, 1964 (reviewed in Central Asian Review, No. 1, 1965, pp. 55–60).

[14] E.g. Izvestiya, 29 April, 1965 and a TASS release of 9 May, 1965.

[15] Pravda, 24 August, 1965.

[16] Official Soviet statements on the Kashmir issue in 1965 are reviewed in Central Asian Review, No. 4, 1965, p. 373.

[17] Radio Moscow, 1 February, 1969.

[18] A. Turanov in New Times, No. 49 (4 December), 1970, p. 17.

[19] Bhutto had denounced the Tashkent agreement in the preceding August, though he had been Foreign Minister

at the time it was negotiated; his position was sharply attacked in a broadcast over Radio Moscow on 27 August, 1970 and his popularity among Leftists was thereafter said to be "visibly declining".

[20] Radio Karachi, 5 May, 1969.

[21] Compare the two communiqués in Pravda, 26 June, 1970 and New China News Agency, 14 November, 1970.

[22] Izvestiya, 3 January and 26 February, 1970.

[23] Pravda, 4 April, 1971.

[24] See his election address at the Bolshoy Theatre, broadcast on Radio Moscow, 9 June, 1971 and the report of his meeting with the Pakistani ambassador in Moscow, broadcast on Radio Pakistan, 24 June, 1971 (both reviewed in USSR and Third World, No. 6, 1971, pp. 297-98). For a comparison of Soviet, Chinese and Indian policies during the East Pakistan crisis, see an article by Zubeida Mustafa in Pacific Community, April 1972, pp. 498-515.

[25] Pravda, 12 August, 1971; see also above, under India.

[26] See Sultan Mohammed Khan's report on his visit following his return; Radio Pakistan, 4 September, 1971.

[27] The TASS denial was carried in Pravda, 11 December, 1971.

[28] This is the total indicated in the Chronology and shown in Table B. Other estimates are: $474 million (U.S. Department of State, RESC-3, 15 May, 1972, p. 4) and $464 million (Radio Karachi, 19 March, 1972).

[29] Radio Karachi, 19 March, 1972.

[30] New China News Agency, 2 February, 1972.

[31] Vneshnyaya torgovlya, No. 11 (November), 1968, p. 17.

[32] Izvestiya, 30 January, 1971, on the occasion of the Soviet-Afghan agreement opening the new roads for transit traffic to and from Pakistan.

[33] According to Joshua and Gibert, Arms for the Third World, p. 71, deliveries included helicopters and trucks;

in addition, a number of Pakistani pilots were sent to the USSR for training.

[34] S.P. Seth, "Russia's Role in Indo-Pak Politics", Asian Survey, August 1969, p. 619, citing Indian and Pakistani newspapers.

[35] See New York Times, 27 July, 1971, citing Indian officials. According to the Institute of Strategic Studies in London, Pakistan possessed the following arms of Russian make in 1970: an estimated 50 tanks (of a total of 400); 80 MIG-19 interceptors (which constituted nearly a third of Pakistan's combat air force); and miscellaneous anti-aircraft guns. See The Military Balance, 1970-1971, pp. 67-68.

[36] New York Times, 27 July, 1971.

[37] Annual draw-downs on American loans, even at the end of the 1960s, were far larger than on Russian and total credits since 1955 were nearly 10 times greater; see The Far East and Australasia, 1970, pp. 305ff. American trade with Pakistan, meanwhile, was five or six times greater than Russian trade through the 1960s. American arms deliveries to Pakistan, until suspended during the Kashmir crisis of 1965, were estimated at $750 million, which made Pakistan the second largest recipient of American arms in the Third World (after Turkey); Joshua and Gibert, op. cit., p. 130.

[38] In a formal address in Islamabad, Kosygin spoke of the urgent need for "relations of friendship and constructive co-operation" among the nations of the sub-continent - especially Pakistan and India; Pravda, 1 June, 1969.

[39] Joshua and Gibert, op. cit., p. 70, citing US news reports.

[40] The Military Balance, 1967-1968, p. 53; New York Times, 5 September, 1967.

[41] Joshua and Gibert, op. cit., pp. 71 and 110.

[42] U.S. Department of State, RSE-120, 14 August, 1968, p. 5.

[43] Pacific Community, April 1972, p. 509.

Soviet policies in the Philippines from 1955 to 1971 were in many respects similar to those in Thailand, with the difference that, in the absence of diplomatic relations, Moscow had less opportunity to press for improved relations when the climate was ripe. Thus the efforts to improve Soviet-Thai relations in the first half of the 1960s (see below under Thailand) have no parallel in the Philippines. Trade between Russia and the Philippines was so slight during the years under review that it was not reflected in the official statistics released by either country. There was of course no Soviet aid. Until 1968 the few "exchanges" were in one direction - Filipino delegations to the USSR.

Soviet commentaries on the Philippines until the mid-1960s tended to be harsh. Philippine "independence", Russian observers argued, was a fiction and would continue to be so as long as Americans continued to dominate the Army, industry and all other features of Filipino life.[1] Manila's reliance on the United States was predictably a constant theme in Soviet commentaries, as it was in the case of Thailand. In 1964 the decision to send 3,000 Filipinos to fight in Vietnam, all costs to be met by the United States, was cited as an example of the Philippines' abject foreign policy.[2] Opposition to these policies was said to exist in the country, but the Russians did not indicate until the latter half of the 1960s where it was to be found. The trade union movement, once considered the mainstay of "progressive" tendencies in the Philippines, was labelled "reformist" after the Second World War and was therefore of little use in combating pro-American policies.[3] Meanwhile, neither the Huk movement, largely confined to central Luzon since the early 1950s, nor the fragmented Communist organization in and around Manila attracted significant attention in Moscow - although both appear to have had a preference for Moscow over Peking into the early 1960s.[4]

From the mid-1960s on, Russia's attitude towards the Philippines, while still critical of Manila's role in Vietnam, softened perceptibly. Less was made of Philippine dependence on the United States and more of growing opposition to the dependency. In May 1966, for instance, N. Savel'yev (the leading Soviet specialist on the Philippines at the time) wrote that for the first time the "national bourgeoisie" in Manila was seeking a change in Filipino foreign policy;[5] an Izvestiya correspondent, the first to be given an entry visa to the Philippines, made a similar report later in the year.[6] These claims persisted. In early 1970 the markedly tougher attitude of the Marcos government towards Washington, according to an Izvestiya correspondent, "reflects the desire of broad strata of the Filipino people to be rid of American control over the economic and political life of the country".[7] The severe student riots at the University of Manila at this time were seen as primarily anti-American in inspiration and their suppression by the government was criticized.[8] Meanwhile, contacts between the USSR and the Philippines multiplied (see Chronology).

The object of this altered policy in the Philippines was clearly the normalization of relations with the last independent state in Asia with which Moscow had no formal ties (not counting South Vietnam, South Korea and Taiwan). The time had long since passed when Soviet diplomats sought to ostracize Third World nations solely because of opposing ideologies or links with capitalist states. "The USSR in no way wants to harm relations of young Asian countries with the Western powers", a Russian spokesman argued in 1971; at the same time co-operation with the socialist countries would allow the Philippines "to take a more independent stand as far as Washington is concerned and to conduct a more independent policy".[9] This, together with the benefits of economic co-operation,[10] continued to be the Russians' principal argument for normal diplomatic relations.

Diplomatic ties, however, eluded the Russians, despite periodic predictions by spokesmen of both nations from 1969 on that they were imminent. In March 1972 something of a climax in the negotiations appears to have been reached, when Madame Marcos visited Russia as her husband's emissary - expressly, as she said, to "explore the normalization of relations" - and when the President himself announced the formal establishment of trade ties.[11] But there was no announcement of diplomatic ties before President Marcos's assumption of emergency powers in September, at which time it was apparent that normalization of relations would be deferred again.

The repeated postponement of normal diplomatic links between Russia and the Philippines was due to indecision in Manila not Moscow, for the Russians were consistently favourable to a formal relationship from the latter part of the 1960s on. The reasons for Filipino indecision are not entirely clear. One consideration may have been the impact of diplomatic relations with Russia on the Philippines' spiralling trade relations with anti-Communist nations in East Asia like South Korea and Taiwan.[12] Another was the encouragement diplomatic ties with Russia might give to the vigorous Marxist (but non-Maoist) elements in Philippine society that persistently harassed the Marcos regime. By 1971 there was a new consideration, stimulated by Sino-American détente: the merits of diplomatic ties with Peking, instead of Moscow. President Marcos, to be sure, explicitly ruled out diplomatic relations with Peking at the time of China's admission to the UN,[13] but this did not prevent a lively unofficial exchange between the two nations during 1971 and 1972 - surely as lively as the unofficial exchange with the USSR. If Chinese diplomats, established in Manila, could urge restraint on the most rebellious Maoist elements in the Filipino resistance movement, this would be a significant gain for the Marcos regime.[14] These considerations, however, had not crystallized sufficiently before the crisis of September 1972 to allow a clear decision on the question of diplomatic relations with Russia or China, or both.

Chronology

(See explanatory note on tables, p. 6.)

	Political		Economic		Cultural
Pre-1966					
July 1946	Independence				
		June 1958	Business delegation in USSR		
				July 1961	Journalist delegation in USSR
		Mar 1963	Delegation in Manila for ECAFE conference		
1966					
		Mar	- Unofficial trade delegation in CPR		
				Sept	- First Soviet correspondent visits Philippines
1967					
		Apr	- Industrial delegation in USSR for trade talks		
June	- Unofficial parliamentary delegation in CPR				
July	- Parliamentary delegation in USSR				
1968					
				July	- Cultural mission in Philippines (first official delegation)
Oct	- House speaker Laurel in USSR				
1969					
		Feb	- First Soviet freighter docks in Manila		
Mar	- Pro-Marxist New people's army formed, dedicated to armed struggle			Mar	- Dance group in USSR
July	- Liberal party leader in USSR				
				Dec	- Dancers in Philippines

PHILIPPINES

	Political	Economic	Cultural
1970			
Aug	– Parliamentary delegation in USSR		
Sept			– Aid to flood victims
Oct	– Government delegation in USSR for exploratory talks on diplomatic relations, trade		– Delegate in Tashkent for Muslim congress
Dec			– Friendship delegation in Philippines – TU delegation in Philippines
1971			
Apr	– Izvestiya correspondent Kudryavtsev heads good will mission to Philippines		
May		– Business, Chamber of commerce missions visit CPR	– TU delegation in Moscow for May Day
July		– Trade delegation in USSR	
Sept	– Senate president in USSR		– Women's, youth delegations in CPR – TU delegation in Moscow for international conference
Nov		– Businessmen in CPR for Canton Fair	– Muslim delegation in Philippines
Dec			– Cultural delegation in CPR

References

[1] A typical argument along these lines is N. Savel'yev, "Archipelago in Imperialist Bondage", International Affairs, No. 11 (November), 1961, pp. 79–84.

[2] See Krasnaya zvezda, 9 November, 1964.

[3] E.g. G.E. Komarskiy, in Problemy Vostokovedeniya, No. 1 (January–February), 1959, pp. 62–69.

[4] This was the impression given the author by the Filipino Communist Jose Lava in interviews in 1961 and 1962; Lava, a former leader of the CPP and brother of the then First Secretary (Jesus Lava), was serving a life sentence for insurrection. (The two interviews, which were concerned mainly with an earlier period in the Philippine Communist movement, are dealt with in Soviet Strategies in Southeast Asia, pp. 294–96 and 419–22).

[5] Mirovaya ekonomika i mezhdunarodnyye otnosheniya, No. 5 (May), 1966, pp. 98–100.

[6] K. Vishnevetskiy, Izvestiya, 20 November and 22 December, 1966. A request for a permanent TASS representative in Manila had been turned down a year earlier; see Radio Manila, 21 August, 1965.

[7] Yu. Popov, Izvestiya, 28 January, 1970.

[8] E.g. Izvestiya, 3 March, 1970.

[9] Radio Moscow, 21 March, 1971 (in English for South-East Asia).

[10] The possibility of Soviet economic aid, including credits, was raised, for instance, in a Radio Moscow broadcast on 23 January, 1970, and dealt with more explicitly by a visiting Russian delegation in December; see Far Eastern Economic Review, No. 50 (12 December), 1970. See also the strong arguments for Soviet-Philippine co-operation by V.L. Kudryavtsev, following his visit to Manila in 1971; Izvestiya, 26 May, 1971.

[11] See USSR and Third World, No. 4, 1972, pp. 201–2 for coverage of Madame Marcos's four-day visit in mid-March and the President's announcement on trade relations on 28 March.

[12]See Far Eastern Economic Review, No. 5 (29 January), 1972, p. 32.

[13]Far Eastern Economic Review, No. 45 (6 November), 1971, p. 4, citing a statement by President Marcos on 27 October.

[14]A Maoist faction of the Philippine Communist movement was organized in December 1968 and for several years thereafter had Peking's open support; see Trends and Highlights, No. 293 (1 February, 1971), No. 299 (1 August, 1970), and No. 306 (1 March, 1971). By 1972, however, officials in Peking were assuring Filipino visitors that the Chinese government had "no intention of interfering in the Philippines' internal affairs"; see Far Eastern Economic Review, No. 10 (4 March), 1972, p. 17. The regular Communists, meanwhile, affirmed their loyalty to Moscow at the time of the Twenty-fourth CPSU Congress and condemned the Maoists as "petty bourgeois adventurists ... who idolize the rifle as the only form of struggle"; Pravda, 10 April, 1971. For a discussion of the Filipino Communist factions, see also Yearbook on International Communist Affairs, 1971, pp. 660-67.

The Russians for many years took it for granted that Malaya and Singapore, when they gained their independence, would be united. They were not greatly surprised, however, as negotiations toward independence proceeded in the mid-1950s, that Singapore was in fact excluded. Singapore, Soviet observers remarked, was too great a prize for England to let go: "This colony is the last major stronghold of British dominion in Asia and is an important link in the SEATO system."[1] Meanwhile, the fact that politics in Singapore were turbulent and the dominant force of the 1955 elections Leftist, while politics in Malaya were relatively calm and dominated by conservative Malay elements, was further reason, Soviet writers argued, for the British to liberate one but not the other.[2] When Malaya was granted independence in 1957 and Singapore kept as a colony, Russian writers continued to condemn the separation and to chide both Americans and English for perpetuating it. The United States, Pravda's correspondent O. Orestov argued in 1958, was gradually "taking over Singapore" to ensure the colony's collaboration with SEATO.[3] England's object, V.S. Rudnev wrote in 1959, was to isolate the "advanced Singapore proletariat" from the more backward population in Malaya proper.[4]

The Russians became less sanguine about the "advanced Singapore proletariat" after the electoral victory of the People's Action Party (PAP) in June 1959. Under Lee Kuan Yew, this party – which Rudnev had described as "progressive and anti-imperialist" before the election[5] – was seen as gradually moving to the Right. Lee's support of Abdul Rahman's 1961 merger plan (see above under Malaysia) was singled out for particularly sharp criticism: merger, it was argued, was a means of overcoming the "serious crisis" in Lee's party, by weakening the "revolutionary forces" in Singapore; Lee sought political security through the "sale" of Singapore to Kuala Lumpur – and thus indirectly to England.[6] Lee stopped briefly in Moscow in September 1962, apparently to seek Soviet good will during his delicate negotiations on merger, but he was unable to persuade the Russians to modify their negative views of his regime. During the two years of Singapore's coexistence with Malaya in the Malaysian Federation, Soviet writers rarely distinguished between Singapore's policies and those of Malaysia as a whole – policies which Russia of course persistently opposed so long as the "confrontation" with Indonesia lasted.

Singapore again became a topic of discussion in the Soviet press after its secession from the Federation in August 1965. The break-away, Russian writers observed, was due to traditional rivalries between Kuala Lumpur and Chinese-dominated Singapore and to Singapore's having been given a disproportionately small voice in the Federation while expected to contribute a large share to the Federation's defence. Soviet sympathies were of course with Singapore and Lee's assertion that Singapore now

sought broader trade relations with all nations, including the USSR, were noted with approval; the only misgivings concerned Lee's agreement to allow the continued use of Singapore's port and shipyard facilities by Malaysia and his hesitation in opening diplomatic ties with Indonesia.[7] Relations between Russia and Singapore now developed rapidly. An exploratory mission to Moscow three months after secession paved the way for a trade agreement the following March. Thereafter trade steadily grew. Technical assistance was provided for the establishment of a clock works and instrument factory and there was discussion of a training programme. A modest programme of cultural exchange was begun following an agreement reached in 1967. In the autumn of 1968, following an agreement on diplomatic relations, a Russian Embassy was opened in Singapore; the Singapore trade mission in Moscow was elevated to Embassy status in 1971. Soviet commentaries on domestic developments in Singapore, meanwhile, were as bland and uncritical as those on developments in Malaysia – precisely as Chinese commentaries, at the height of the Cultural Revolution, grew more acid.

It is clear that improved Soviet relations with Singapore, as with Malaysia, were accelerated by the end of Indonesia's policy of konfrontasi after the fall of Sukarno. But this policy, which the Russians officially supported as long as it lasted, was aimed at the concept of a Greater Malaysia, not at Singapore per se. Singapore's secession from the Federation, therefore, opened the way for a détente with Moscow which would presumably have progressed even had the Malaysian-Indonesian impasse continued. Russia's interest in Singapore was not identical with the interest in Malaysia. In Malaysia, it was trade that attracted the Russians, especially the annual rubber crop; in Singapore, it was the port and harbour facilities, serviceable for shipping in all directions. Even Malayan rubber, after all, was shipped to Russia via Singapore. From 1967 on, according to Soviet sources, 500 Russian ships or more stopped annually in Singapore[8] – a measure of Moscow's interest in good relations with this city-state. Meanwhile the gradual evacuation of the vast British naval base in Singapore, in keeping with London's reduced commitments "east of Suez", opened up the prospects of Russia's use of these vacated facilities. Perhaps one day vessels of the Soviet Pacific or Indian Ocean fleets would refuel and be repaired at the former British base. The position of Lee Kuan Yew's government on the servicing of Russian naval vessels was unclear through 1971, but agreement was apparently reached on the repair of other shipping and the first Russian ships were overhauled in Singapore in early 1972.[9] It requires little imagination to see that a central object in Soviet strategies in Singapore was to make available the extraordinary facilities in this port to Russia's far-flung merchant and naval fleets.

Chronology

(See explanatory note on tables, p. 6.)

	Political		Economic		Cultural
Pre-1965					
June 1959	People's action party under Lee Kuan Yew wins elections after Singapore becomes self-governing				
Sept 1962	Lee Kuan Yew stops in Moscow en route to London				
Sept 1963	Singapore merges with Malaya in Malaysian Federation				
1965					
Aug	– Singapore withdraws from Federation				
Nov	– Deputy premier in USSR for exploratory talks				
1966					
				Jan	– TASS office set up in Singapore
				Feb	– Cultural group in Singapore for performances at national theatre
Mar	– Deputy foreign minister Zarubin in Singapore	Mar	– Trade delegation in Singapore: first agreement		
1967					
				Jan	– TU delegation in Singapore
				Apr	– First Soviet tourists in Singapore
				May	– TU delegation in USSR
		Aug	– Trade delegation in USSR: protocol on 1966 agreement		
				?	– Cultural agreement
		Oct	– Economic delegation in Singapore for aid talks		
1968					
		Feb	– Shipping agreement		
				Apr	– TU delegation in Singapore

SINGAPORE

	Political	Economic	Cultural

1968 (cont.)

	Political	Economic	Cultural
June	– Diplomatic relations established		
Sept	– Parliamentary delegation in USSR		
Nov			– TU delegation in USSR for anniversary
Dec	– Lee stops in USSR en route to USA		

1969

	Political	Economic	Cultural
Jan	– LEE IN USSR on 3-day visit		
Feb		– Air services agreement – Foreign trade minister Patolichev in Singapore	
May		– Aviation officials in Singapore to open air service	
Aug			– Ballet group in Singapore
Sept		– Communications minister in USSR for aviation talks	– TU delegation in Singapore

1970

	Political	Economic	Cultural
Jan			– Ballet troupe in Singapore
Mar			– Soviet film festival in Singapore
Apr			– TU delegation in Singapore
Sept	– LEE IN USSR for 8-day visit		

1971

	Political	Economic	Cultural
Apr		– Exhibition of Russian industrial equipment in Jurong – Shipping delegation in Malaysia	
May			– TU delegation in Moscow for May Day
June	– Lee Kuan Yew stops in Moscow en route to Helsinki – Malaysian trade mission in Moscow raised to embassy		

Political	Economic	Cultural

1971 (cont.)

July   - Destroyer stops
          at Singapore

Oct   - Chamber of commerce
         trade mission in CPR
       - Deputy foreign trade
         minister in Malaysia
         for Soviet trade fair

References

[1] International Affairs, No. 12 (December), 1956, pp. 138-39.

[2] E.g. International Affairs, No. 6 (June), 1956, pp. 121-23.

[3] Pravda, 24 August, 1958.

[4] Sovremennyy Vostok, No. 1 (January), 1959, pp. 27-28; see also Mirovaya ekonomika i mezhdunarodnyye otnosheniya, No. 9 (September), 1959, pp. 131-33.

[5] See the review of a 1959 volume by Rudnev, entitled (in translation) Outline of Recent Malayan History, 1918-1957, in Yuva Newsletter, October, 1962, pp. 2-9.

[6] International Affairs, No. 1 (January), 1962, pp. 118-20.

[7] See Y. Bochkaryov, in New Times, No. 34 (25 August), 1964, pp. 4-6 and A. Nikolaev, in International Affairs, No. 10 (October), 1965, pp. 98-100.

[8] Izvestiya, 8 October, 1968; Pravda, 9 August, 1970; and Izvestiya, 13 March, 1971.

[9] Radio Moscow, 29 February, 1972, announcing completion of work on a Russian whaler. Lee Kuan Yew was reported to have said in March 1971 that Singapore would have no objections to Russian naval vessels using the facilities of the former British base in peacetime; The Times, 30 March, 1971. In November, however, he was reported to have said Soviet naval ships would not have access to these facilities; Radio Kuala Lumpur, 4 November, 1971.

If Soviet relations with Thailand were subdued during the years reviewed here, this was more the consequence of Thai policies than Russian. Successive Thai leaders since the Second World War held persistently to their alliance with the United States, despite Bangkok's traditional capacity to switch sides as the fortunes of one or another Great Power rose and fell in the area.

Diplomatic relations were established between Moscow and Bangkok in 1946, as one of the conditions for Soviet acquiescence in Thai membership in the United Nations (the other condition was repeal of the 1933 anti-Communist legislation), and the missions were raised to embassies in 1956. Economic and cultural relations, however, remained minimal. Thai exports to the Soviet Union to the end of the 1960s rarely exceeded one per cent of total exports; imports averaged about a third of one per cent of all Thai imports.[1] Soviet aid to Thailand was confined to a cobalt charge given for medical uses in 1964. Cultural co-operation was negligible – a few academic exchanges, an occasional troupe of Russian performers and various film showings and exhibitions within the Soviet Embassy compound; a TASS correspondent was attached to the Embassy, but was not permitted by Thai authorities to distribute news.[2] The few Russian visitors to visit Bangkok came as a rule to attend international conferences and consulted with Thai officials incidentally (if at all). There were apparently no official Thai visits to Moscow before 1969.

Soviet commentaries on Thai developments varied slightly over the years, depending on the political climate of a given period, but were consistent on most issues. Thailand's dependence on the United States was predictably the main theme of Russian commentary and criticism here was constant. Occasionally Soviet observers pretended to discover growing popular resistance in Thailand to the government's foreign policy, but there was too little evidence in support of this argument to persist in it. Another theme in Russian commentaries was the tendency in Bangkok to pin the "Communist" label on anyone opposing the government's policies. "McCarthyism" was rampant in Thailand, one writer charged in 1961, despite the fact that no Communist "menace" existed;[3] the arrest of "Communists" at the time of the American landings in Thailand in 1962 and the execution without trial of one known Communist (Ruam Wongphan) were the subject of contemptuous reports in Pravda.[4] Soviet observers, meanwhile, persistently supported Cambodia's claim over Thailand's regarding the disputed border between the two nations – a posture which did not improve relations with Bangkok.

Russian-Thai diplomatic relations, however, were not always as strained as Soviet commentaries might lead one to believe. Early in the 1960s, for instance, there were efforts on both sides to improve the relationship – by the Russians, to lessen Bangkok's persistent dependency on the United States, and by the Thai, to vent displeasure over certain American policies in South and South-East Asia (such as rice sales to India, a traditional Thai market; an insufficiently firm posture, by Bangkok's lights, in Laos; and, in 1962, arms shipments to Cambodia following a decision by the World Court against Thailand in its boundary dispute with Phnom Penh).[5] Marshal Sarit held two widely publicized talks with the Soviet ambassador, in November 1960 and December 1961, during which

trade and cultural agreements were discussed. A Soviet specialist on South-East Asia, V. Pavlovskiy, argued in mid-1961 that Thailand appeared at last to be swinging to a neutralist position in international affairs.[6]

Russian-Thai relations did not necessarily grow more intimate, or Bangkok more independent, as a result of this mood of détente in 1960 and 1961, but the mood persisted. Khrushchev's son-in-law Alexey Adzhubey, for instance, was reported to have held cordial conversations with Thai leaders, including the King, during a visit to Bangkok in November 1963.[7] Moscow exchanged friendly greetings with the new government of Thanom Kittikachorn following Sarit's death in December.[8] In the spring of 1964 two Pravda correspondents, the first to visit Thailand since the 1950s, reported sympathetically on their findings and emphasized the desire of many Thai leaders for better relations with Moscow.[9] Meanwhile the informal trade agreement proposed in 1960 was concluded in May 1964.

The escalation of the war in Vietnam in 1965, and Thailand's steadfast support of the United States, led inevitably to a cooling of Soviet-Thai relations. Despite the warm reception given a Soviet variety troupe that performed at Chulalonghorn University and elsewhere in Thailand in January 1966,[10] Soviet commentators were by this time critical of all aspects of Thai behaviour. "Thailand has always carried out wars against neighbouring countries", a Russian broadcaster said in May 1966, commenting on a new episode in the perennial Cambodian-Thai border conflict, "in order to seize the territory and property of others."[11] A Soviet trade representative in Bangkok was expelled for espionage later in the year.

The Thai were meanwhile taken sharply to task for their growing involvement in fighting in Indochina. Not only were Thai airfields freely available to American bombers but under the terms of a secret agreement concluded in 1965, according to Soviet commentators, as many as 12,000 Thai troops were fighting in Vietnam by 1970 and another 5,000 in Laos. "Ruling circles in Thailand, regardless of the national interests of their people, have increasingly tied their country to the military machine of the Pentagon."[12] When Thai troops joined American and South Vietnamese in the invasion of Cambodia in May 1970, Russian observers charged Bangkok with undertaking a "punitive expedition" to recover Cambodian areas occupied by Thailand under Japanese protection during the Second World War.[13] Occasionally Russian journalists and broadcasters – as they always had – noted signs of popular dismay in Thailand at the nation's policies,[14] but so long as the policies persisted the bulk of official and unofficial comment in the Soviet press was critical.

If Thai-Soviet relations grew no worse than they did after 1965, it was due in part to Bangkok's growing uneasiness over Chinese activities in Thailand, against which Soviet friendship might one day prove useful. In the latter half of the 1960s unrest in the north-east provinces, and subsequently in the north, was increasingly traced to Chinese agitation. Peking openly praised Thai Communists and their allies, the Thai Patriotic Front, for adhering to "the revolutionary road of using the countryside to encircle the cities and seizing political power by force of arms".[15] The Chinese press repeatedly hailed the accomplishments of the Thai insurgents and urged them on to further victories, both during and after the Cultural Revolution. In August 1971 articles and broadcasts

marking the sixth anniversary of the Thai insurrection re-
joiced that the insurgents, "under the wise leadership of
the Communist Party", had killed more than 6,000 government forces, destroyed 150 aircraft and established a "relatively consolidated revolutionary base area" in Northern
Thailand.[16] The fear that Peking might follow its own
propaganda with active intervention led Bangkok to keep
the door open to possible rapprochement with the USSR.
A new round of contacts between Russia and Thailand in
1969 and 1970 served this purpose - including the first
"officially" invited Soviet delegation to visit Bangkok.[17]
The first formal trade agreement between the two nations
was signed in 1970, an agreement which foreign observers
felt had more political than economic significance.[18]

Whether or not this modest relaxation in diplomatic
ties would lead to further détente depended upon the
course of events in South-East Asia and, in particular,

upon any change in the impasse between Bangkok and
Peking. There was ambiguity in Thai government circles
during 1971 concerning relations with China. The Foreign
Minister, Thanat Khoman, apparently wished to open
trade talks with Peking and to this end instructed government news agencies in May to refrain from anti-Chinese
propaganda.[19] Thanom, on the other hand, stated bluntly
in the autumn that there would be no trade with China in
the forseeable future.[20] His coup and dismissal of Thanat
in November indicated that no change in relations with
China was imminent - a circumstance that presumably
encouraged the rapprochement with Russia. The Russians,
meanwhile, responded mildly to Thanom's coup[21] and put
no obstacle in the way of rapprochement. It had, after
all, been Bangkok's choice over the years, not Moscow's,
to keep Soviet-Thai relations as unproductive as they
had been.

Chronology

(See explanatory note on tables, p. 6.)

	Political	Economic	Cultural
Pre-1956			
Dec 1946	Agreement on diplomatic relations (first Soviet minister in Thailand May 1948)		
1956			
Feb	- Informal delegation in CPR; arrested on return		
May	- Missions raised to embassies		
Sept	- Pibulsonggram overthrown; Sarit emerges as leader		
Nov	- Parliamentary group in Bangkok for international conference		
1957			? - Academic delegation in Thailand for conference
1958			
July	- Parliamentary delegation in USSR		
1959			
Oct	- Soviet attaché and correspondent expelled		
1960			
1961			

THAILAND

	Political	Economic	Cultural
1962			
May	– US troops land in Thailand during Laos crisis		
1963			
		Feb – Foreign trade minister Patolichev in Thailand	
Nov	– Adzhubey (Khrushchev's son-in-law) in Thailand for editors conference; political, economic talks with Thai leaders		
Dec	– Sarit dies; Thanom Kittikachorn succeeds as premier		
1964			
		Jan – Delegation in Thailand for ECAFE conference	
Feb	– Uzbek leader in Thailand for UNESCO conference	Feb – Gift of cobalt for medical use	
		June – Informal trade agreement	
Nov	– Deputy foreign minister Firyubin in Thailand		
1965			
Aug	– Beginning of insurgency in Thailand		
1966			
			Jan – Variety troupe in Thailand
Sept	– Soviet trade representative expelled		Sept – Cultural delegation in USSR
		Nov – USSR takes part in Bangkok trade fair	
1967			
			Mar – Princess leads women's delegation to USSR
1968			
		Jan – Government delegation in Bangkok for ECAFE meeting	

	Political	Economic	Cultural
1969			
May		– Delegation in USSR to discuss increased trade, economic co-operation	
June	– Foreign office aide Kapitsa in Thailand		– First cultural delegation in Thailand
July	– President Nixon in Thailand for 3 days		
Oct			– Education minister heads cultural delegation to USSR – Press delegation in USSR
1970			
Feb		– Civil air delegation in Bangkok	– Buddhist delegation in Thailand
Mar		– First formal trade agreement initialled (signed in December)	
Aug		– Agricultural official attends conference in Minsk	
Sept		– Foresters' delegation in USSR	
Dec			– Cultural delegation in Thailand
1971			
May		– Agreement on air service	
June		– Minister of economic affairs in USSR for trade talks	
Aug	– Soviet diplomats in Thailand restricted after trip to northern provinces		
Nov	– Government-led coup strengthens Thanom regime	– Soviet trade mission established in Bangkok	

References

[1] Paul R. Shirk, "Thai-Soviet Relations", Asian Survey, September 1969, p. 688.

[2] U.S. Department of State, RSE-25, 7 May, 1969, p. 108.

[3] E.g. Pravda Vostoka, 29 July, 1961.

[4] Pravda, 18 and 28 May, 1962; see also "Soviet Writing on Thailand", Yuva Newsletter, October 1962, pp. 14-23.

[5] See Donald E. Nuechterlein, Thailand and the Struggle for Southeast Asia (Ithaca: Cornell University Press, 1966), pp. 178, 222, 255 and Paul R. Shirk, op. cit., pp. 690-91.

[6] New Times, No. 28 (17 May), 1961, pp. 18-19.

[7] See Izvestiya, 5 December, 1963.

[8] Pravda, 27 December, 1963 and Izvestiya, 3 January, 1964.

[9] Pravda, 10 May, 1964.

[10] Paul R. Shirk, op. cit., p. 692.

[11] Radio Moscow, 20 May, 1966.

[12] M. Il'inskiy in Izvestiya, 1 April, 1970.

[13] Ivan Shchedrov in Pravda, 2 June, 1970.

[14] See, for instance, A. Filippov in Pravda, 11 August, 1970, noting growing opposition among the business community; a broadcast over Radio Peace and Progress on 17 November, 1970, noted opposition in Parliament and increasingly in the government itself.

[15] E.g. New China News Agency, 30 October, 1967.

[16] New China News Agency, 6 August, 1971; for coverage of Chinese commentary on the Thai insurgency, see also Trends and Highlights, No. 277 (October, 1968); No. 301 (1 October, 1970); and No. 313 (1 September, 1971).

[17] See Izvestiya, 4 July, 1969.

[18] E.g. Denis Horgan in Far Eastern Economic Review, No. 2 (9 January), 1971.

[19] Financial Times (London), 18 May, 1971 (cited in USSR and Third World, No. 5, 1971, p. 236); see also Far Eastern Economic Review, No. 21 (22 May), 1971, p. 85.

[20] Radio Bangkok, 1 November, 1971.

[21] See, for instance, the analysis of the coup by V. Shurygin in Pravda, 20 November, 1971; Shurygin relies mainly on Western commentaries for his view of the coup as essentially pro-American.

TABLES

TABLE A

SOVIET POLITICAL RELATIONS WITH ASIAN STATES*

COUNTRY	(a) POPULATION	(b) INDEPENDENCE	(c) Diplomatic Relations USSR	(c) Diplomatic Relations CPR	(d) EXCHANGES 55	56	57	58	59	60	61	62	63	64	65	66	67	68	69	70	71	(e) Total Major Exchanges State	Other
Afghanistan	15.9	1919	1919	1/55	1/ 1/	1/ 2/1	1/ 1/2	1/ 2/	1/ 4/1	1/ 3/	1/ 3/3	1/ 3/1	1/ 1/	1/ 5/2	2/ 1/2	1/ 4/4	1/ 2/1	2/ 4/1	1/ 5/5	12/4	1/ 4/3	11/7	58/27
Burma	25.2	1948	1948	1949	1/1 1/1	1/ 2/1	3/	3/1	/2	1/ 1/	1/2	3/1	5/3	1/ 1/	1/	1/3	2/1	5/1	2/	2/3	2/2	2/4	32/20
Cambodia	5.7	1953	5/56	7/58	1/ 1/	1/ 1/	3/		/2	/1	1/2	1/	5/3	1/2	2/	2/4	2/	1/1	2/3	2/3		3/	17/12
Ceylon	11.9	1948	2/57	9/56			2/1	2/	1/1		2/1	1/2	2/ 1/	2/3	/3	1/1	1/	3/2	2/1	2/	1/1	1/	17/17
India	511.0	1947	1947	1950	1/1 /3	1/ 3/3	2/4	9/3	10/3	1/2 4/1	2/1 4/1	6/3	6/4	1/1 4/7	6/3	2/1 4/5	1/1 4/3	2/8	17/16	8/9	10/9	11/8	99/85
Indonesia	118.0	1949	1950	1950(1)		3/	2/4	4/	4/3	5/2	6/2	7/4	10/7	1/1 4/2	6/4	2/ 1/	2/	2/8	/2	3/	2/	3/4	60/26
Laos	2.8	1953	10/60	6/62		3/	2/				1/ 1/	3/	2/1 3/1	1/ 1/	1/		1/		/1	/1		5/	10/2
Malaysia	10.1	8/57	3/67														1/1	5/2	1/3	2/	1/3		11/9
Maldive Is.	.1	7/65 (2)																					
Nepal	9.4	3/55	7/56	8/55				1/		1/ 1/		1/	1/ 1/	1/	1/3	2/1	1/2	5/2	2/1	1/	1/	3/1	12/7
Pakistan	93.6	1947	1947	1950		1/ 1/1	4/	1/1		1/		/2	2/	3/3	2/1	1/2	3/3	5/5	8/8	2/2	3/2	4/3	37/30
Philippines	35.8	1946									1/						2/	1/1	1/	1/1	2/1		9/3
Singapore	2.0	9/63	6/68							2/6		1/			1/	/2	1/	2/1	1/2	1/1	1/2	2/	7/8
Thailand	33.7		1946				1/1	1/	1/		1/1		/2	3/4		1/	1/	3/2	1/2	/1	1/		7/6
TOTALS: STATE					2/3	3/3	15/5	23/5	19/10	15/3	20/10	26/14	30/17	21/21	20/16	19/22	22/13	28/22	44/44	33/19	28/23	45/27	
OTHER					3/3	10/5																	376/252

143

Notes to Table A

*The columns include the following information:

Column (a) – Estimated population (in millions); this is to facilitate comparison of activity in nations of different size – in this and the following tables.

Column (b) – Date of independence or statehood (month/year).

Columns (c) – Date of diplomatic relations with the USSR and China (not necessarily the date of exchange of embassies).

Columns (d) – The upper figures refer to heads of state exchanges by year – that is, Presidents, Premiers, Kings etc.; Mikoyan's visits are also counted here because of his unique position in the USSR (though he was Chief of State for only a portion of the 17 years covered). Unofficial visits by heads of state – for instance, in transit – are not counted unless they have unique political significance. The lower figures refer to other major exchanges – including important parliamentary, ministerial, governmental and military missions, as well as major economic and cultural delegations and delegations of ruling parties; each delegation is counted as one, even though it may include representatives of several of these categories. Exchanges of lesser missions, such as trade union delegations and minor economic and cultural delegations (including many listed in the chronological tables), are not counted.

/Note: Figures to the left of the stroke represent visits to the USSR; figures to the right of the stroke represent Soviet visits to the given Asian country: to USSR/to Asian country. The count of other major exchanges is admittedly somewhat arbitrary, reflecting the author's judgment as to what constitutes a "major" visit at a given juncture; a relatively low-ranking mission might be considered "major", for instance, in the case of a country which had few exchanges with the USSR, where it would not be judged so elsewhere. /

Columns (e) – Total major exchanges with the USSR, heads of state and other, from 1955 to the end of 1971.

/Note: The data in Table A are drawn from the chronological tables; for an estimate of the reliability of these data, see Note on Chronological Tables, p. 6. /

(1) Indonesia suspended relations with China in October 1967.

(2) The USSR established diplomatic relations with the Maldive Islands through its embassy in Ceylon after independence; the date is unknown.

TABLE B

SOVIET ECONOMIC AID TO ASIAN NATIONS*

	55	56	57	58	59	60	61	62	63	64	65	66	67	68	69	70	71	Total: USSR	Total: CPR
Afghanistan	6(1)	100	15		129		195	20	39 17		11	1	5	127		3	5	673	30
Burma		10	5															15	88
Cambodia				11					12		4							27	56
Ceylon				30												8		38	71
India		125 125			375 20 25	125					225	550 16						1586	
Indonesia		100			18	250					3							371	103
Nepal					7					8								15	66
Pakistan						30					52	84		66	20		209	461	310
TOTAL	6	460	20	41	574	405	195	20	68	8	295	651	5	193	20	11	214	3186	724

Notes to Table B

*The sums shown are in US dollars and rounded to the nearest million. They represent the author's best estimate of Soviet credits extended to Asian nations, based on both Russian and Western sources. The dates of the credit agreements and the purposes for which credits were extended (where known) are shown in the Chronologies above; a brief discussion of the credits to individual nations normally appears near the end of the section dealing with the nation in question.

(1)
The estimated $6 million credits to Afghanistan were extended in 1954.

TABLE C

SOVIET TRADE WITH ASIAN STATES*

	1st Trade Agr.	1955 Im	1955 Ex	1960 Im	1960 Ex	1965 Im	1965 Ex	1966 Im	1966 Ex	1967 Im	1967 Ex	1968 Im	1968 Ex	1969 Im	1969 Ex	1970 Im	1970 Ex
Afghanistan	1950	10.7	13.4	16.7	31.6	20.0	51.0	20.6	72.6	21.1	56.1	30.7	39.3	30.6	44.8	34.3	40.0
Burma	7/55	16.6	.2	4.9	3.7	13.4	5.2	.3	5.2	4.6	4.8	.3	1.9	3.7	2.6	1.6	3.3
Cambodia	5/57							.6	2.4	.7	1.3	2.1	.7	0	.7	1.6	.3
Ceylon	2/58			8.4	1.0	18.9	21.1	17.2	21.1	10.6	20.0	16.1	11.7	14.4	8.3	13.3	5.6
India	12/53	4.4	7.2	67.7	46.6	186.3	212.9	189.2	191.4	179.0	160.7	181.1	181.5	221.4	171.3	269.6	135.9
Indonesia	8/56	3.6	.1	16.0	31.1	31.6	53.9	30.5	4.7	24.1	5.2	18.9	5.2	23.8	3.6	27.8	5.0
Laos	12/62													0	0	0	2.1
Malaysia	4/67	21.5	0	110.4		111.5	0	124.3	0	95.6	.1	99.4	.1	121.8	1.7	123.3	1.8
Nepal		0	.1					.3	1.2	.4	.9	.6	.9	1.1	.9	.7	.8
Pakistan	6/56	0	.3	4.4	2.4	3.8	13.0	29.0	38.6	26.7	39.1	11.0	36.4	23.7	39.4	31.4	35.7
Singapore	3/66							0	2.8	.1	5.3	2.0	6.8	1.1	6.2	3.2	6.1
Thailand	6/64							0	2.4	.9	3.7	.4	3.3	.3	2.8	.9	2.9
TOTAL		56.8	21.3	228.5	116.4	385.5	357.1	412.0	342.4	363.8	297.2	362.6	287.8	341.9	282.3	507.7	239.5

Note to Table C

*All sums, expressed in millions of US dollars, are taken from official Soviet trade statistics. The Soviet totals do not always correspond exactly to sums shown in official summaries prepared by Russia's trading partners in Asia but they are never far from them. The intent of Table C is to indicate the general volume and direction of trade with Asian nations over the years reviewed, especially in the latter part of this period; students of Soviet trade requiring more detailed figures should consult the annual Soviet compilations and breakdowns in Vneshnyaya torgovlya SSSR za – god, articles in the Soviet journal Vneshnyaya torgovlya and the official trade statistics of the Asian nations concerned.

Where no figure is shown, there was no trade reported in Soviet compilations. Zero (0) indicates true totalling less than $50,000. The Maldive Islands and the Philippines had neither trade agreement nor trade with the USSR by the end of 1971 and are therefore not included in the table.

SOVIET MILITARY RELATIONS WITH ASIAN STATES*

	(a) 1st Agr.	(b) Total	(c) Types	(d) Military Exchange				(e) Naval Visits
				55-59	60-64	65-69	70-71	
Afghanistan	8/56	400	Fighter planes, including advanced models (MIG-21s); tanks; artillery; small arms in large quantity	1/	1/1	3/2	5/	
Burma					2/2			
Cambodia	9/63	10	Fighter planes; artillery		1/	3/		1
Ceylon	5/71	7	Fighter planes					1
India	10/60	1100	Bombers and fighter planes, including advanced models (MIG-21s, SU-7s); tanks; submarines; missiles; artillery; small arms	1/1	3/2	4/2	1/2	5
Indonesia	2/57	1300	Planes, including some advanced models (MIG-19s, MIG-21s), but only 10 percent operational in 1970; a few missiles; naval craft; artillery – all delivered prior to September 1965	1/	14/4	2/	1/	2
Laos	11/60	5	Artillery and small arms – delivered to neutralist forces in 1960-61		3/			
Nepal							1/	
Pakistan	8/68	150	Planes (chiefly MIG-19s) and tanks				2/1	4
TOTAL		2972		3/1	24/9	14/5	8/2	13

Note to Table D

*Data on Soviet military relations with Asian countries are meagre and often unauthenticated; they must therefore be treated with care. The data available are organized as follows:

Column (a) – Date of initial arms agreement or, if no agreement is reported, the date of earliest known arms deliveries.

Column (b) – The estimated value of Soviet military credits or sales in millions of US dollars, to the end of 1970. /Note: It is not usually clear whether reported sums of Soviet military aid represent cash transactions or credits extending over several years; the figure shown, then, is the total commitment, whether actual or projected. The estimates are mine, drawn from a variety of sources. Among them are the following (see Bibliography for full listings): Joshua and Gibert, Arms for the Third World (covering Soviet military aid to 1967 and bringing up to date an earlier study by Stephen Gibert published in Orbis (Fall 1966, pp. 839-58); Uri Ra'anan, The USSR Arms the Third World (especially for early shipments to Indonesia); The Military Balance, published annually by the Institute of Strategic Studies in London; the same

Institute's Adelphi Papers, No. 28 (October 1966); also periodic summaries by military correspondents, e.g. New York Times, 5 September, 1967; Washington Star, 14 September, 1969; and Christian Science Monitor, 3 April, 1970. 7

Column (c) – The major types of arms transferred. /Note: These data came principally from The Military Balance; the quantity of different Soviet arms reported on hand in 1970 is indicated in the country studies above. 7

Columns (d) – Exchanges of major military delegations, not including those attached to Presidential parties; also left out of the count are Soviet military missions assigned to a given Asian nation for a period of time and groups of military personnel going to the USSR for specialized training. /Note: Figures to the left of the stroke represent Asian delegations visiting the USSR; figures to the right of the stroke are Soviet delegations visiting the country concerned. These exchanges are included in Table A, column (d) ("Other Exchanges"). 7

Column (e) – Visits to Asian nations by Soviet naval units. /Note: Apart from a 1959 call in Indonesia, these visits all took place after 1967. 7

147

This Bibliography lists selected monographs, journal articles, yearbooks and other materials relevant to a study of Soviet policies in Asia; also included are a small number of key studies which related to Moscow's Third World policies more generally. For materials relating to Soviet policies in India and Indonesia, see the Special Bibliographies at the end of the sections dealing with these two countries. Source references for other countries may be found in the footnotes following each section.

Russian sources listed in the bibliographies are restricted to those which shed direct light on Soviet relations with Asian states; a wider listing of Soviet commentary on these nations during the years under review would quickly run to many hundreds – even thousands – of items. Unless otherwise indicated, all Russian volumes listed were published in Moscow.

Adelphi Papers. See Institute of Strategic Studies, below.

Barnett, A. Doak, ed. Communist Strategies in Asia. New York: Praeger, 1963.

Berton, Peter and Alvin Z. Rubinstein. Soviet Works on Southeast Asia: A Bibliography of Non-Periodical Literature, 1946-1965. Los Angeles: University of Southern California Press, 1967.

Bibliografiya Yugo-vostochnoy Azii, 1960.

Boyd, R.G. "Soviet and Chinese Involvement in Southern Asia", Canadian Slavonic Papers, Vol. XII, No. 2 (1970), pp. 175-94.

Carrére d'Encausse, Helene and Stuart R. Schram. Le Marxisme et l'Asie, 1853-1964. Paris: Armand Colin, 1965; translated into English as Marxism and Asia, Penguin, 1969 (documents on Russia's Eastern policy, chiefly before 1955).

Carter, James R. The Net Cost of Soviet Aid. New York: Praeger, 1971.

Chertkov, D.G., R.N. Andreasyan, I.I. Mozhayev. SSSR i razvivayushchiyesya strany (sotrudnichestvo v razvitii ekonomiki i kul'tury). 1966, 106 pp.

Duncan, W. Raymond, ed. Soviet Policies in Developing Countries. Waltham, Mass.: Ginn-Blaisdell, 1970 (views of Soviet policies by 13 Western scholars).

Ekonomicheskoye sotrudnichestvo Sovetskogo Soyuza s ekonomicheski slaborazvitymi stranami, 1962.

The Far East and Australasia: a Survey and Reference Book of Asia and the Pacific. London: Europa Publications, 1969, 1970 (an annual, useful especially for aid and trade statistics drawn from official sources).

Gibert, Stephen P. "Wars of Liberation and Soviet Military Aid Policy", Orbis, Fall 1966, pp. 839-58 (estimates of Soviet aid are based on the findings of a research project conducted at Georgetown University, entitled "Soviet Military Programs as a Reflection of Soviet Objectives", June 1965).

Goldman, Marshall I. Soviet Foreign Aid. New York: Praeger, 1967.

Gurtov, Melvin. China and Southeast Asia – the Politics of Survival. Lexington, Mass.: Heath, 1971 (Chinese policies in Thailand, Burma and Cambodia).

Guseynov, K.A. Internatsional'nyye svyazi profsoyuzov SSSR s profsoyuzami stran Azii i Afriki. 1965, 180 pp. (also in English, entitled Trade Union Association: USSR, Asia and Africa, 1967).

Holbik, Karel. The United States, the Soviet Union and the Third World. Hamburg, 1968.

Institute of Strategic Studies (London).
Adelphi Papers (published irregularly). The following were of use in the present volume:
No. 28 (October 1966). John L. Sutton and Geoffrey Kemp, "Arms to Developing Countries, 1945-1965".
No. 87 (May 1972). Geoffrey Jukes, "The Indian Ocean in Soviet Naval Policy".
The Military Balance (published annually since 1958; includes detailed estimates of the armed strength of all countries).

Joshua, Wynfred and Stephen P. Gibert. Arms for the Third World: Soviet Military Aid Diplomacy. Baltimore: Johns Hopkins Press, 1969 (this updates Mr. Gibert's earlier estimate of Soviet military aid; see above).

Kirsch, Marion P. "Soviet Security Objectives in Asia", International Organization, Summer 1970, pp. 451-78.

Knigi glavnoy redaktsii vostochnoy literatury izdatel'stva "Nauka", 1957-1966: annotirovannyy katalog, 1968, 304 pp. (lists about 1,400 major Orientalist works, with brief notes on contents).

Korneyev, S.G. Nauchnyye svyazi Akademii nauk SSSR so stranami Azii i Afriki, 1969, 315 pp. (detailed summary of cultural ties between Russian and Afro-Asian scholars).

Kovner, Milton. The Challenge of Co-existence; a Study of Soviet Economic Diplomacy. Washington: Public Affairs Press, 1961.

Lavrichenko, M.V. Ekonomicheskoye sotrudnichestvo SSSR so stranami Azii, Afriki i Latinskoy Ameriki, 1961, 144 pp.

Literatura o stranakh Azii i Afriki; yezhegodnik 1963, 1967 (though intended as an annual, published irregularly; this volume – listed as the third – was the only one consulted).

London, Kurt, ed. Unity and Contradiction: Major Aspects of Sino-Soviet Relations. New York: Praeger, 1962.

, ed. New Nations in a Divided World. New York: Praeger, 1963 (the above volumes include papers read at international conferences - respectively, at Lake Kawaguchi, Japan in 1960 and in Athens in 1962; a number of the papers deal with Sino-Soviet strategies in Asia).

McVey, Ruth T. Bibliography of Soviet Publications on South-east Asia. Ithaca: Cornell University Press, 1959 (most titles listed are pre-1955).

The Military Balance. See Institute of Strategic Studies, above.

Müller, Kurt, ed. The Soviet Bloc and the Developing Countries. Hannover: Forschungsinstitut der Friedrich-Ebert-Stiftung, 1964 (articles by German scholars on aspects of Soviet Third World policy).

Na novom puti, 1968, 491 pp. (third and last volume of a series entitled Natsional'no-osvoboditel'noye dvizheniye v Azii i Afriki, prepared by the Institute of the Peoples of Asia under the general editorship of B.G. Gafurov; the "new course" is the path of non-capitalist development).

Nollau, Günther and Hans Jürgen Wieke. Russia's South Flank: Soviet Operations in Iran, Turkey and Afghanistan. New York: Praeger, 1963 (translated from German).

Noveyshaya istoriya stran Azii i Afriki, 1965, 593 pp. (a reference work prepared at Moscow University; includes brief accounts of Soviet relations with Afro-Asian nations).

Pajak, Roger Frank. "Soviet Military Aid: an Instrument of Soviet Foreign Policy toward the Developing Countries", American University doctoral thesis, 1966.

Perera, S.B. "The Russian Presence in the Region", The Asia Magazine, 20 February, 1966 (the "region" is South-East Asia).

Prokhorov, G.M., ed. Problemy sotrudnichestva sotsialisticheskikh i razvivayushchikhsya stran, 1966.

Ra'anan, Uri. "Moscow and the 'Third World'", Problems of Communism, January-February 1965, pp. 22-31.

. "Tactics in the Third World: Contradictions and Dangers", Survey, No. 57 (October 1965), pp. 26-37.

. The USSR Arms the Third World: Case Studies in Soviet Foreign Policy. Cambridge: Massachusetts Institute of Technology Press, 1969 (early Soviet military policies in Egypt and Indonesia).

SSSR i strany vostoka; ekonomicheskoye i kul'turnoye sotrudnichestvo, 1961, 140 pp.

Samylovskiy, I.V. Nauchnyye i kul'turnyye svyazi SSSR so stranami Azii i Afriki, 1963, 68 pp. (a summary prepared by the Institute of the Peoples of Asia).

Sawyer, Carole A. Communist Trade with Developing Countries, 1955-65. New York: Praeger, 1966.

Scalapino, Robert A., ed. The Communist Revolution in Asia: Tactics, Goals and Achievements. Englewood Cliffs, N.J.: Prentice-Hall, 1965; 2nd edition, 1969.

Shaffer, Harry G. and Jan S. Prybyla, eds. From Underdevelopment to Affluence: Western, Soviet and Chinese Views. New York: Appleton-Century-Crofts, 1968 (collection of articles on different Third World problems; mainly by Western scholars but including some Russians).

Tansky, Leo. "Soviet Foreign Aid to the Less Developed Countries", prepared for the Subcommittee on Foreign Economic Policy of the Joint Economic Committee, Congress of the United States: 89th Congress, 2nd Session, "New Directions in the Soviet Economy", Part IV, 1966, pp. 947-74.

. U.S. and U.S.S.R. Aid to Developing Countries: a Comparative Study of India, Turkey and the UAR. New York: Praeger, 1967.

Thornton, Thomas Perry, ed. The Third World in Soviet Perspective: Studies by Soviet Writers on the Developing Areas. Princeton: Princeton University Press, 1964 (an Introduction by Mr. Thornton reviews Soviet scholarship on the Third World to the end of 1962).

The USSR and Developing Countries (economic cooperation). Moscow, 1965, 88 pp. (though insignificant in appearance, this pamphlet gives considerable detail on Soviet economic activity in 25 Afro-Asian nations).

United States Department of State, Bureau of Intelligence and Research. Research Memorandum (called Research Study after 1969). The following in particular were relevant to the present study:
  "Soviet Diplomatic Relations and Representation".
    RSE-70, 9 September, 1969.
  "The Sino-Soviet Economic Offensive" (title varies: "Communist Governments and Developing Nations: Aid and Trade").
    No. 8426, 21 March, 1961.
    RSB-182, 12 December, 1962.
    RSB-43, 18 June, 1964.
    RSB-50, 17 June, 1966.
    RSB-80, 21 July, 1967.
    RSE-120, 14 August, 1968.
    RSE-65, 5 September, 1969.
    RECS-5, 9 July, 1970.
    RECS-15, 22 September, 1971.
    RECS-3, 15 May, 1972.
  "Educational and Cultural Exchanges between Communist and non-Communist Countries" (title varies slightly).
    RSB-46, 29 March, 1963.
    RSB-85, 4 November, 1964.
    RSB-49, 1 June, 1965.
    RSB-10, 25 January, 1967.
    RSB-40, 12 May, 1967.
    RSB-65, 31 May, 1968.
    RSE-25, 7 May, 1969.
    RSES-35, 12 August, 1970.
    RSES-34, 30 August, 1971.
    RESS-57, 31 August, 1972.

_____. World Strength of the Communist Party Organizations (published annually; indicates activity as well as legal status and strength of all Communist parties).

Vasil'yev, D. and K. L'vov. Torgovlya Sovetskogo Soyuza so stranami Yugo-vostochnoy Azii, 1959, 157 pp. (also in English).

Vneshnyaya torgovlya SSSR: staticheskiy sbornik, 1918-66, 1967 (in addition to periodic trade summaries such as this volume, the Ministry of Foreign Trade publishes an annual summary, Vneshnyaya torgovlya za - god, which includes a detailed breakdown of trade with some 60 Afro-Asian nations).

Walters, Robert S. American and Soviet Aid: a Comparative Analysis. Pittsburg: University of Pittsburg Press, 1970.

Yearbook on International Communist Affairs. Stanford: Hoover Institution Press, 1966, 1968, 1969, 1970, 1971 (this annual includes extensive detail on the World Communist movement as well as on individual parties).

Periodicals

Aziya i Afrika segodnya (journal of Institut Afriki and Institut narodov Azii, Akademiya nauk SSSR, March 1961 to present; monthly; for popular consumption).

British Information Service (comprehensive world monitoring service prepared in London, comparable to the American Foreign Broadcast Information Service; issued daily in several regional series).

Central Asian Review (published by Central Asian Research Centre, London, from 1953; quarterly; merged with Mizan in 1969; included coverage of Soviet activities in India, Pakistan and Afghanistan).

Current Digest of the Soviet Press (published by the American Association for the Advancement of Slavic Studies, 1949 to present; weekly, indexed quarterly; translations cover all major statements on Soviet foreign policy, but coverage of Third World affairs is irregular).

Foreign Broadcast Information Service (comprehensive world monitoring service of US Government; issued daily in six regional volumes).

International Affairs (English edition of Mezhdunarodnaya zhizn'; principal Soviet journal on world affairs for foreign readers; 1955 to present; monthly).

Joint Publications Research Service (translations from world press prepared by US Government; issued daily in several series; includes many items from Soviet publications).

Kommunist (organ of the Central Committee of the CPSU, 1924 to present; published 18 times a year).

Mirovaya ekonomika i mezhdunarodnyye otnosheniya (organ of Institut mirovoy ekonomiki i mezhdunarodnykh otnosheniy, Akademiya nauk SSSR, 1955 to present; monthly; next to Narody Azii i Afriki, provides most significant scholarly coverage of Afro-Asian affairs).

Mizan (published by the Central Asian Research Centre, London, 1959 to 1972; monthly at outset, later bi-monthly, merged with Yuva Newsletter in 1965 and with Central Asian Review in 1969; Supplements A, covering the Near East and Africa, and B, covering South and South-East Asia, were published separately from 1967 to the end of 1970; replaced in 1971 by USSR and the Third World).

Moscow News (organ of Union of Soviet Societies of Friendship and Cultural Relations with Foreign Countries, 1956 to present; weekly; useful for information on cultural exchange with Asian nations, especially to mid-1960s).

Narody Azii i Afriki (principal journal of Institut Afriki and Institut narodov Azii, Akademiya nauk SSSR, 1961 to present; bi-monthly; replaced Problemy Vostokovedeniya).

New Times (English edition of Novoye vremya, 1945 to present; weekly; popular journal on international affairs, mainly for foreign readers).

Novaya sovetskaya i inostrannaya literatura po stranam Azii i Afriki (an important bibliographic source, mid-1960s to present; monthly).

Problems of Peace and Socialism (alternative title of World Marxist Review; see below).

Problemy Vostokovedeniya (journal of Institut Vostokovedeniya, Akademiya nauk SSSR, 1956-61; bi-monthly; replaced by Narody Azii i Afriki).

Sovremennyy Vostok (journal of Institut Vostokovedeniya and later Institut Afriki, Akademiya nauk SSSR, July 1957-February 1961; monthly; replaced by Aziya i Afrika segodnya).

Trends and Highlights (published by South-East Asia Treaty Organization in Bangkok, mid-1950s to present; fortnightly at outset, later monthly; though strongly biased against Leftist and Communist movements, contains useful data from obscure local sources in South-East Asia).

USSR and the Third World (see Mizan).

Vneshnyaya torgovlya (official organ of the Soviet Ministry of Foreign Trade; monthly).

World Marxist Review (English edition of Problemy mira i sotsializma, unofficial organ of the international Communist movement; published in Prague, September 1958 to present; monthly; includes both Russian and divergent views on world Communist developments).

Yuva Newsletter (published by Central Asian Research Centre, London, 1962-1965; quarterly to 1964, then bi-monthly; covers Soviet commentary on South-East Asia).